Inside the World
of Harry Potter

ALSO FROM CHRISTOPHER E. BELL
AND FROM MCFARLAND

*Wizards vs. Muggles: Essays on Identity
and the Harry Potter Universe* (2016)

*From Here to Hogwarts: Essays on Harry Potter
Fandom and Fiction* (2016)

*Hermione Granger Saves the World:
Essays on the Feminist Heroine of Hogwarts* (2012)

*American Idolatry: Celebrity, Commodity
and Reality Television* (2010)

Inside the World of Harry Potter

Critical Essays on the Books and Films

Edited by CHRISTOPHER E. BELL

McFarland & Company, Inc., Publishers
Jefferson, North Carolina

LIBRARY OF CONGRESS CATALOGUING-IN-PUBLICATION DATA

Names: Bell, Christopher E., 1974– editor.
Title: Inside the world of Harry Potter : critical essays on the books and films / edited by Christopher E. Bell.
Description: Jefferson, North Carolina : McFarland & Company, Inc., 2018 | Includes bibliographical references and index.
Identifiers: LCCN 2018034412 | ISBN 9781476673554 (softcover : acid free paper) ∞
Subjects: LCSH: Rowling, J. K.—Criticism and interpretation. | Rowling, J. K. Harry Potter series. | Potter, Harry (Fictitious character) | Children's stories, English—History and criticism. | Literature and society. | Civilization, Western.
Classification: LCC PR6068.O93 Z73365 2018 | DDC 823/.914—dc23
LC record available at https://lccn.loc.gov/2018034412

ISBN (print) 978-1-4766-7355-4
ISBN (ebook) 978-1-4766-3413-5

BRITISH LIBRARY CATALOGUING DATA ARE AVAILABLE

© 2018 Christopher E. Bell. All rights reserved

No part of this book may be reproduced or transmitted in any form or by any means, electronic or mechanical, including photocopying or recording, or by any information storage and retrieval system, without permission in writing from the publisher.

Front cover image © 2018 Redakie/Shutterstock

Printed in the United States of America

McFarland & Company, Inc., Publishers
  Box 611, Jefferson, North Carolina 28640
   www.mcfarlandpub.com

For Liv,
Always.

Acknowledgements

As always, if you're not in the mood to read a bunch of thanks issued to people who almost certainly are not you, feel free to skip to the Introduction. You're not hurting my feelings if you do.

Thank you forever to the great loves of my life, Megan and Liv and H and K and S. I love you as much as anyone has ever loved anything ever. I love you like the sun loves the mountain, and the mountain loves the tall trees, and the tall trees love the mountain lion, and the mountain lion loves the flavor of the unwary hiker.

Thank you and thank you to my research assistant, Rachel Menkhus, who always works so hard on what always seems to be such short notice.

Thank you to all of my friends and family, who continue to listen to me talk about Harry Potter long after they, perhaps, were as interested as I am.

Thank you to our home in the Southwest Popular/American Culture Association, for continuing to support and nurture what has become the greatest collection of *Harry Potter* scholars on Earth.

Finally, as always, thank you to J.K. Rowling for giving us an ever evolving set of texts by which to explore this confusing world in which we find ourselves.

Table of Contents

Acknowledgments	vi
Introduction	
Christopher E. Bell	1
Gone but Not Forgotten: The Missing Mothers of the Wizarding World	
Kate Fulton *and* Alicia L. Skipper	7
"Beyond the veil": The Narrative Functions of Death	
Samantha J. Vertosick	21
"I don't think you're a waste of space": Activity, Redemption and the Social Construction of Fatness	
Tolonda Henderson	33
Of the Patil Twins	
Soma Das	44
Time Travel and the *Cursed Child*	
Elizabeth Morrow Clark	59
Frisky, Risky Firewhisky: The Rhetorical Function of Alcohol	
Lauren Camacci	76
Pure-Bloods, Half-Bloods and Mudbloods	
Camilla Schroeder	92
"You have your mother's eyes": Inheritance and Social Class	
Alison Baker	103
The First Gift: Owls as Paragons of the Non-Human	
Keri Stevenson	116

Dangerous Depictions of Adoption in Rowling's
  Wizarding World Narratives
    Tara Moore   130
Harry Potter and the Paradoxes of Fidelity
    Jelena Borojević   147
What Is a Hero?: An Analysis of Legacy Symbolism
    Marley Stuever-Williford   161

About the Contributors   177
Index   181

Introduction

CHRISTOPHER E. BELL

This being the fourth book of *Harry Potter* scholarship I have had the privilege of editing, I believe it is fair for me to make an observation, here, at the outset. I often find myself at a loss for words when attempting to introduce a new collection of essays. In the past, I have used this space to "make a case" for the collection, whether that is to justify selecting Hermione Granger out of the entire, wide cast of characters to solely focus upon (2010), or to delineate real-world applications of the scholarship contained within (2016). I think we, as a community of scholars, are in a space now where such justifications are no longer necessary. You have picked up this volume and made the decision to read it—my guess is that I do not have to convince you of the societal value of the texts at hand. *Harry Potter* has proven to be an invaluable artifact in the study of real-world application of fictional texts. In a very real way, we can understand the world around us by using Harry's world as a guide. In another, equally real way, some of the best scholars among us are also some of the biggest traditional fans of the Potterverse. Indeed, for nearly every scholar in this volume (and the hundreds of scholars who have joined us in academic fellowship over the six years of our existence as a formal scholarly organization), fandom and serious academic research go hand in hand.

In 2002, the term "acafan" began to surface in academic scholarship via Matt Hills, who essentially coined the term in his book *Fan Cultures* (Hills 2002). Hills differentiated between acafans (scholars who happened to be fans of the artifact) and fan scholars (fans with an academic interest in the artifact)—motivation was a key, important factor in the categorization. Hills drew heavily upon the work of Henry Jenkins of the University of Southern California in conceptualizing acafandom (Jenkins 1992). The acafan straddles the line between researcher and fan, each of which serves a particular societal function that, until relatively recently, was entirely separate. Acafandom requires not only intimate knowledge of the academic theories and concepts endemic to particular disciplines, but also intimate knowledge of the artifact and surrounding fandom communities in order to properly perform both functions. A true acafan must be not only an outstanding researcher, but also a dedicated fan and legitimate member of the fandom community. This last piece cannot be overstated. There is a long-standing mistrust of university researchers who enter into fan communities in anthropological, ethnographic ways; fan communities are (often rightly) wary of academics coming in to "study the natives" to produce condescending reports of what's happening in the "freaks and mom's-basement-dwellers" community. Acafans circumvent this in an important way:

> Knowledge travels within the fan community, from fans to acafans, then from acafans to other academics.... Fan knowledge thus circulates in two circuits, one involving the fan community alone and another involving both fan and academic communities, in which the acafan plays a crucial role.... The acafan represents a crucial node where knowledge from the community is passed on into the academic world. Academic knowledge may eventually seep back into fan communities, with or without the aca-fan's input ... but the acafan is best-placed to structure and transmit knowledge from (as well as about) the fan community [Cristofari & Guitton, 2016, 718].

The acafan simply has more access than the traditional academic, both to the artifact and its varying interpretations, and to the fandom community that generates an *enormous* amount of knowledge—knowledge that is largely closed off from the academy.

For example, while Harry Potter studies is a growing and vibrant, but relatively new, community within academic circles, online fan communities like *Mugglenet* and *The Leaky Cauldron* have been actively engaged in all levels of *Potter* scholarship for more than a decade. Thousands of fans have poured theories, interpretations, and histories into these online repositories, yet few *Potter* scholars within traditional academic research have used these repositories as a resource. Acafans recognize the wealth of knowledge available in these non-traditional sources and are able to bring those voices to the table, serving as mediating forces—academic translators, if you will—for both the fan community and the academic community. In short, "being a fan of a fandom that one also studies professionally means being respectful of the various components of that fan world—components that can be fraught with stigma" (Ingram-Waters, 2010).

Why is this categorization—the acafan—necessary at all? As someone who has just come through a tenure and promotion process, I can relate the answer with authority: because the academy, by and large, believes in "objective" research, and acafandom rejects the very notion of objectivity. Jenkins, considered by most to be the "founding father" of acafandom, relates:

> [Film and media studies] as a discipline had to define ourselves in opposition to fans and buffs in order to gain admission to the academy. That is, if you're going to be

taken seriously, and you're writing about popular culture, the last thing you want to do is be accused of being a fan. Right? You want to say, I am an academic.

I'm studying this just like you study art history and you study music history, and you study literature. And you push away those personal implications of this stuff in your own life, and you devalue them. ... It's only now that there is a secure base for film and media studies within the academy that it is possible for people like me to go through graduate school publicly as a fan, to assert to out myself as a fan ... and I've in fact heard very negative things from some academics as a result of that. I was quoted in *Lingua Franca* as saying that I'm a fan first and an academic second, which is actually a misquote. It was a chronological statement; it wasn't a statement of priority. But I said that the things I write about grow out of things that I care about as a fan, and that I choose to write about them and engage with them as an academic as well. But I got a lot of ribbing and uncomfortable remarks from other academics because of that statement. But I think it is now possible to be a fan academic in the infrastructure of the academy as it's now evolved [Jenkins 1993].

In a nutshell, it is the very *subjectivity* of acafan research that produces its intrinsic value. That makes the research output immediately suspect to those who value "distance" in research. Never mind that there is literally *no such thing* as objectivity when dealing with human behavior, and that there are countless studies intricately detailing the inherent human bias in even the most "empirical" of scientific work—the *appearance* of objectivity matters. In truth, objectivity is merely subjectivity willfully made invisible. I wish that what Jenkins asserts was entirely true, but in reality, I have lost count of the number of Harry Potter studies colleagues who have been challenged, marginalized, or outright threatened because of their publication and scholarship in this area. "Serious" scholars do not engage in acafandom. "Serious" scholars do not write about *Harry Potter*.

This myopic view of academic pursuit, and its attendant lack of self-reflective understanding about the role of the academy in contemporary society, is backward and counterproductive. There is not only a place for, but also a *dire* necessity for academics who are trained in their individual disciplines, yet also highly media literate and schooled in media criticism, who also actively engage as media consumers. As the walls between universities and the public at large grow higher and higher, those of us working in acafandom can serve as a much-needed bridge to the "outside world"—ironically, in our case, through the Wizarding World.

There is, admittedly, quite the truckload of discursive baggage surrounding the terms "fandom" and "acafan" that are beyond the scope of this introduction. There are certainly those within even the acafandom community who believe we should stop using the term altogether, as it positions the work that we do in ways that are not always constructive. However, the clear necessity for terminology that describes the heretofore taboo unification of personal and professional pursuits outweighs the potential stigma attached to the word. Acafandom *matters*; it matters profoundly, and those of us actively engaged in these endeavors must continue to fight for our rightful place within the academy, despite the slings and arrows of our more traditional colleagues. Serious scholars do, in fact, write about *Harry Potter*—in ways that can deeply critique the society in which we live to the benefit of everyone.

For example, in the collection's first essay, Kate Fulton and Alicia L. Skipper deal directly with parenthood, particularly with motherhood, in the Wizarding World. These considerations are later echoed in by Tara Moore in her exploration of the highly problematic way adoption is treated throughout the texts. Samantha J. Vertosick's musings on the functions of death, Elizabeth Morrow Clark's examination of the functions of time travel, and Camilla Schroeder's taxonomy of the functions of blood status use the *Potter* texts to explain facets of traditional literature and the real world. Tolonda Henderson, Soma Das, and Lauren Rose Camacci, delineate Rowling's use of body size, skin color, and alcoholism (respectively) to indicate moral or social failure. Borojević Jelena critiques notions of adaptation from book to film, and Marley Stuever-Williford expands upon a theory of mine, regarding the number three, from several collections ago. Alison Baker discusses the role of inheritance and social class in the Wizarding World, and Keri Stevenson has penned one of the most interesting *Potter*-related pieces I have read in some time—I won't spoil it for you here.

Feel free to enjoy the volume in any order you wish. Grab a pen and a highlighter and mark up the work. Scribble down questions, furiously underline passages, and use the work in this volume as a jumping-off point for your own acafandom study. If something particularly catches your eye, shoot me an email at dr.christopher.bell@gmail.com. I make no promises that I will be able to respond to everything, but I shall do my best. If you really want to immerse yourself in this community, please join us at our next conference—check out http://southwestpca.org for details. For now, jump on in. The water is fine.

Naming Conventions

For the ease of reading and for the sake of consistency, in this volume, the titles of the books/films will be abbreviated as follows:

Harry Potter and the Sorcerer's/Philosopher's Stone—*SS* or *PS*
Harry Potter and the Chamber of Secrets—*CoS*
Harry Potter and the Prisoner of Azkaban—*PoA*
Harry Potter and the Goblet of Fire—*GoF*
Harry Potter and the Order of the Phoenix—*OotP*

Harry Potter and the Half-Blood Prince—HBP
Harry Potter and the Deathly Hallows—DH, or DH1/DH2

REFERENCES

Cristofari, C., & Guitton, M.J. (2016). "Aca-Fans and Fan Communities: An Operative Framework." *Journal of Consumer Culture*, 17(3), 713–731.
Hills, M. (2002). *Fan Cultures*. London: Psychology Press.
Ingram-Waters, M. (2010). "When Normal and Deviant Identities Collide: Methodological Considerations of the Pregnant Acafan." *Transformative Works and Cultures*, 5.
Jenkins, H. (1992). *Textual Poachers: Studies in Culture and Communication*. Abingdon-on-Thames: Routledge.
Jenkins, H. (1993). As quoted in *Fanlore*. https://fanlore.org/wiki/Acafan.

Gone but Not Forgotten
The Missing Mothers of the Wizarding World
Kate Fulton *and* Alicia L. Skipper

Throughout the texts of J.K. Rowling's wizarding world, readers encounter characters who are either parentless or raised without mothers. Orphans are a common trope, most familiar in fairytales, and found in many classic novels and films. J.K. Rowling readily uses the orphan trope throughout her *Harry Potter* series and in her most recent full-length work, the screenplay for *Fantastic Beasts and Where to Find Them* (2016). The families of Harry Potter, Tom Riddle, Luna Lovegood, Neville Longbottom, and Credence Barebone stand as a stark contrast to the enviable, loving, and intact Weasley family, spearheaded, of course, by super-mom Molly Weasley. Even Death Eaters can claim a caring mother in Narcissa Malfoy, a matriarch who puts Draco ahead of everything, including her loyalty to Lord Voldemort. Like many writers/storytellers before her, J.K. Rowling employs the trope of the orphaned child in many of her characters. Certainly the missing mothers in the *Harry Potter* series and in Rowling's *Fantastic Beasts and Where to Find Them* gain prominence in absentia. Their absence in the lives of their children influences not only the storylines of the works but also the development of the characters themselves.

Rowling's preoccupation with orphans and the vulnerability of orphans is reflected not only in her literature, but in her charitable work as well. In 2004, Rowling started the foundation *Lumos*, named for the spell that enables a witch or wizard to produce light. Rowling's endeavor in starting the foundation is to end the institutionalization of children throughout the world. In an op-ed Rowling penned for *The Guardian* (2014), she explains the impact of institutionalization on children:

> Damage is done very early, and it is lasting. Cut off from society, institutionalized children return to the world with their chances of a happy, healthy life greatly

impaired, often unable to find employment, excluded from the community and more likely to enter into a lifetime of poverty and dependency [Rowling 2014].

Certainly her characters do not suffer the neglect and debilitating conditions that exist in the real world, the world beyond magic, but examining the impact and struggles of fictional characters certainly helps to reflect the obstacles experienced by those who are without the protection and stability of a family.

One of the most logical reasons to create child characters who are missing the protection of the mother is to highlight the vulnerability of the orphaned or motherless child. According to Sarah Boxer, "The dead-mother plot is a fixture of fiction, so deeply woven into our storytelling fabric that it seems impossible to unravel or explain" (2014). In spite of this seemingly impossible task, many scholars have their own view of the function of the orphan trope. For example, in examining the orphans in 19th Century British novels, Professor John Mullan (2014) notes that aside from making a child vulnerable, the plight of being an orphan also opens characters up for adventure:

> The orphan is therefore an essentially novelistic character, set loose from established conventions to face a world of endless possibilities [and dangers]. The orphan leads the reader through a maze of experiences, encountering life's threats and grasping its opportunities. Being the focus of the story's interest, he or she is a naïve mirror to the qualities of others. In children's fiction, of course, the orphan will eventually find the happiness to compensate for being deprived of parents [Mullan, 2014].

Readers of the *Harry Potter* series will certainly notice that this "compensation" occurs in many of the characters, and that being free from the confines of a watchful parent certainly enables them to seek adventures that would be otherwise forbidden. This is exemplified when Molly Weasley endeavors to keep Ron, Hermione, and Harry apart in *The Deathly Hallows* (2008), as they attempt to plot their escape from The Burrow and embark upon their quest for the horcruxes.

Yet, there may be a more practical purpose for implementing the orphan trope. As author Liz Moore reflects, "I think there is a practical or functional component to writing about orphans. The orphan character—especially one who is an orphan before the novel begins—comes with a built-in problem, which leads to built-in conflict. And, as I am constantly telling my creative writing students, conflict is all" (Moore, 2016). Moore ascribes the commonality of the trope to convenience, but also points out that the end result is to create a message of empowerment:

> If I can attempt to make an excuse for myself, and for all the writers from Charles Dickens to J.K. Rowling who find themselves drawn, over and over again, to the orphan trope, it might sound like this: For me, at least, writing about orphans is a

way to write through the terror of being alone in the world. My characters offer a vision of a future beyond a catastrophic event. Whether these characters are better-off or worse-off at the end of my books, they have, at least, moved beyond their orphandom. It is no longer the central, controlling problem in their world. And generally they have become empowered in some way [Moore, 2016].

For better or for worse, Harry, Luna, Neville, Tom Riddle and Credence all become empowered at the end of their journeys. For Harry, Luna, and Neville, that empowerment is achieved through acceptance, self-love, and the creation of stable environments. For Tom Riddle and Credence, that empowerment comes from destructive forces: the development of the alter-egos of Lord Voldemort and the Obscurus.

There has been quite a bit of research into the impact of losing a parent, particularly a mother, on children. The outcomes and process of grieving depend on many factors, including the age at which the loss happened, the support systems in place for the child after the loss occurs, and how the loss is experienced, re-experienced, and processed as subsequent developmental stages are reached. The age of the child when the loss occurs is important because the stage of development dictates both the level of understanding of the loss and the emotional ability to process the loss. The child will revisit the loss as development progresses, using new cognitive and emotional skills that evolve (Granot, 2005). Important factors that influence how a child will cope are:

- whether the loss occurred at a very young age
- who cared for the child after the loss
- what the child was told
- what kind of support was provided
- what did the child understand about what happened [Granot, 2005].

Outcomes for children who lose parents range from positive resilient growth to addiction, crime, and other forms of psychopathology. Tom Riddle, Harry Potter, Luna Lovegood, Neville Longbottom and Credence Barebone all lost their mothers at different developmental stages and in different manners. The impact of those losses and the influence of their mothers throughout their lives is experienced in very different ways.

Erik Erikson said that at each stage of development, there is an "interaction of opposites" (Feist&Feist, 2009, p.249) that results in either an ego strength or core pathology to emerge. However, a child needs to experience both sides of the equation in order have balance—too much or too little of one quality can lead to problems. Children usually form their first relationships with their parents. During the first year of life, if their needs are met, they develop trust. If they have too much trust, they can become vulnerable or taken advantage of. If they develop too much distrust, they may become angry, depressed or hostile (Feist, 2009). If the proper balance between these two attitudes is achieved, the ego strength of hope emerges. If the scale tips in favor of distrust, the core pathology of withdrawal occurs. An infant who withdraws from the world can travel down a road toward psychopathology. While the outcomes may vary, it is undisputable that the loss of a parent, especially the mother, has a profound impact upon the development of a child, and readers/viewers see this impact reflected in J.K. Rowling's characters.

Harry Potter

First we begin with the most famous of all of the characters, Harry Potter. Harry loses his parents, Lily and James, to Lord Voldemort when he is just a baby. He grows up with his maternal aunt and uncle, Vernon and Petunia Dursley, who feel nothing but disdain for Harry because his parents, unbeknownst to him, were magical. Harry is mistreated at the Dursleys' and is expected to perform menial tasks, like cooking breakfast and cleaning the house. He sleeps in a small room under the stairs and wears only hand-me-down clothing from his older and abusive cousin, Dudley. It does not take much of a leap to make the connection between Harry's plight and the plight of Cinderella. Cinderella, of course, is mistreated by her stepmother and stepsisters, who are jealous of her beauty, and ultimately, her ability to win the Prince. Yet according to Ming-Hsun Lin's (2016) "As Fitting the Glass Slipper: A Comparative Study of the Princess's Role in the Harry Potter Novels and Films," it is Petunia's jealousy of Lily that prompts her mistreatment of Harry, much like it prompted the wicked stepmother in *Cinderella*. Readers later learn in the series that Petunia had desired the magical ability that both Lily and Harry possess, even writing to Dumbledore, unsuccessfully requesting admittance into Hogwarts when she was a young girl. Lily's abilities, and their parents' pride at them, fueled Petunia's contempt for Lily and, by extension, Harry. This is revealed fully in *SS* (1998) when Petunia finally admits the truth about Lily and James, that they were not killed in a car crash. Because Petunia harbors jealousy and resentment, she cannot care for Harry, and as a result, she and her family abuse him and make him feel worthless.

It is not only the physical mistreatment of not having enough to eat and being denied proper boarding and essentials, but also the verbal abuse that has an impact upon Harry until he, like Cinderella, is rescued by magic. In Perrault's version of "Cinderella," Cinderella's rescuer takes the form of a fairy godmother who uses magic to transform Cinderella. In the Grimm version of the tale, Cinderella receives her beautiful clothing by visiting the tree at her mother's grave:

Cinderella went to her mother's grave under the hazel tree and said "Shake your branches, little tree, Toss gold and silver down on me." The bird tossed down a dress of gold and silver, with slippers embroidered with silk and silver [Grimm and Grimm, p 119].

More than the typical Perrault version that most of us are familiar with due to the animated film from Walt Disney, the Grimm version highlights the impact of the loss of Cinderella's mother. She returns to her mother's grave and looks to the tree as representative of her mother to rescue her from her plight. Because of magic, it works, and ultimately she weds the prince and lives "happily ever after." Harry is not able to visit the grave of his parents; indeed, he is even unaware of the truth of their deaths until the Hogwarts groundskeeper, Hagrid, tracks him down and presents Harry with his letter of acceptance to Hogwarts. Because he inherits his mother and father's magical traits, Harry is rescued from his abusive situation. He is saved by magic. Hagrid acts as a courier in the same way that Perrault's Cinderella has a fairy godmother and Grimm's Cinderella had a magical tree. But despite the rescue, the impact of not having parents has a profound impact on Harry's development.

Harry was 15 months old when Voldemort killed his parents. It appears, through stories told by other characters and a letter Harry finds in *DH* (2007), that Harry was a well loved and cared for infant/toddler. His parents met his needs and provided him with the opportunity to develop trust and hope. In a letter Harry finds in *DH*, from Lily to Sirius, Lily thanks Sirius for buying a toy broom for Harry's birthday and sends a picture of Harry zooming around the house on the broom (pp 180–81). It appears Harry had already moved on to Erickson's second stage, autonomy vs. shame and doubt, in which a child balances budding independence and self-expression (think "Me do" or "NO!") with feelings of uncertainty and self-consciousness. Again, there must be experiencing of both, but the scales that tip in favor of autonomy result in development of the basic ego strength of will.

A child who loses a parent during these early stages of development may have difficulty developing trusting relationships. Their sense of trust and hope is shaken. This may be mitigated by the presence of another involved loving parent or caregiver. While research suggests that children do not carry distinct memories from infancy into adulthood, the child still experiences the pain and confusion of the loss of the loving caregiver. Harry, at 15 months old, was old enough to feel the loss of his parents, their sudden disappearance from his life, but not to comprehend what had happened (Granot, 2005). His loving world had been destroyed, and he did not have a loving family to care for him afterward.

John Bowlby's research on attachment underscores the need for an infant to receive loving, consistent care. This allows a child to develop confidence and a secure base from which to explore the world (Feist, 2009). This attachment relationship is a two way street between infant and caregiver and becomes the model for future friendships and relationships. The caregiver and infant respond to each other and influence each other other's behavior. Harry had this opportunity with his parents, but it was ripped from him with no suitable replacement. Object relations theory supports the idea that a young child such as Harry needs to have others in his life who can keep the memory of the lost parents alive for them. An object becomes the internalized image or memory of the lost parent. Stories, pictures, clothing (or invisibility cloaks) become representations of the lost parent and help the child identify with that parent. It is important that the parent is portrayed accurately or they may become idealized and difficult to identify with (Granot, 2005). Harry was not told the truth about his parents' death and was not treated in a loving, caring manner. When he finally learns the truth, he is given those opportunities to connect and identify with his parents through stories, pictures and items (cloak). This helps explain Harry's obsession with the Mirror of Erised and the importance of the pictures Hagrid collects for him at the end of SS. Harry is able to reconnect with the early experience of trust, hope and will through his new family at Hogwarts. He does initially idolize his father, leading to difficulties in his own identity, when he learns James could be a bully, sometimes arrogant, and cruel (Rowling, 2003).

Children revisit the loss of a parent at each subsequent developmental stage. They may travel through magical thinking that a parent will return to the sadness and hopelessness of knowing that the loss is forever. As their cognitive and social emotional growth unfolds, they may re-experience the loss. Harry experiences this upon learning his parents died protecting him, and throughout the series, as he encounters further loss and feels the void of not having his family. He attempts to fill the void through friendships and relationships with other parental figures but still has the feeling of being detached and different from others. This feeling of being "other" or different is common in children who experience the loss of a parent in childhood (Granot, 2005). He is comforted knowing he was loved so deeply, and his ego strengths of hope and will are played out throughout the series. In this way, he differs from his nemesis, Lord Voldemort.

Tom Riddle/Lord Voldemort

There are many similarities highlighted between Tom Riddle and Harry Potter, and at the most basic, the fact that both are orphans who find a home at Hogwarts is one that first stands out both to readers and to Harry. Yet unlike Harry, Voldemort does not have any family to take him in, begrudgingly or not. He is left at an orphanage until he, like Harry and the fairytale princess, Cinderella, is saved from his existence by magic. Unlike Harry, however, Tom Riddle revels in his loneliness. He is excited and not surprised to learn that he is a wizard. He knows he is destined for greatness. When Dumbledore reveals to Riddle that he is a wizard in *HBP* (2007), he responds, "I knew I was different, I knew I was special. Always, I knew there was something" (p. 271). Despite his meager beginnings, Tom Ridldle has no difficulty believing that he is destined for something great, that in spite of being abandoned and alone, he is "special." His lack of parents and his circumstances would normally make him a sympathetic figure, but instead it sets up the conditions from which he becomes Lord Voldemort.

Tom Riddle can be easily compared to another famous orphan, Luke Skywalker in the *Star Wars* series. It is true that there have been arguments that Harry and Luke have parallels, which is also viable since Tom Riddle and Harry have similarities. Yet, we contend that Skywalker and Riddle have more commonalities. Both are born to mothers who die in childbirth and quite possibly as a result of their grief. Padme Amidala and Merope Gaunt are both desperately in love with husbands who abandon them. Anakin Skywalker and Tom Riddle, Sr., abandon the mothers of their children. Anakin abandons Padme because he has given himself over to darkness. Merope Gaunt lifts her enchantments in the hopes that Tom Riddle did actually love her, when in fact, he did not. Ultimately he abandons her and her unborn child. In the orphanage, Mrs. Cole explains to Dumbledore the circumstances of Merope's last words:

> I remember she said to me "I hope he looks like his papa," and I won't lie she was right to hope it, because she was no beauty—and then she told me he was to be named Tom, for his father, and Marvolo, for her father and she said the boy's surname was to be Riddle. And she died soon after that without another word [Rowling, 2005, p. 266].

Likewise, Padme Amidala lives long enough to name her children and then she dies. Unlike Tom Riddle, Luke Skywalker is raised by a loving aunt and uncle; he still is not satisfied with his circumstances and, like Tom Riddle, feels he is destined for greatness. While Tom Riddle shows that he has powers and abilities that foreshadow the development of a great wizard, Luke Skywalker is strong in his abilities with "the Force" and achieves greatness in his powers as a Jedi.

Both Luke Skywalker and Tom Riddle are also destined to seek out their fathers. In Joseph Campbell's monomyth of the hero's journey, he explains the significance of the quest for the father:

> The finding of the father has to do with your own character and destiny. There's a notion that the character is inherited from the father, and the body and very often

the mind from the mother. But it's your character that is the mystery, and your character is your destiny. So it is the discovery of your destiny that is symbolized in the father quest [Campbell, 1988. p. 209].

Campbell's words are true for both Tom and Luke. Tom Riddle seeks out his father and kills him and his grandparents. Of course, in the process he also kills his matrilineal uncle. He seeks vengeance on those who abandoned him. Yet, in killing his father, he attempts to kill the muggle side of himself. He chooses his destiny of evil and rises to become a powerful Dark Wizard. Luke Skywalker also confronts his father and is faced with a life and death struggle in that confrontation. However, he does not kill his father, and instead brings out the remaining goodness in him, allowing him to look upon him as Anakin before he dies. Like Lord Voldemort, Luke Skywalker achieves greatness, but it is as a great and enlightened Jedi instead of an evil and powerful wizard. What is it in their development that makes them have different destinies? Both had evil in their genetics, but achieved different outcomes.

Tom Riddle's mother, abandoned by the love of her life while she was pregnant, arrived at an orphanage on New Year's Eve during a bitter cold snowstorm. She gave birth to Tom Riddle and died an hour later, not using magic to save herself (Rowling, 2005). Tom was raised in the orphanage with no contact from either parent's family, never knowing the father whose name he carried. Tom was abandoned by his father before he was born and by his mother an hour after his birth. He never knew the love, support, encouragement or wisdom of a parent. Unlike Harry, he did not experience the early consistent care of a loving parent or caregiver. While his basic needs were met by the orphanage staff, he did not have the opportunity to experience enough trust in his caregivers to develop an ego strength of hope. His experience seemed to develop more along the lines of Erickson's core pathology of withdrawal, or Bowlby's description of the detached infant who grows into a child who may superficially play or appear sociable, but who show little emotion and warmth. If detachment is used as a defense mechanism, a child may also experience difficulty in learning self-control and may exhibit cruel behavior and a preoccupation with violence (Granot, 2005). This describes Voldemort quite well. He does develop an attraction to objects, but these objects represent power, whether the belongings of the children in the orphanage or the objects that represent power and become the vessels that house the pieces of his soul. The ring and locket were objects from his family, but are representations not of the lost parent, but of the power that fills the void left by the death of his mother and abandonment of his father. Unlike Harry, he is unable to form close, trusting relationships with others. People are pawns in his plan, not sources of support, love, and friendship.

There is research to suggest that some young children who lose parents have a greater chance of developing mental health issues, addiction or criminal behaviors. Voldemort's behaviors as an adolescent and adult fit the description of psychopathy, which has a biological basis but can be mitigated by a loving, supportive environment. Tom Riddle had the biology of Marvolo and Morfin Gaunt and the environment of the orphanage. Even Harry has moments of sympathy for Riddle, upon learning that his mother did not fight to live for him and that Riddle cannot experience love. Love is what saved Harry, not only as an infant but many other times in the series. It is apparent that while both Harry and Riddle lost their mothers, the influence of their mothers and consequences of that loss were experienced in different ways. One tried to rule and destroy while the other used love and sacrifice to save and protect others. Riddle dismissed his mother as weak and unworthy while Harry embraced the memory and legacy of his mother. The two characters illustrate the experience of growth versus destruction.

Luna Lovegood

One of the most beloved motherless characters in the *Harry Potter* series is Luna Lovegood. Luna is the quirky and independent character who lost her mother, Pandora, and is raised by her doting father, Xenophilius Lovegood. Luna is teased by her classmates; even Hermione refers to her as "Loony Lovegood," but Luna remains unphased and seems to be quite comfortable being herself. Luna's character is reminiscent of the character Pippi Longstocking from Astrid Lindgren's beloved children's book, and Beauty from "Beauty and the Beast." In terms of Pippi Longstocking, Luna appears to be equally matched in terms of her quirkiness. In *OotP*, Harry encounters Luna for the first time, and his description of her sets the tone for how Luna is perceived:

> The girl gave off an aura of distinct dottiness. Perhaps it was the fact that she had stuck her wand behind her left ear for safekeeping or that she had chosen to wear a necklace of Butterbeer caps, or that she was holding a magazine upside down [p. 185].

Like Luna, Pippi comes to be associated with her quirky dress of striped stockings, unconventional clothing, and behavior that defies social norms. Unlike Luna, however, Pippi is left mostly to her own devices. She sometimes takes voyages with her sea captain father but mostly chooses to remain with her friends, Tommy and Annika. Luna, too, values her friendships, as is revealed in *DH* when Harry discovers the paintings of Harry, Ron, Hermione, and Neville upon her bedroom ceiling.

Yet, in spite of her love for her friends, Luna's relationship with her father mirrors that of Beauty and her unnamed father in "Beauty and the Beast." In that story, Beauty sacrifices herself by taking her father's place as Beast's prisoner as a penalty for picking a rose from his garden. However, Beauty's father is upset at the sacrifice, and his longing for beauty drives him to become deathly ill. The same scenario plays out in *Harry Potter*. Luna Lovegood is imprisoned in Malfoy Manor because her father has been writing articles against the Death Eaters and the Ministry. Luna is sacrificed for his deeds, just as Beauty is sacrificed. Xeniophilus is driven to near madness in his quest to rescue his Luna, betraying his beliefs and Harry, just as Beauty's father is driven to sickness. The underlying theme of this development is that being motherless makes one more vulnerable, for as is true with Harry, the mother is the ultimate protector. Luna's characteristic quirkiness and her attachment to her father, which can be compared to both Beauty and Pippi, are linked to losing her mother, leaving her with only a father to parent her. Xenoiphilius Lovegood emerges as a doting father.

Luna experiences the death of her mother at age 9. She has a distinctly different experience from Harry and Riddle in that she was raised by loving parents and is at a developmental stage in which she understands that death is final. She has had the opportunity to securely attach, develop trust, will, purpose and competence. She is immediately in the care of a loving, protective father. While she may have experienced greater personal care from her mother, she has emotional support from her father. Research suggests that a surviving parent lost in their own grief may unintentionally neglect a child's needs, leading to feelings of not only loss, but abandonment. It is important for children this age to be given a clear understanding of what happened to the parent who died. Luna tells Harry that her mother was a gifted witch who died when a new spell she was experimenting with went wrong. She tells him she was sad, but that we will see those we love again, as they are just "beyond the veil" (Rowling, 2003). One study of mourning in children said that children aged 9–11 could talk about the parent who died, but also may withdraw, become messy, and immerse themselves in school activities. They may retain an image of the parent as protector, teacher, and coach. They may also show a tendency to intellectualize grief (Christ, 2000). Luna seems to have accepted what happened to her mother and appreciate her father, who is willing to go to any lengths to save her from the Death Eaters, even betray Harry. She appears to be secure in herself, quirkiness and all, and accepts others as they are as well.

Neville Longbottom

Neville is another prominent character in the *Harry Potter* series who does not have a mother. Raised by his patrilineal grandmother, Neville is depicted throughout the early series as inept and not very talented. Neville even admits that his family was relieved to learn he was not a squib as they suspected. His grandmother does not have pride in him and constantly reminds him that he is inferior and unworthy of his auror parents. Neville initially presents as incompetent and forgetful, but has the strength and bravery of his parents when he stands up to Harry, Ron and Hermione in *SS*. When he learns Bellatrix has escaped from Azkaban, he works harder and makes more progress than any member of Dumbledore's Army.

He has to grieve the loss of his parents in a different way. Their continued life must have been confusing for him as a younger child—if they are alive, why aren't they taking care of me? He learns to internalize their bravery and, in the end, stands up to Voldemort. He accepts that we live, love, and experience loss, but we carry those we have lost in our hearts and grow stronger from them. Neville has a different experience from the other characters in that his parents are still alive but unable to care for him. He, like Harry and Luna, had the early love and care of his parents and the opportunity to develop secure attachment. Unlike Harry, he has someone, his grandmother, who is able to keep the memory of his parents alive as she constantly reminds him that he does not measure up to them. He is able to see them, but not interact in a long-term, meaningful way. His mother obviously has some memory of her connection to him, as she gives him candy wrappers as an object when he visits her. Neville keeps the candy wrapper his mother gives him, an object that represents their connection to one another.

Neville's situation is similar to the character Paikea in the book *Whale Rider* (2002). Paikea's mother and her twin brother do not survive childbirth, disappointing Pai's grandfather Koro, who is chief of the Maori people and wants a male heir. Pai's grandfather and grandmother raise her, and Pai is constantly on a quest to please her grandfather and convince him to allow her to learn the cultural ways of the Maori people, despite her being a female. Like Pai, Neville constantly tries to prove himself to his grandmother, who does not deem him worthy of the Longbottom name. However, in the end, both Pai and Neville triumph. Pai becomes the leader of her people and Neville's bravery instills Augusta Longbottom with pride for her grandson. He finds his place in his family and in the wizard community, killing the basilisk during the Battle of Hogwarts and even becoming a professor at Hogwarts later in life.

Credence Barebone

J.K. Rowling's most recent foray into the world of orphans is found in *Fantastic Beasts and Where to Find Them*. In this work, Mary Lou Barebone, the crusader against the hidden world of witches, is reminiscent of Charles Dickens' portrayal of Victorian-era workhouses in *Oliver Twist*. Instead of auctioning the children off to various means of employment, Mary Lou Barebone adopts them to do her bidding in her quest against witchcraft in the city, but the neglect and abuse found in the Dickensian world of orphans and in the Second Salem Church of Mary Lou Barebone bear stark similarities. During one scene in the Second Salem Church, children crowd around Chastity and Mary Lou Barebone, with empty bowls outstretched in hopes of receiving a thin-looking soup. Mary Lou Barebone's adopted children are all mistreated, but as Tina Goldstein explains to Newt, "His mother beats him. She beats all of those kids she adopted, but she seems to hate him the most" (Rowling, 2016, p. 192). It seems that Mary Lou Barebone may have suspected that Credence was harboring some magical ability because when she mistakenly believes that Chastity toy wand is his, she says, "I am not your ma! You're ma was a wicked unnatural woman! (Rowling, 2016, p. 204). As a result of this abuse and his desire to contain his magical abilities, Credence develops an obscurus, which is defined by Newt Scamander as a "dangerous parasitic force" (p. 160). Credence's desire to be loved by anyone leads him to befriend the wrong person in the form of Mr. Graves, a.k.a. Gellert Grindewald, and his ultimate betrayal unleashes the violent force of the Obscurus. Credence's repression of the trauma he has experienced is reminiscent of those suffering from Post Traumatic Stress Disorder. According to a study of repression, "Nevertheless, consistent with the original concept of repression, it has been suggested that the psychopathology involved with PTSD is likely related to physiologic processes to some degree inaccessible through normal cognitive processes" (Boscarino & Figley, 2009). According to the study, repression may have some protective qualities, but may also result in psychological distress. Credence most certainly experiences psychological distress in trying to obtain acceptance and love and in his experiences of rejection and abuse.

Readers do not have enough information about Credence to ascertain at what stage in his development he was adopted by Mary Lou Barebone. Based upon his desire for acceptance and love, one can determine that he is without the support systems present in the lives of the previously discussed characters. In fact, Credence still seeks out acceptance from Mary Lou and does not run away from his abusive situation in spite of his trauma. Sullivan and Lasley (2010) examined the brain development of rats to determine the connection between neuroprocess and attachment:

> But when the parent and the nest are themselves sources of danger, the suppression of fear circuits in the amygdala unfortunately still works. The fear, avoidance, and even memories associated with pain are extinguished—explaining why an abused child, even while trying to escape pain, will later seek contact with the abuser [Sullivan and Lasley].

Because he does not attempt to escape and tries to repress his feelings of rage and depression, he becomes an Obscurial. Credence does not appear to know how to grieve for himself or for his missing parents. In "What Harry and Fawkes Have in Common" (2006), Misty Hook examines Harry's resilience and his ability to develop secure attachments as providing him with the ability to overcome his trauma in a positive manner; whereas, Voldemort does not. Hook notes:

> Characteristics of people who are insecurely attached include: an inability to develop and maintain friendships; alienation from and opposition to parents, caregivers, and other authority figures; anti-social attitudes and behaviors, aggression and violence; difficulty with genuine trust, intimacy, and affection; a lack of empathy, compassion, and remorse [p. 101].

Credence the Obscurial, like Lord Voldemort exhibits these characteristics, while Credence sans Obscurial does not. He lashes out with violence when he is upset, damaging property, killing Senator Shaw and Mary Lou Barebone. Ultimately, he, like Voldemort, is destroyed as the result of his power. Yet Credence, unlike Voldemort, did not intentionally set out to obtain power or revenge. He was simply unable to control the dark forces that welled up as the result of repression.

The love, trust, and secure attachment Harry, Luna and Neville experience with their mothers shape the courageous, good people they become. The emphasis placed upon resilience and the significance of developing secure relationships is embodied in these three characters. They truly carry their lost mothers in their hearts and grow stronger from them in a way Lord Voldemort and Credence cannot. The missing mothers of the Wizarding World are key in both plot development and in the emotional/social/cognitive development of the characters. By examining the impact of their absence, one can understand why Rowling would embrace such a commonly used trope and make it her own.

References

Boscarino, J.A., & Figley, C.R. (2009). "The Impact of Repression, Hostility, and Post-Traumatic Stress Disorder on All-Cause Mortality: A Prospective 16-Year Follow-Up Study." *The Journal of Nervous and Mental Disease, 197*(6), 461–466. http://doi.org/10.1097/NMD.0b013e3181a61f3e.
Boxer, S. (2014) Why Are All the Cartoon Mothers Dead?" *The Atlantic.* Retrieved from https://www.theatlantic.com/magazine/archive/2014/07/why-are-all-the-cartoon-mothers-dead/372270/.
Campbell, J. (1988). *The Power of Myth.* New York: Anchor Books.
Christ, G.H. (2000). "Impact of Development on Children's Mourning." *Cancer Practice,* 8(2), 72–81.
Dickens, C. (2002) *Oliver Twist.* New York: Penguin.
Feist J., & Feist, G. (2009) *Theories of Personality.* New York: McGraw-Hill.
Granot, T. (2005). *Without You: Children and Young People Growing Up with Loss and Its Effects.* London: Jessica Kingsley Press.

Grimm, Jacob W., & Grimm, Wilhelm K. (ND). *Grimm's Complete Fairy Tales*. Garden City, NY: International Collectors Library.

Hill, M. (2006). "What Harry and Fawkes Have in Common." N. Mullholland. (Ed). *The Psychology of Harry Potter*. (pp. 91–104). Dallas, TX: BenBella Books.

Ihimaera, W. (2003). *The Whale Rider*. New York: Harcourt.

Lin, M. (2010). "Fitting the Glass Slipper: A Comparative Study of the Princess's Role in the Harry Potter Novels and Films (2001–2005)." P. Greenhill & S. Matrix (Eds). *Fairy Tale Films: Visions of Ambiguity*. (pp. 79–98). Logan, UT: Utah State University Press.

Lindgren, A. (1978). *Pippi Longstocking*. New York: Viking Press.

Moore, L. (2016). "Why Do We Write About Orphans So Much?" *Literary Hub*. Retrieved from http://lithub.com/why-do-we-write-about-orphans-so-much/.

Mullan, J. (2014). "Orphans in Fiction." *British Library*. Retrieved from https://www.bl.uk/romantics-and-victorians/articles/orphans-in-fiction#authorBlock1.

Otowa, T., York, T., Gardner, C., Kendler, K., & Hettema, J. (2014). "The Impact of Childhood Parental Loss on Risk for Mood, Anxiety and Substance Use Disorders in a Population-Based Sample of Male Twins." *Psychiatry Research*, 220(1–2), 404–409. doi:10.1016/j.psychres.2014.07.053.

Rowling, J.K. (2016) *Fantastic Beasts and Where to Find Them: The Original Screenplay*. New York: Arthur A. Levine.

Rowling, J.K. (1999). *Harry Potter and the Chamber of Secrets*. New York: Scholastic.

Rowling, J.K. (2007). *Harry Potter and the Deathly Hallows*. New York: Scholastic.

Rowling, J.K. (2005). *Harry Potter and the Half Blood Prince*. New York: Scholastic.

Rowling, J.K. (2003). *Harry Potter and the Order of the Phoenix*. New York: Scholastic.

Rowling, J.K. (1998). *Harry Potter and the Sorcerer's Stone*. New York: Scholastic.

Rowling, J.K. (2014) "Isn't It Time We Left Orphanages to Fairytales?" *The Guardian*. Retrieved from https://contribute.theguardian.com.

Sullivan, R., & Lasley, E.N. (2010). "Fear in Love: Attachment, Abuse, and the Developing Brain." *Cerebrum: The Dana Forum on Brain Science*, 2010, 17.

"Beyond the veil"
The Narrative Functions of Death
Samantha J. Vertosick

The death of a friend or family member is an extremely difficult time for an adult, let alone a child or teen that may be experiencing death for the first time. "Children are old enough to grieve if they are old enough to love" and so they are sometimes the "forgotten grievers" when tragedy strikes (Kübler-Ross & Kessler, 2005). Adults often struggle when forced to explain death and loss to a young person, and to someone young, conceptualizing the thought of someone or something ceasing to exist is terrifying in its uncertainty. There still seems to be a lack of interest and a level of mistrust concerning the capacity of literature to provide socially relevant information about death (Teodorescu, 2015). "Until recently, children's books did not address sensitive topics such as death, divorce and bullying, and in the past few decades there have been more books published dealing with non-traditional issues" (Lowe, 2009). Primary educator Danielle F. Lowe claims that, "Real life does indeed call for real books: books that provide information, comfort, and models for coping with life's difficult times" (2009). There many books for children and young adults that deal with death as a part of the plot, but very few books for young people contain as much character death as found within the realm of J.K. Rowling's hugely popular *Harry Potter* series.

Although the thought of so much death in a work of young adult literature may seem to be too much for a young reader, the actual result is meant to be comforting and equips children and teens with the tools to discover what death is to them and what death means to those left living. Through the many major character deaths in the *Harry Potter* series, both Harry Potter and the reader learn about what it means to live and die through the complex narrative function of death. As opposed to the usual ambiguous answers that adults provide children, this narrative function affords young people the opportunity to develop themselves and come to terms with various forms of death on their own and within the safety of the novel. Bruno Bettelheim writes, "The fairytale is the primer from which the child learns to read his mind ... and must learn to be responsive to it, if he is to become master of his soul" and this is true in the *Harry Potter* universe as well (1976).

Outi Hakola and Sari Kivistö in *Death in Literature* highlight what the presence of death may do in a work of fiction. They explain that people "need to encounter the death experience" with the help of fiction to imagine "how it will feel," and "what we seek in fiction is the knowledge of death that is denied to us in the real life" (2014). No one is denied this knowledge of death more than a child typically is. As a narrative event, death both affects characters and leads the story in some direction (Hakola & Kivistö, 2014). When death occurs in a work of fiction, it then not only affects characters and the story, but also provides the reader a personal encounter with death. This encounter then enables the young reader to not only imagine how death will feel, or to gain an idea of what death may entail, but to also have a taste of the various feelings and responses death brings to the survivors who are left to grieve, react, and recover. In the case of the *Harry Potter* series, it is then what the young reader chooses to psychologically do regarding their interaction with literary death that will determine the functionality and effectiveness of the selected novels.

Martha C. Nussbaum's *Cultivating Humanity: A Classical Defense of Reform in Liberal Education* etches out the beginnings of what Danielle F. Lowe would later refer to as "bibliotherapy" or therapeutic reading. The imagined young reader of Rowling's novels, when encountering death in each book, is participating in therapeutic reading even if they are unaware of it at the time. Nussbaum writes, "When a child and a parent begin to tell stories together, the child is acquiring essential moral capacities ... they learn to attribute life, emotion, and thought to a form whose insides are hidden. These stories interact with their own attempts to explain the world and their own actions in it" (2012). While Nussbaum mostly frames her text for her own argument, the argument that reading could create better future leaders through empathy, she uses the tragedy to frame her argument and its impact on young adults. Nussbaum states, "Tragedies acquaint the young citizen with the bad things that may happen in a human life, long before life itself does so" (2012). Rowling's novels are not the tragedies Nussbaum had in mind at the time, but they do include protagonists who must deal with tragic situations very early on in life, which is where therapeutic reading plays a larger role in interpretation.

Both Danielle F. Lowe and Bruno Bettelheim advocate for the reading of what some may consider "difficult" or "dark" material in order to help children either cope with a loss or to prepare for inevitable loss. Bettelheim has noticed that many "fairy stories" begin with the death of a mother or father and "in these tales the death of the parent creates the most agonizing problems, as it (or the fear of it) does in real life" (1976). *Harry Potter*, of course, features the title character whose parents were murdered during his infancy. Although death has touched Harry's life early on and will continue to do so throughout the series, he must also face true evil, and possibly his own death. Bettelheim believes that in the fairy story, once the hero has overcome their challenge, they can "dissipate the fear of death," which *Harry Potter* strives to do within the realms of its own narrative (1976).

There are countless examples in the *Harry Potter* series where families are torn apart by death, much like reality. The first set of characters who perish in the series are Harry's parents, Lily and James Potter. Maria Nikolajeva, in "Harry Potter and the Secrets of Children's Literature," explains, "The removal of parents is the premise of children's literature" and it is the premise of this series as well (2009). This lack of parental authority "allows the space that the fictive child needs for development and maturity," which Harry will do plenty of (Nikolajeva, 2009). Harry's young parents are killed by Lord Voldemort while he is just a baby, as a result of their support for The Order of the Phoenix during the First Wizarding War, which pitted the Order against Voldemort and his loyal Death Eaters. In the *Harry Potter* series, there are two great Wizarding Wars, both of which involves the Order of the Phoenix battling against Lord Voldemort and his Death Eaters.

One could expect only malevolent deeds to come from a character named Voldemort—his name literally translating to "flight of death" in French and the stem word "Morte" meaning "death" in Latin. Voldemort's primary goals were to use magic against muggles (non-magical humans), to become immortal, and to master the Dark Arts. Voldemort's hatred for muggles, his hunger for power, admiration for "pure-blooded" wizards, and his organization of loyal "followers" begins to construct him as a fascist figure at war, which would therein make Harry's parents casualties of war. If Harry's parents are casualties of war, then Harry is an orphan of war at a very early age. Harry is reminded of his parents' sacrifice by the lightning shaped scar on his forehead, and he longs to be reunited with his parents throughout the entire series. His is a longing so strong, that he clings to any bit of new information about his parents that he receives. As readers know, Harry will come face to face with Voldemort, but it is not this confrontation with him that acts as consolation. Harry will lose many more friends, family, and even his childhood pet to Voldemort and his followers before he finds peace, or begins to properly grieve—taking the reader along for the ride.

The series frequently utilizes death to depict to the reader "symbolic journeys into separation from the parent" or parental figures to become an independent, mature self (Kokorski, 2015). While the death of Harry's parents serve to display the horrors of war upon the family, there are many more casualties in the Second Wizarding War that affect both Harry and the reader deeply. These casualties are of characters the reader has grown attached to over the course of seven lengthy novels and have even acted as pseudo-parental figures for Harry, depicting that continuous journey to master one's self.

One specific scene from *Harry Potter and the Deathly Hallows* and described by Rowling, is a scene played out all too often on television and from news sources online. She writes, "The survivors stood in groups, their arms around each other's necks.... The dead lay in a row in the middle of the Hall"—a scene reminiscent of survivors banding together while a news camera pans over a row of sometimes covered bodies after a large-scale tragedy (Rowling, 2009). It is in this moment that Harry learns his father's friend and his own teacher, Remus Lupin, has died. In addition, Lupin's wife, Nymphadora Tonks, is also killed in the battle. When Harry sees their bodies lying side-by-side Rowling writes, "He yearned not to feel.... He wished he could rip out his heart, his innards, everything that was screaming inside him" (Rowling, 2009). Harry's intense reaction is not only due to the fact he has lost two good friends and mentors, but because they left behind a baby boy—a case of Harry's own history literally repeating itself. This act of history repeating itself gives off a feeling of failure; that Harry could fight Voldemort as much as he wanted, but never actually stop him or that he was responsible for all of this suffering by being "The Chosen One." Lupin and Tonks' deaths not only remind the reader of Harry's dark and tragic history, but also shows that death does not discriminate. Although "Lupin, Tonks, and many others die a violent death in the Battle of Hogwarts, Rowling depicts their dead bodies as 'peaceful-looking, apparently asleep' and thus follows the custom of soothing the reader's prospective pain," by showing a form of peace in death (Kokorski, 2015). The image of a peaceful sleep may lessen the sting of death, but it does not completely soften its impact, especially to Harry, who feels responsible.

Rowling writes the death of Fred Weasley in a way that seems as though she is trying to lessen the immediate shock for Harry and the reader as well. Fred, who perishes during the Battle of Hogwarts, is said to have "the ghost of his last laugh" on his face, which once again reflects the idea of the body being at peace (Rowling, 2009). Although Fred's body is not asleep, as Tonks and Lupin appear, he is in death, doing what he loved to do in life—laughing. When Fred dies during the Battle of Hogwarts, there is too much going on to properly grieve him. Harry must feel the agony of losing someone who was practically family throughout a large portion of his life, and the pain is doubled when the reader thinks of Fred's twin, George, who is left behind.

Popular culture presents the audience with stories of twins sharing a special and close bond, but this bond has been broken by death. Understandably, Percy Weasley is frantic at Fred's demise, and it is during this moment that Harry is mimicking the words of Lupin when Sirius Black died. Harry tells Percy that there is nothing that can be done and that they must continue forward. He does pause, however, to help ensure Fred's body is hidden away in a safe place before the group presses on. Fred's body is hidden in an alcove where a suit of armor had been, ensuring that his body is safe and will be damaged no further.

The death of Severus Snape, however, is violent and he does not achieve the same tranquility Fred, Lupin, and Tonks do in death. Serving as a type of "double agent" throughout the entire series, Snape dies at the hands of Lord Voldemort and his snake, Nagini. Throughout the *Harry Potter* fandom, Snape's character is the source of much debate; some argue that he was heroic in his actions, while others condemn his lifelong infatuation with Harry's mother Lily Evans and his poor treatment of Harry. In 2015, Rowling herself shed light on the subject via Twitter. She wrote, "You can't make [Snape] a saint: he was vindictive & bullying. You can't make him a devil: he died to save the wizarding world" and in honoring Snape by naming a son after him, Harry "hoped in his heart that he too would be forgiven. The deaths at the Battle of Hogwarts would haunt Harry forever" (jk_rowling, 2015). Although there may be debates in the fandom about Snape, his intentions, and his status as "hero," Rowling views Snape as walking the line between good and evil, but ultimately providing another way for Harry to both grieve and atone for the grief of others, which he perceives as his fault. While Snape gives Harry the power to both forgive others and begin to forgive himself, there are plenty of other lessons the remaining deaths of the series teach Harry and the reader, especially when it comes to the mass casualties of the Second Wizarding War.

Large-scale tragedies tend to be different in origin, whether it be from war, or a natural disaster, among other reasons, but they are similar in that they "cause large numbers of deaths and injuries and wide paths of destruction in a community" (Kübler-Ross & Kessler, 2005). So while it is easy to root for one's own country in a war, narrative death instructs that war is not so simple. On either side, there are innocent adults and children suffering for the acts of others, as illustrated through the deaths of Harry Potter's parents, Fred, Lupin, and Tonks, among the many other casualties of the Wizarding Wars.

Even Harry's beloved pet owl, Hedwig, cannot escape the horrors of war and is struck dead in an aerial battle. Hedwig had been Harry's cherished pet since he began school at Hogwarts, and so her death furthers this point of war affecting the innocent of both sides. Hedwig's death also teaches a young reader that no amount of magic can save a childhood pet—they too will die, although probably not as violently as Hedwig. The reader, however, does get to see that life goes on after the death of a pet. It may seem like a terrible thing, but Harry and the reader must press on.

Hedwig's tragedy is not the only death of a magical creature to illicit strong audience sympathy though. Although the status of "creature" does not exactly fit, Dobby is most definitely a wandless, magical being. Peter Dendle, in "Monsters, Creatures, and Pets at Hogwarts," speaks on the status of house elves in the wizarding world. He acknowledges that Harry treats house elves kindly, but people such as Sirius did not because he never saw elves as having feelings close to a human's. Dendle also highlights the irrefutable parallel of the treatment of house elves to historical slavery, further illustrating that house elves are just as sentient as human beings in this world, even if they have been treated as lesser. Maria Nikolajeva brings up a compelling argument though, in that the only free elf dies and Kreacher, inherited from Sirius, still does work in the large Potter household; "there is, in other words, no indication of equal rights" (2009). Regardless of one's opinions on the status of house elves, it is undeniable that Dobby's death in final book greatly disturbed both Harry and readers alike. From his humble beginnings, readers were with Harry as he freed Dobby from the Malfoys and watched him grow into his own identity. Although Dobby sometimes treated Harry as a savior, it was clear that Harry saw Dobby as a friend, which made his death all the more tragic to both Harry and the reader.

When Harry is faced with Dobby's body, the audience sees Harry think back to his experience with Dumbledore, since he had to face the body of a deceased person then. From his experience with Dumbledore, Harry learned that funerals are customary and provide closure, and so it is important to him that he buries Dobby. While Dobby's funeral is not as grand as Dumbledore's, it provides Harry, Ron, Hermione, Luna, and Dean with closure. Harry's ability to give Dobby a headstone, stating he died a free elf, is also Harry's way of making sure Dobby's efforts to be free were not in vain. Perhaps, Dobby's self-sacrifice is what also sets an example in Harry's mind when he is willing to die at the hands of Voldemort at the end of the series; a sacrifice that is made for both Harry's living friends and those that have died before him, such as Colin Creevey and Cedric Diggory.

Both Hogwarts students Colin Creevey and Cedric Diggory fall victim to Voldemort in the *Harry Potter* series, not only to show the impact of a fellow student's death, but to also further illustrate Voldemort's willingness to kill anyone for his cause. While Colin Creevey dies at the Battle of Hogwarts, Cedric Diggory is killed by Voldemort earlier on in *Harry Potter and the Goblet of Fire* during the Triwizard Tournament. Despite there being many casualties in *Harry Potter and the Deathly Hallows*, Cedric Diggory's death provokes one of those most intense reactions from both Harry and those at

Hogwarts because it occurs at a time when death is less familiar. Cedric's death also "draws attention to Voldemort's inhumane and murderous behavior, and therefore the very serious threat he poses to the wizarding society" (Kokorski, 2015).

Cedric is just sixteen years old when he dies at the Triwizard Tournament in front of fourteen-year-old Harry Potter. Rowling describes the scene: "For a second that contained an eternity, Harry stared into Cedric's face, at his open gray eyes, blank and expressionless as the windows of a deserted house, at his half-open mouth, which looked slightly surprised" (Rowling, 2002). Modernity not only "'denies' death … but it also isolates it from 'polite society,' not showing it 'before the children'" (Douglas, 2015). Harry and the reader encounter Cedric's death in a way that is atypical today, by seeing him die and then by having to face the deceased body afterwards. It is a method that rejects today's treatment of death—one that "is deeply embedded in a consumer-based culture of longevity" that replaces real images of death with "versions of material immortality" (Douglas, 2015). To summarize, Rowling forces the readers and Harry to see death for what it truly is. In a reaction true to life, Harry is further said to have a hard time accepting what he is seeing due to his mind being clouded with numb disbelief.

What is so unusual about Cedric's death is that, like Sirius Black's, Harry is able to see Cedric again and interact with him. When Harry and Voldemort's wands are fused in a fight shortly after Cedric's death, the ghostly figures of those Voldemort's wand killed are ejected from it and are able to speak with Harry. It is unclear what these figures are, but seeing as ghosts do exist in Harry's world, this is a possibility. Cedric's apparition is at least sentient enough to request that Harry take his body back to his parents. Naturally, Harry fulfills this request, but at the cost of his own mental stability, since as mentioned before, today's people are not used to such interaction with the dead anymore as a result of shifting cultural norms.

When Harry reappears at the school with Cedric's body, he is in so much shock that he has to be physically pried from Cedric. Dumbledore understands Harry's shock and tries to reason with him, by insisting that there is nothing Harry can do now and that he must let Cedric go. It is here that Dumbledore acts as a support to Harry in these trying moments, and he also serves as the reader's voice of reason. The next scenes are chaotic and any verbalized comments are only presented in snippets. Harry's surroundings are described in blurs and as being fuzzy, but he can hear screams and exclamations over Cedric's death. This is true shock and Harry's first direct interaction with the death of a friend. While he was technically present for his parents' deaths, this is the first murder Harry sees up close and it is that of a friend who should not have died so young.

Harry's shock is clearly troublesome and understandably so. The full extent of the damage is seen when Mrs. Weasley tries to give Harry his winnings from the tournament and he refuses the prize, since he believes it should have been Cedric's. When thoughts of Cedric are brought back to the surface by the mention of this prize money, Harry finds himself emotionally overwhelmed again. It is in this moment that Harry calls for more of the potion he has been kept on to heal his body and mind—a potion that induces dreamless sleep. The sensation is described as not only a dreamless sleep, but as ceasing all thought completely. Harry's grief is so overwhelming, it could be described as a death itself, or a glimpse of depression and shock.

By the time there is a memorial service at Hogwarts for Cedric, Harry is able to be present to hear Dumbledore's speech—one of the most moving speeches in the entire series and a speech that embodies the spirit of this essay. Dumbledore begins by telling Hogwarts students that the Ministry of Magic and many parents do not wish for them to hear the truth due to their young age or because they do not believe Voldemort has returned. In his speech, Dumbledore adds, "…the truth is generally preferable to lies, and that any attempt to pretend that Cedric died as the result of an accident, or some sort of blunder of his own, is an insult to his memory" (Rowling, 2002).

The beginning of Dumbledore's speech speaks to the issue of adults imposing upon children what they think is appropriate. Just as Bettelheim writes, "Many parents believe that only conscious reality or pleasant and wish-fulfilling images should be presented to the child—that he should be exposed only to the sunny side of things. Such one-sided fare nourishes the mind only in a one-sided way, and real life is not all sunny" (1976). Dumbledore is aware that the Ministry and parents will want to shield children from this tough subject matter, but this is not true to actual life. Even today, there are plenty of real "Ministry of Magic" type institutions and parents that challenge or ban books and try to shield children from the truth if it isn't positive, which Rowling attempts to combat through her books and Dumbledore's own criticism of such institutions.

Dumbledore continues, "…in the light of Lord Voldemort's return, we are only as strong as we are united, weak as we are divided" (Rowling, 2002). It is here that the reader is reminded that this is a world at war where innocent, young lives will be lost, which is only too familiar today. To drive the point home, Dumbledore concludes by saying that should the time come, "…when you have to make a choice between what is right and what is easy, remember what happened to a boy who was good, and kind, and brave, because he strayed across the path of Lord Voldemort" (Rowling, 2002).

While Harry was greatly affected by Cedric Diggory's death, it is the deaths of his godfather Sirius Black and headmaster Albus Dumbledore that draw out strong, personal emotions. In *Harry Potter and the Order of the Phoenix*, the reader learns of "The Veil," which separates the living world from the dead and cannot be traveled freely. While there has been a definite "decline in adherence to orthodox religion," the decline "does not detract from the beliefs and experiences of people who believe in life after death" (Howarth, 2007). It is in this way that The Veil in *Harry Potter* acts as a comfort to both Harry and the reader. Despite varying religious backgrounds and beliefs, The Veil provides a neutral view what life after death may look like.

During a fight with Voldemort's Death Eaters, Harry and his friends witness Sirius Black get hit with a curse from his own cousin, Bellatrix Lestrange, and pushed into The Veil. Harry's reaction is much like his reaction to Cedric's death—full of panic and denial. In this moment, Harry panics and assumes he can simply pull Sirius back out, but it takes Lupin to bring Harry back to reality. Lupin echoes Dumbledore during Cedric's death when he tells Harry that there is nothing he can do and that Sirius is gone. Harry still wishes to deny Sirius is dead, but as he slowly comes to realize that Sirius never kept him waiting, meaning he was gone, he immediately turns to anger—a rational response, especially when considering that the second stage of the Kübler-Ross grief model is anger. When Sirius dies, Harry is a year older than he was when Cedric died. His response to his godfather's death may be similar, but it has matured in that there is less shock and denial.

In the next book, *HBP*, Harry has mentally matured a little more, but will mourn Dumbledore in much the same way he did Sirius, as they were both authority or parental figures in his life. His thoughts are more melancholic though, and can be seen when Fawkes, Dumbledore's phoenix, leaves the school. Harry, somehow, knows that Fawkes had left for good "just as Dumbledore had left the school, left the world ... had left Harry" (Rowling, 2005). As mentioned, it is with Dumbledore's death that the reader sees what normal grieving looks like, or more mature grieving. Perhaps because Dumbledore was old, and it is natural for the old to die, Harry is finally able to better prepare himself and reflect on his own thoughts.

Before Dumbledore's funeral, Harry inwardly admits he had never attended a funeral because there was no body to bury with Sirius' death. Due to this, he has no idea what to expect and expresses anxiety at how he would feel about the funeral. Rowling writes that Harry "wondered whether Dumbledore's death would be more real to him once the funeral was over" (2005). Despite this internal contemplation, Harry also acknowledges that he had not desperately looked for a way that Dumbledore may have survived or would come back. It is in this private admission that the reader sees how Harry has matured in his grief. He is more realistic in his expectations, just as the reader will one day have to be as well.

A child who experiences the death of a loved one loses his or her innocence quickly by learning life doesn't hold guarantees, which makes them feel as though they cannot count on anything (Kübler-Ross & Kessler, 2005).

With Dumbledore's death, or the loss of his "last and greatest protector," Harry matures and he sheds "the illusion he ought to have lost at the age of one, that the shelter of a parent's arms meant that nothing could hurt him" (Rowling, 2005). While Dumbledore's death is tragic, it "leaves Harry unprotected, vulnerable, but matured and able to make his own decisions and live with the consequences" (Kokorski, 2015). Dumbledore's death prepares Harry for the eventual loss of his many loved ones during the events of *Harry Potter and the Deathly Hallows*. Also worth noting is that Dumbledore is the one who guides Harry in his fight against Voldemort when he is stuck in between life and death and "only through the acceptance of his own death is Harry able to overpower Voldemort, a character who is obsessed with death" (Kokorski, 2015).

As readers know, Voldemort's obsession with death is so serious that he split his soul seven times, six intentionally, in an attempt to cheat death. As "The Tale of the Three Brothers" instructs, death cannot be cheated, only welcomed, for it is inevitable, which is exactly what Harry does. Towards the end of *DH*, when Voldemort has "killed" Harry, he is transported to a version of King's Cross Station where he is able to speak to Dumbledore. During his time with Dumbledore, it is confirmed that the events are playing out in Harry's mind, although not making it any less "real." While the reader is unsure if the events actually happen or not, it is confirmed that Harry is able to master death this time because he was willing to die. His self-sacrifice, despite having all three Deathly Hallows, enables Harry to beat Voldemort's killing curse. It appears as though, when Voldemort strikes Harry with the curse, he only serves in weakening the fragment of his own soul that lives inside Harry. This is confirmed in the flayed, small, and shivering child that is seen in Harry's vision. "Rowling's message is clear: only souls which are unmarred by evildoing are able to continue their existence in the afterlife, while the ripped and burdened souls die … which is a punishment worse than death" (Stojilkov, 2015). So by accepting death, as Karin Kokorski stated in her chapter titled "Death Is But the Next Great Adventure: Representations of Death and the Afterlife in Fantastic Literature for Children and Young Adults," Harry is able to overpower Voldemort, who fears it (2015).

Although the common thought is that ridding the Wizarding World of Voldemort will bring peace, the actual events only cause more death—the deaths of Lupin, Tonks, Fred, Colin Creevy, and over fifty others, to be exact. It is the aftereffects of the great battle that are truly therapeutic for Harry and his close friends. In the epilogue, we are shown the trio as adults with their own families and jobs, sending their children to Hogwarts. Some may criticize the ending as being too close to that of a generic fairy tale ending, and Rowling has even seemed apprehensive about her choices now as well, but it shows that what truly quells grief is moving on. It is as Neil Gaiman says in the epigraph of *Coraline*, "Fairy tales are more than true—not because they tell us dragons exist, but because they tell us dragons can be beaten" (Gaiman 2002).

This essay has merely skimmed the surface of the functionality of character death for both Harry and the reader in the *Harry Potter* series, mainly due to the fact that there is simply so much of it to be found within the texts and so much to be said about death itself. All of the deaths in Rowling's books are unique in their meanings, but each is comforting in its own way that real life is often unable to fulfill and affords the reader a chance to cognitively process death. Interacting with death is relieving to both young and old readers who now live in a society where talking about death is taboo (Anthony, 1972). The amount of character death in Rowling's series can be upsetting to both characters and readers, but both eventually find relief, too—relief that those who die will not be lost, and that there is hope beyond earthly life, perhaps beyond The Veil, or that forgiveness can be found in the future; that one can atone after living. Both Harry and the reader learn that it is within the living that the spirit of the dead continue to live, as seen in both Harry's scene with Dumbledore at King's Cross and in the epilogue, with the names of Harry and Ginny's children: Albus Severus, James Sirius, and Lily Luna Potter. The children's names act as living memorials to the deceased and are proof that good came out of the Second Wizarding War; showing that good can indeed come from real wars as well—that tragedy, no matter how terrible, is not truly the end.

References

Anthony, Sylvia (1972). *The Discovery of Death in Childhood and After.* New York: Basic Books.
Bettelheim, Bruno. (1976) *The Uses of Enchantment: The Meaning and Importance of Fairy Tales.* New York: Knopf.
Dendle, Peter. (2009). "Monsters, Creatures, and Pets at Hogwarts." Animal Stewardship in the World of Harry Potter. In E. Heilman (Ed.), *Critical Perspectives on Harry Potter.* Abingdon-on-Thames: Routledge.
Douglas, Cristina. (2015). "Understanding Death During Childhood: Cultural and Psychological Dimensions." In A. Teodorescu (Ed.), *Death Representations in Literature: Forms and Theories.* Newcastle upon Tyne, UK: Cambridge Scholars Publishing.
Gaiman, Neil. (2002). *Coraline.* New York City: Scholastic.
Hakola, Outi, and Sari Kivistö (Eds.). (2014). *Death in Literature.* Newcastle upon Tyne, UK: Cambridge Scholars Publishing.
Howarth, Glennys. (2007). *Death & Dying: A Sociological Introduction.* Cambridge: Polity Press, 2007.
jk_rowling. (2015, November 27). Snape is all grey. You can't make him a saint: he was vindictive & bullying. You can't make him a devil: he died to save the wizarding world. [Tweet]. https://twitter.com/jk_rowling/status/670176159561326592?lang=en.
jk_rowling. (2015, November 27). In honouring Snape, Harry hoped in his heart that he too would be forgiven. The deaths at the Battle of Hogwarts would haunt Harry forever. [Tweet]. https://twitter.com/jk_rowling/status/670178875406729216?lang=en.
Kokorski, Karin. (2015). "Death Is But the Next Great Adventure: Representations of Death and the Afterlife in Fantastic Literature for Children and Young Adults." In Adriana

Teodorescu (Ed.), *Death Representations in Literature: Forms and Theories*. Newcastle Upon Tyne, UK: Cambridge Scholars Publishing.
Kübler-Ross, Elizabeth, and David Kessler. (2005). *On Grief and Grieving: Finding the Meaning of Grief Through the Five Stages of Loss*. New York: Scribner.
Lowe, Danielle F. (2009). "Helping Children Cope through Literature." *The Forum of Public Policy*, 2009 (1), 1–17.
Nikolajeva, Maria. (2009). Harry Potter and the Secrets of Children's Literature. In E. Heilman (Ed.), *Critical Perspectives on Harry Potter*. Abingdon-on-Thames: Routledge.
Nussbaum, Martha C. (2012) From *Cultivating Humanity: A Classical Defense of Reform in Liberal Education*. In Vincent B. Leitch (Ed.), *The Norton Anthology of Theory and Criticism*. New York City: W.W. Norton & Company.
Rowling, J.K. (2009). *Harry Potter and the Deathly Hallows*. New York: Scholastic.
Rowling, J.K. (2002). *Harry Potter and the Goblet of Fire*. New York: Scholastic.
Rowling, J.K. (2005). *Harry Potter and the Half-Blood Prince*. New York: Scholastic.
Rowling, J.K. (2003). *Harry Potter and the Order of the Phoenix*. New York: Scholastic.
Rowling, J.K. (1999). *Harry Potter and the Sorcerer's Stone*. New York: Scholastic.
Stojilkov, A. (2015). "Life (and) Death in *Harry Potter*: The Immortality of Love and Soul." *Mosaic: A Journal for the Interdisciplinary Study of Literature* 48(2), 133–148. Retrieved September 12, 2017, from Project MUSE database.
Teodorescu, Adriana (Ed.). (2015). *Death Representations in Literature: Forms and Theories*. Newcastle Upon Tyne, UK: Cambridge Scholars Publishing.

"I don't think you're a waste of space"
Activity, Redemption and the Social Construction of Fatness

TOLONDA HENDERSON

When we encounter Dudley Dursley in *DH*, he is a very different person than the one we knew in *SS*. Far from bullying Harry at every opportunity, this new Dudley expresses concern for Harry's well-being. Dudley even goes so far as to contradict Harry's assessment of how the Dursleys feel about him when he declares that he doesn't think Harry is a "waste of space" (*DH*, p. 40). Fans have referred to this transformation as a redemption of Dudley's character.[1] A careful reading of the text, however, reveals that Rowling has not only radically reoriented Dudley's moral compass, she has also changed how she talks about Dudley's body and its size. Early in the series, the narrator refers to Dudley as fat, but in *DH* he is described instead as "large" and "muscular" (*DH*, p. 30). Similarly, Horace Slughorn is described as fat (*HBP*, p. 64) when he doesn't want to be associated with Dumbledore and the Order of the Phoenix, but no mention is made of his size when he demonstrates loyalty to Harry's quest to defeat Voldemort. Even Neville Longbottom begins the series as a "round-faced boy" (*SS*, p. 94) who isn't good at magic before transforming into a substitute hero whose body size is simply not discussed by the end of the saga. In this essay, I use a fat studies lens to critique Rowling's choices in the social construction of fatness in the *Harry Potter* series. In particular, I focus on the ways in which fatness is written into the background as Dudley, Slughorn, and Neville engage in physical activity that repositions them within the saga of The Boy Who Lived. While none of these characters are described as losing weight, Rowling chooses to de-emphasize their fatness as they move closer to the center of the story. This renders fatness and fat bodies invisible as the series approaches a climax: when good triumphs over evil, thin-thinking replaces the presence of fatness in Rowling's fictional universe.

In their introduction to the groundbreaking anthology *The Fat Studies Reader*, Solovay and Rothblum (2009) describe fat studies as "an interdisciplinary field of scholarship marked by an aggressive, consistent, rigorous critique of the negative assumptions, stereotypes, and stigma placed on fat and the fat body" (p. 2). Part of that critique is the rejection of the assumption that there is a direct causal connection between lower body weight and increased health or longer life (Campos, 2004, p. xxv). Because the field "offers no opposition to the simple fact of human weight diversity, but instead looks at what people and societies make of this reality" (Wann, 2009, p. x), fat studies opens the door to examining understandings of fatness as social constructions rather than as received truths. My use of the phrase "the social construction of fatness" in the title of this essay is intended to highlight and raise awareness of the fact that ideas about fatness are not inevitable (Hacking, 1999, p. 6–7). The meaning of fatness is not pre-established but rather is manufactured and agreed upon within specific communities. The fat studies understanding of fatness is itself a social construct, but it is one that I privilege because it "offers a crucial corollary to fat pride community and fat civil rights activism" (Wann, 2009, p. x). In other words, fat studies is grounded in the lived experience of fat people, a stance which is crucial in any theory about a marginalized group. As such, fat studies provides a unique lens through which to experience and critique a story written by a thin author and manifest through the experiences of a thin protagonist.

Of central concern to any fat studies analysis is the language used to describe fat bodies. While Rowling is fond of euphemisms such as pudgy, portly, round, beefy, and plump, I will use the word fat, which is a neutral descriptor of body size (Wann, 2009, p. xii). Moreover, I will not use terms such as "overweight" or "obese." The term "overweight" implies that each body has a weight that it must maintain or else be considered in excess, while the term "obese" implies that medical intervention is necessary. Both terms suggest that such fat bodies are problems in need of a solution, a position that is both echoed by many authors of books for children and young adults (Averill, 2016; Flynn, 2013; Quick, 2008; Rabinowitz, 2003; Webb, 2009) and objected to by fat studies. By reclaiming the word fat to talk about bodies which are, in fact, fat, I hope to highlight the ways in which Rowling de-emphasizes fatness when she stops using the word.

By including fat characters in her fictional universe, Rowling has entered into a longstanding conversation in Western culture about who fat people are and who they are allowed to be. The choices she has made about how to construct ideas about fatness do not echo the tolerance and embrace of diversity for which her novels are famously known (Vezzali 2014). If they did, we would expect fat people to be complex—even central—characters and for their fatness to be an unquestioned part of who they are. Instead we get moral judgments about flat stereotypes or characters whose fatness is deemphasized as they transform and grow. Rowling's construction of fatness, then, is built on what Lindsey Averill (2016) refers to as "thin-thinking" (p. 15). Thin-thinking is pervasive and often unexamined in Western culture, which holds that being thin is morally superior to being fat. Over the course of seven novels, Rowling presents a world in which "fat is not understood as normal or regular, but rather it is envisioned as a catastrophic failure or weakness, which must be addressed and corrected" (Averill, 2016, p.16). Even though she does not correct fatness through weight loss, Rowling addresses the failures and weaknessess she wrote into Dudley, Slughorn, and Neville as fat characters by failing to remind the reader that these characters are fat late in the series. This underscores the fact that fat characters need to be normalized before they can be truly relevant to Harry's journey.

One of the first things we learn about Harry's cousin Dudley is that he "was very fat and hated exercise" (p. 20). Rowling describes his size in detail, adding the word fat to mention of his wrist (*SS*, p. 45), his arm (*CoS*, p. 6), his legs (*CoS*, p. 8), his face (*CoS*, p. 9), his fist (*PoA*, p. 22), his head (*SS*, p. 21; *PoA*, p. 22), and his bottom (*SS*, p. 59; *CoS*, p. 9; *OotP*, p. 21). Rowling also uses euphemisms to describe Dudley's fatness: his shoulder, hands, and whole body are described as porky (*PoA*, p. 13; *GoF*, p. 41; *CoS*, p. 4) and he is described as large in whole and in part—specifically his feet, head, and hand (*HBP*, p. 51; *HBP*, p. 47; *DH*, p. 42). Looking very much like his "beefy" father (*SS*, p. 1), Dudley takes up a great deal of space in direct contrast to Harry who "had always been small and skinny for his age" (*SS*, p. 20). This difference is underscored when Rowling tells us that being forced to wear Dudley-sized hand-me-downs meant that Harry "looked even smaller and skinnier than he really was" (*SS*, p. 20). In other words, Dudley's fatness is constructed in direct contrast to Harry's thinness.

This contrast between thin protagonist and fat anti-hero builds on a long tradition of oppositional stereotypes in British literature for and about boys (Webb, 2009, p. 109). In particular, the *Harry Potter* series is a fantastical twist on the school story, a genre which typically follows a pattern whereby "the new scholar learns first to understand, then to accept, and finally to excel at, the ways of the strange world he or she is entering" (Reimer, 2009, p. 224). Harry's re-entry into the wizarding world is mediated through his experiences at Hogwarts, positioning him as the new scholar to which Reimer points. Like *Harry Potter*, school story novels are often published in series and included extended description of the protagonist's childhood before school.

Extra-curricular adventures, especially those that involve rule breaking and the possibility of expulsion, are privileged over academics. Also, school stories tend to spend time exploring the relationship between the headmaster and the protagonist and prominently feature sports such as Quidditch in the life of the school and as an area in which the main character excels (Galway, 2012).

Harry's thinness is informed by the values of the early British boarding school story and Dudley's fatness emerges in counterpoint. According to Webb (2009), within the tradition of British stories written for boys, "a 'space' was created for those characters who were not physically proficient and athletic to be stereotyped with a range of negative personality traits" (109). Such negative personality traits include being greedy and lazy, two clear aspects of Dudley's character in the early books of the series. Speaking of Billy Bunter of *The Greyfriars School Stories*, Webb (2009) observes that "the audience/reader is 'invited' to focus on his physicality as the source and manifestation of his unattractive and negative traits" (p. 109). The same can be said of Dudley, whose fatness is not presented as part of a natural variation in body sizes, but rather as an outward sign of his inner failings. Dudley fills up the space left by Harry both in terms of size and in terms of character.

Dudley's fatness is not simply a detail of his physical appearance but rather serves a symbol of the type of household that Harry grew up in but was not allowed to participate in. As Flynn (2013) observes, Dudley "acts as a spoiled foil to Harry's initial humility, and this contrast is conveyed through their very different bodies" (p. 213). Aunt Petunia and Uncle Vernon indulge Dudley's every whim in the first three books of the series. For example, when Dudley is on the verge of throwing a tantrum because he has been given fewer birthday gifts than the previous year, he is not only promised more gifts by his mother, he is encouraged in this sort of behavior by his father (*SS*, p. 22). Harry has no reason to expect the same sort of treatment. He is expected to do chores while Dudley never contributes his labor to the household (Flynn, 2013, p. 214). When important houseguests arrive, Harry is not only expected to make no noise but also to pretend he isn't even there (*CoS*, p. 6). Moreover, in his aunt and uncle's house, Harry was never "allowed to eat as much as he liked" (*SS*, p. 123). He was given smaller portions than Dudley (*GoF*, p. 27) and if there was anything he particularly wanted to eat, Dudley would take it "even if it made him sick" (*SS*, p. 123). Harry's skinny features are at least in part inherited from his father (*OotP*, p. 641), but his size is also constructed as a reflection of the neglect and maltreatment he experiences in his aunt and uncle's house. Dudley's fatness, then, is part of how Rowling invites the reader to sympathize with her thin protagonist.

Scholars disagree about whether it is important to assign blame for Dudley's fatness. Placing Dudley in the tradition of Roald Dahl's Augustus Gloop,

Webb (2009) states that "the parental lack of the exercise of discipline and social and moral training are symbolized by the children's greed" (p. 114). For Webb, then, a child's body size is directly linked to the way they have been brought up by their parents. In this context, Dudley's body is a site of "intense scrutiny and regulation," inviting not only scorn but also a narrative of how it came to be fat (Mosher, 2005, p.62). In a thin-thinking world, fatness needs to be explained if it is to be reversed: case history precedes diagnosis which precedes treatment (Mosher, 2005, p.61). Fat studies, however, "eschews the search for causes of, and solutions to, fatness" (Flynn, 2013, p. 14) because it understands variation in human weight to be a normal part of human existence. Flynn (2013) notes that it is the text itself that emphasizes "Vernon and Petunia's poor parenting" (p. 219) and that Rowling constructs the fact of Dudley's fatness as, in part, "the outcome of parental abuse" (p. 220). In other words, we do not know why Dudley is fat. What we know is that Rowling strongly suggests that the Dursley's parenting style has resulted in a fat child. That particular construction of fatness is not inevitable but rather serves a specific purpose in Rowling's narrative, namely to create a contrast to humble and thin Harry.

Another way that Rowling constructs Dudley as a fat character early in the series is to depict him as "a body out of control" (Averill, 2016, p. 18). Emboldened by the permissive home environment that Rowling has created for him, Dudley is simply disinterested in moderating his physical desire. When Dudley is first expected to constrain himself, moreover, he is unable to do so. At the beginning of *Goblet of Fire*, Aunt Petunia and Uncle Vernon have placed Dudley on a diet after having received a letter from the nurse at Smeltings, Dudley's private boarding school, explaining that no one made school uniforms big enough for him. Faced with a breakfast consisting of only a grapefruit quarter—albeit a bigger one than Harry's—Dudley snatches up his father's portion as soon as Uncle Vernon has left the room and Aunt Petunia's back is turned (*GoF*, p. 29). Like many fat characters in young adult literature, Dudley is portrayed here as both a "physical and moral failure" (Averill, 2016, p. 19). Not only is he physically too large for his school uniform, Dudley's morals—if he ever had any—take a back seat to his hunger and greed.

Dudley does not, however, remain a physical and moral failure. His attitude towards Harry changes drastically by the seventh book. When Harry steps on a cup of cold tea outside his bedroom door at the beginning of *Deathly Hallows*, he assumes that his cousin has set some kind of booby trap (p. 13). This would be in character for the Dudley who threatened to shove Harry's head in a toilet (*SS*, p. 32), rubbed in the fact that Harry hadn't received any letters from his friends (*CoS*, p. 9), and taunted him about having nightmares after the death of Cedric Diggory and the return of Voldemort

(*OotP*, p. 15). Harry soon discovers, however, that his cousin is no longer intent on tormenting him. As the Dursleys prepare to go into hiding because Lily Potter's protective charm on their house is about to break, Dudley expresses confusion that Harry isn't joining them (*DH*, p. 39). Assured that Harry does not want to join him and his parents, Dudley asks where his cousin is going to go. This sets up an exchange that reveals just how deep Dudley's transformation has been. When Hestia Jones, one of the people who will be hiding the Dursleys, expresses astonishment that the Dursleys don't know where Harry is going, Harry explains that his aunt, uncle, and cousin think that he, Harry, isn't worth worrying about. Dudley immediately contradicts him—"I don't think you're a waste of space" (*DH*, p. 40)—and then acknowledges for the first time that Harry saved him from the dementors. This is an awkward moment for the cousins: Dudley turns "red" and Harry is "embarrassed" (*DH*, p. 40). Harry explains to Hestia that Dudley may as well have said "I love you," words Harry had certainly never heard addressed to him in that house. Dudley doesn't simply stop being mean to Harry; he demonstrates concern for his well-being through both word and deed. *Deathly Hallows* Dudley is a cousin we can like, maybe even respect. This is a Dudley who has been redeemed.

According to the Oxford English Dictionary, a person is redeemed when they "make amends" for "an error, sin, or failing" (OED). In the scene described above, Dudley aligns his morals with, instead of against, goodness and compassion. He shows empathy for another person rather than always putting himself first. What is significant here is that this moral realignment follows a physical one. We learn at the beginning of *Order of the Phoenix* that while Dudley's size could still be described as "vast," the fact that he had dieted "hard" and discovered a talent for boxing "had wrought quite a change in his physique" (p. 11). Dudley is still a bully after learning to box, beating up neighborhood children for giving him "cheek" (*OotP*, p. 13). The more immediate change in the wake of his boxing career is how his body is described. Once the reader learns that Dudley is an athlete, the narrator never uses the word fat to describe him again. In the remainder of the series, when Dudley shows up, he is described as large rather than fat. Rowling has already used the word large to describe Dudley in *Sorcerer's Stone* (p. 18), but that instance is quickly followed by the word fat as described above. In *Deathly Hallows*, however, Dudley is not only large, he is "muscular" (p. 30). The word fat, then, carries moral weight in the *Harry Potter* series. It applies to Dudley when he is gluttonous and lazy, but is not used at all in the scene where he shows concern for Harry's well being. It is a dieting and physically active Dudley that comes close to thanking Harry for saving his life. More to the point, it is a dieting and physically active Dudley whose life is saved. Whether or not Rowling did this intentionally is less important than its possible effect, especially on young readers. Dudley's redemption and even value as a person worth saving are tied up with him moving away from gluttony and laziness towards the disciplined athleticism of boxing.

Another fat character redeemed through physical activity is Professor Horace Slughorn. Because he is not introduced until *Half-Blood Prince* and because Harry, Ron and Hermione are not Hogwarts students in *Deathly Hallows*, Rowling has less time to build and then transform the relationship between Slughorn's character and his fat body size than she does with either Dudley or Neville. Nevertheless, Rowling's construction of Slughorn as a fat character does shift over time. The first description of Slughorn labels him as "enormously fat" (*HBP*, p. 64) and as the book continues, our attention is drawn to various fat parts of Slughorn's body: his thumbs (*HBP*, p. 73), his cheeks (*HBP*, p. 491), and especially his belly (*HBP*, p. 64). Slughorn's belly is "great" (*HBP*, p. 146), "big" (*HBP*, p. 166), and "enormous" (*HBP*, p. 233). It is a defining characteristic that fills spaces (*HBP*, p. 142), casts noticeable shadows (*HBP*, p. 166), and is the first thing seen when Slughorn goes through doorways (*HBP*, p. 183).

Slughorn is not only fat, he is morally ambiguous, a perfect example of Sirius' declaration that "the world isn't split into good people and Death Eaters" (*OotP*, p. 302). For example, Slughorn declares that Harry's mother was his favorite student but then expresses surprise that this should be so given that Lily was a Muggle-born witch (*HBP*, p. 70). Slughorn is not outwardly cruel like Dudley in the early books, but he also does not want to be aligned with the anti–Voldemort movement (*HBP*, p. 72). Former head of Slytherin house, Slughorn is a living example of Phineas Nigellus' declaration that Slytherins will save themselves over others when given the option (*OotP*, p. 495). His reluctance to give Dumbledore the true memory of his conversation about horcruxes with Tom Riddle because it shows him in a bad light (*HBP*, p. 371) suggests that he cannot be relied upon to always do the right thing. Even when Slughorn does relinquish the true memory, he expresses concern that Harry not think poorly of him after seeing it (*HBP*, p. 491). Just before the Battle of Hogwarts, McGonagall informs Slughorn that "The time has come for Slytherin House to decide upon its loyalties" (*DH*, p. 602). In that moment, Slughorn chooses to leave the castle with the other Slytherins, implying that his loyalties do not lie with the school, with Dumbledore, or with Harry.

Slughorn has difficulty moving at speed. When Harry convinces Professor McGonagall to evacuate the school in advance of the Battle of Hogwarts, Slughorn is the last of the heads of house to arrive on the scene: "There were heavy footfalls behind them, and a great deal of puffing: Slughorn had just caught up" (*DH*, p. 599). The text goes on to describe him "massaging his immense chest" (*DH*, p. 599), tying his difficulty with physical activity with his size. Furthermore, when Slughorn speaks, ellipses indicate the pauses he must take to catch his breath (*DH*, p. 600). Just as he was reluctant to align himself with the Order of the Phoenix in the beginning of *Half-Blood Prince*, at the end of *Deathly Hallows* Slughorn is hesitant to defy Voldemort (*DH*, p. 601).The implication is that Slughorn is unable to keep up with his colleagues, both physically and morally.

Slughorn manages, however, to overcome both limitations by the end of the Battle of Hogwarts. As giants battle in front of the castle and stampeding centaurs push Death Eaters and defenders of Hogwarts alike back into the entrance hall, a swarm of reinforcements makes its way over the boundary walls and across the Hogwarts grounds. While it is not surprising that families and friends of Hogwarts students would rally alongside the residents of Hogsmeade, it is surprising that Horace Slughorn is among them (*DH*, p. 734). By placing himself in harm's way when he could have easily saved himself, Slughorn reveals that his loyalties are with the school after all. Even more noteworthy here is where Slughorn is positioned in relation to the crowd. Given his earlier huffing and puffing when running to the meeting of the heads of house, the reader could reasonably expect to see him bringing up the rear of the group, if not falling far behind it. Instead, Rowling tells us that Slughorn is at the front of the mass of new fighters. Indeed, the only one of the reinforcements to reach the castle faster than Slughorn is Charlie Weasley. Given that Charlie has been working with dragons for years, his speed is completely in character. Slughorn's speed, however, defies expectations. Most importantly, Rowling does not describe him as huffing or puffing in this scene. In this moment of choosing sides—of choosing the *right* side—Slughorn has been redeemed. No longer hiding from both Voldemort and Dumbledore by disguising himself as an armchair, Slughorn shows that his loyalties lie with Hogwarts. By running across the grounds, his morality becomes less ambiguous and as a redeemed character, the impact of his size on his ability to run is irrelevant. Slughorn's fatness takes a back seat to his contribution to the fight against Voldemort, just as Dudley is no longer described as fat when he shows concern and compassion for Harry.

Rowling spends less time describing Neville's fatness than she does describing Dudley's or Slughorn's. She often reminds the reader that Neville is "round faced" (*SS*, p. 104; *CoS*, p. 86; *PoA*, p. 55; *GoF*, p. 167; *HPB*, p. 136), but further mention of him as plump (*OotP*, p. 513), pudgy (*GoF*, p. 168), or even fat (*SS*, p. 148) are rare. When Neville is described in a scene, especially early in the series, the reader is more likely to be presented with evidence of him as a bumbling oaf than with reminders of his body size. For example, he runs off while still wearing the sorting hat (*SS*, p. 120), has a reputation for causing "devastation with the simplest spells" (*CoS*, p. 193), breaks tea cups in Divination class (*PoA*, p. 105), and is so forgetful his grandmother sends him a memory aid (*SS*, p. 145). Neville's comic inability to smoothly navigate space or perform magic stands in for descriptions of his physical size. In this way, Rowling has managed to eat her cake and have it too, creating a fat character and then rendering that fat invisible (Mosher, 2001, p. 171).

The arc of Neville's character development is one of the most dramatic in the series. He transforms from a boy who is "forgetful, timid, quick to cry, and of ostensibly poor magical ability" (Camacci, 2015, p. 35) into a very competent young man who fulfills the role of rabble rouser in school and "bold, rebellious hero" (Camacci, 2015, p. 35) on the battlefield when Hogwarts is under siege. In other words, Neville is redeemed from his early failings and ineptitude when he steps up in Harry's absence. He, Ginny, and Luna led an underground rebellion at Hogwarts, but he had to go it alone when first Luna and then Ginny didn't return to the school (*DH*, p. 575). In one class, Neville asks a Death Eater teaching at Hogwarts how much Muggle blood is in her family tree. This is the height of daring because of the hatred that Death Eaters carry for Muggles and Muggle-born witches and wizards. Harry, Ron and Hermione are shocked when they learn Neville has spoken out like this, but Neville insists they would have done the same thing. In particular, he points to the hope everyone garnered from Harry's willingness to speak out against injustice (*DH*, p. 574). In other words, Harry's role as disruptor in the face of repressive school administrators does not go unfilled just because he is physically absent from the school. Even Neville's beheading of Voldemort's snake Nagini happens in Harry's absence, as everyone thinks Harry is dead when it happens (*DH*, p. 730; *DH*, p. 733).

As with Dudley, Rowling has stopped using words like round, plump, and pudgy to describe Neville by the seventh book. Even though she does not say that he has lost any weight, lack of description in a thin-thinking world invites readers to assume that Neville is now thin. Readers may think that Neville would be emaciated after living in the Room of Requirement for several weeks, but Rowling's comments about his appearance as he emerges from behind the portrait of Ariana Dumbledore are focused on the abuse he has suffered rather than whether or not his face is still round (*DH*, pp. 570–571). Again, this may or may not be a deliberate choice of the author, but the impact is the same: when Neville is a bumbling oaf, he is described as fat and when he is redeemed as a competent substitute hero, he is not.

In the movies adaptations of the *Harry Potter* series, Neville's arc from bumbling oaf to substitute hero is paralleled by a change in body size from fat to thin, now known as Longbottoming. The Urban Dictionary defines "Neville Longbottomed" as "when a non-attractive person goes through puberty and becomes very attractive as a result" and goes on to say that the term "refers to [actor] Matthew Lewis's battle and victory over puberty" (n.p.). Another way of putting it is that to Longbottom is "to suddenly go from

Durmstrang cold to dragon-fire hot" (Nudd, 2015, n.p.) The idea is that the change is fast and somewhat unexpected. Fans, then, were struck by the difference in Matthew Lewis' appearance in the first movie to his appearance in the eighth. What most fans don't know, however, is that one reason the difference is so noticeable is that in the third through seventh films, Lewis was wearing a fat suit (McPhee 2011, n.p.). In an interview on his website, Lewis shares that after the second movie he "simply grew taller and thinned out" but that the fat suit—along with bits of plastic behind his ears to make them stick out and a contract not to have his teeth fixed until after filming for all eight movies was complete—"help[ed] with the whole image of Neville.... He's not supposed to look like Brad Pitt, the character is described in the book as being very round-faced" (McPhee, n.p.). Rowling never describes Neville's ears as sticking out or his teeth as crooked; these visual details were added by studio executives. Fans became accustomed to seeing them, only to be shocked by the change in Neville/Lewis' appearance in the eighth film. Lewis reveals, however, "in the last film, Neville's got no fat suit, no false teeth, no plastic behind his ears" (Hill, n.p.). In other words, the concept of Longbottoming is based on a visual fiction. Lewis' "sudden" transformation came when studio executives filmed the body he had been developing and that they had been hiding since the third film. Both Rowling and studio executives contribute to fans' perception of Neville as a thin character by the time he destroys Voldemort's last defense death, Nagini. Neville has always been on Harry's side, so he does not need to be redeemed from being a bully like Dudley or morally ambiguous like Slughorn. He does, however, grow from a boy who cannot get into portrait hole entrance to Gryffindor Tower without help (SS, p. 130) to a young man who destroys a piece of Voldemort's soul. Redeemed from early incompetence into a central player in the fight against evil, Neville's fatness disappears from the text just as Dudley's has.

There are a lot of disappearing acts in *Harry Potter*, but from the perspective of fat studies, the most significant is the way the word fat disappears from Rowling's descriptions of characters such as Dudley, Slughorn, and Neville as the series progresses. If Rowling believed, as fat studies scholars do, that the word fat is a neutral descriptor of body size, such an absence would not be necessary. It is the thin-thinking context with which Rowling has constructed the muggle and wizarding worlds that requires the word fat to be stripped away from those who become compassionate, loyal, and heroic as good triumphs over evil.

Notes

1. I am indebted to my friend songquake, facilitator of the LiveJournal fanfic festival entitled "Dudley Redeemed," for this perspective on what happens here.

REFERENCES

Averill, L. (2016). "Do Fat-Positive Representations Really Exist in YA? Review of Fat-Positive Characters in Young Adult Literature." *Fat Studies*, 5(1), 14–31. doi:10.1080/21604851.2015.1062708.

Camacci, L.R. (2016). "The Prisoner of Gender: Masculinity in the Potter Books." In Bell, Christopher E. (Ed.), *Wizards vs. Muggles: Essays on Identity and the Harry Potter Universe* (pp. 27–48). Jefferson, NC: McFarland.

Campos, P. (2004). *The Obesity Myth*. New York: Gotham Books.

Flynn, K.E.R. (2013). *Constructions of the Fat Child in British Juvenile Fiction (1960–2010)* (Doctoral dissertation). University of Worcester, Henwick Grove, UK.

Galway, E.A. (2012). "Reminders of Rugby in the Halls of Hogwarts: The Insidious Influence of the School Story Genre on the Works of J.K. Rowling." *Children's Literature Association Quarterly*, 37(1), 66–85. Retrieved from http://muse.jhu.edu/journals/childrens_literature_association_quarterly/v037/37.1.galway.html.

Hacking, I. (1999). *The Social Construction of What?* Cambridge, MA: Harvard University Press.

Hill, Erin. (2011). "Matthew Lewis: 'I'm ready to say goodbye to Neville Longbottom.'" Retrieved from https://parade.com/95957/erinhill/matthew-lewis-harry-potter-deathly-hallows/.

McPhee, R. (2011). "Exclusive Interview with Harry Potter Star Matthew Lewis." Retrieved from http://www.yorkshireeveningpost.co.uk/news/exclusive-interview-with-harry-potter-star-matthew-lewis-1-3547202.

Mosher, J. (2001). "Setting Free the Bears: Refiguring Fat Men on Television." In J.E. Braziel, & K. LeBesco (Eds.), *Bodies Out of Bounds: Fatness and Transgression* (pp. 166–193). Berkeley: University of California Press.

Mosher, J. (2005). Survival of the Fattest: Contending with the Fat Boy in Children's Ensemble Films. In M. Pomerance, & F. Gatward (Eds.), *Where the Boys Are: Cinemas of Masculinity and Youth* (pp. 61–82). Detroit: Wayne State University Press.

"Neville Longbottomed." *Urban Dictionary*. Retrieved from http://www.urbandictionary.com/define.php?term=Neville%20Longbottomed.

Nudd, T. (2015,-05–12T15:15:00+00:00). "Neville's Nerdiness Was—Gasp!—Fake, Says Matthew Lewis' Harry Potter Costar." PEOPLEwww. Retrieved from http://people.com/movies/matthew-lewis-neville-longbottom-in-harry-potter-was-always-handsome-costar/.

Quick, C.S. (2008). "Meant to be huge": Obesity and Body Image in Young Adult Novels. *The ALAN Review*, 35(2) doi:10.21061/alan.v35i2.a.8.

Rabinowitz, R. (2003, Sep 1,). "Fat Characters in Recent Young Adult Fiction." *Kliatt*, 37, n.p.

Reimer, M. (2009). "Traditions of the School Story." *The Cambridge Companion to Children's Literature*. Grenby, M.O., and Immel, Andrea (Eds.), 209–225.

Solovay, S., & Rothblum, E. (2009). "Introduction." In E. Rothblum, & S. Solovay (Eds.), *The Fat Studies Reader* (pp. 1–7). New York: New York University Press.

Vezzali, L., Stathi, S., Giovannini, D., Capozza, D., & Trifiletti, E. (2015). "The Greatest Magic of Harry Potter: Reducing Prejudice." *Journal of Applied Social Psychology*, 45(2), 105–121. doi:10.1111/jasp.12279.

Webb, J. (2009). "'Voracious appetites': The Construction of 'Fatness' in the Boy Hero in English Children's Literature." In K.K. Keeling, & S.T. Pollard (Eds.), *Critical Approaches to Food in Children's Literature* (pp. 105–121). Abingdon-on-Thames: Routledge.

Of the Patil Twins

Soma Das

> "I can't say I have suffered for my politics. SF and fantasy slip under the wire a lot.... People just aren't looking for radical thought in a field the respectable critics define as escapist drivel."
>
> —Le Guin, 2008

Race in literature, played at multifaceted levels, is significant and has ramifications for culture, both past and contemporary. Welch (2016) points out the lack of characters of color in children's books in "Missing Adventures: Diversity and Children's Literature." She quotes figures and facts about lack of proper representation of children of color in children's literature and media. This bolsters this essay's discussion of the narration of the Patil twins in the *Harry Potter* texts.

The world of Harry Potter introduces myriad ideas alongside the preconceived notions of race. Muggles, wizards, witches, half bloods, derogatorily termed mud bloods, giants, half giants, goblins and house elves—this list is by no means exhaustive, but enumerates some different ideas of race that the texts weave into the fabric of the story. This works along with the preconceived notions of the foreign-sounding people such as Fleur Delacour and Viktor Krum, the thick west country accent of Hagrid and, the smooth talking hints at the manor-owning, aristocratic Malfoys.

If *Harry Potter* is read as a text that belongs to the genre of fantasy, can the politics within the stories be dismissed? Is it okay to overlook the racial politics within the texts on the grounds that this is children's literature or books aimed at young adults, apparently in order to encourage readership (Rowling & Fry, 2005). What are the consequences of the Patil twins' narration if readers choose to align themselves with the implied meaning of the text? Cocks (2004, p. 94) discusses the real and implied meanings of texts.

He posits that Chambers (1990) suggests "an author creates a relationship with a reader 'in order to discover the meaning of a text' instead of the text having an 'intrinsic quality.'"

What are the underlying implications of narrating a pair of British Indian girls as minor characters? If racial politics are to be read here, how is this radical or innovative? The Patils are not there for the purpose of comic relief, unlike the Weasley twins. This essay argues that the Patil twins cannot be read as characters that introduce any radical positive changes in terms of racial representation of brown minor characters. They can be read working within the premise of maintaining status quo, reinforcing gender and racial stereotypes, and tokenism.

Presenting the Patils

The Patil twins' introduction is framed by the sentence and the prerequisite that "There weren't many people left now" (Rowling & Kay, 2015). The twins seem to be accorded a bit of an elevated status when, instead of just going over their last names, the detail "…then a pair of twin girls…" is mentioned. However, the narration seems to not accord any more importance to them, as their forenames are left out. Their sorting ceremony is part of a list which tapers down unceremoniously to only the last names of the students. The penultimate name in this part of the list is detailed in its full form, and the list ends with the eponymous hero, Harry Potter's, name being exclaimed out. His sorting ceremony is, of course, then detailed with much fanfare.

The narrative premise of the texts seems to follow a similar trajectory for the twins in most places. They are important insofar as they are mentioned. However, that importance quickly trails off. They are almost always in the periphery of Harry Potter or other characters. The narration gives a sense that they are good, but always with a potential of being outshone. In the Yule Ball (Rowling, 2000), they are specified as "the best looking girls in the year." However, the perspective then turns and Hermione outshines them. The quintessential white girl hogs the limelight by her magical transformation from the proverbial ugly duckling to the beauty. Guin (2004) opines about fantasy, "If black kids, Hispanics, Indians both Eastern and Western, don't buy fantasy—which they mostly don't—could it be because they never see themselves on the cover?"

The *Potter* texts have been sold, bought, and read by many people in different nations. Is it not worth considering why the Patil twins are never allowed to shine brilliantly, on their own, by being narrated in terms of any of the qualities that the texts seem to endorse? For instance, they cannot really be read in terms of their exceptional valor or adventures, individually.

A reader's potential experience through attempt at association of identification of the self, with these British Indian girls, can then be read as, even if a character of color has the potential to be the best at something (for instance, "best looking"), they will be outshone by a white character. The terms of narration of these Indian kids are thus not cover page material.

The contrast is even starker in the *GoF* movie (Newell, 2005), where the Patils are dressed in brightly colored Indian clothes while attending a traditional English ball. This is a definite statement in racial representation. Are the clothes a claim to racial identity? They are wearing Indian *lehenga*s in an English ball. This is conspicuous when these girls clearly look like this culture is not alien to them. In school uniforms, they're similar to the other kids; however, when it comes to the Ball, it was deemed fit for their attire to be stereotypically Indian. This is a definite diversion from the books. *GoF* specifically mentions that Parvati is dressed in robes of "shocking pink" and Padma in robes of "bright turquoise" (*GoF*, 412). So, not only are the color schemes of the clothes in the movies a diversion, the robes in the book are not Indian by any specificity. The visuals make a long lasting impact. The idea behind such a cinematic representation is to make the ethnicity loud and clear. Doesn't matter how much it doesn't correspond to the text, it has been able to pass on without much hue and cry. Is this ok because the twins are narrated to be British Indians, and why should there be a fuss if they're being painted stereotypically? At least accusations of whitewashing can't be made.

Said's *Orientalism* (2014) discusses,

> ...a long tradition of.... Orientation(,) a way of coming to terms with the Orient that is based on the Orient's special place in European Western experience. The Orient ... (as) the place of Europe's greatest and richest and oldest colonies ... its cultural contestant, and one of its deepest and most recurring images of the other [p. 1].

The Patil girls can be read as "The Other." According to the book, the twins are dressed in robes just as Hermione is. But the diversion in the movie brings out the contrast between the girls as the racial Other. It caters to certain preconceived notions of racial stereotypes and maintains the status quo. The books do not abstain from the aforementioned either. Parvati is narrated in terms of "her long dark plait braided with gold, and gold bracelets glimmering at her wrists" and Padma in terms of her "dark eyes" (*GoF,* 412).

Clothes as a marker of cultural representation work as a leitmotif in the *Harry Potter* movies. In the scene where Fleur and Bill's wedding is being celebrated, there is a lady lurking behind, out of focus, in the scenes. She is brown skinned and wearing a *sari*. This can be viewed as an example of tokenism. A tokenistic representation of racial and cultural diversity works under the assumption that it doesn't matter if the wedding is in England, or it is a French bride and an English groom; in the 21st century, apparently if there is a brown skinned woman guest, she'll be in a *sari*. So, this must be cinematically represented at the periphery, in order to include (while at the same time highlighting) the exclusion of the margins. The brown skinned woman seems to be doubly marginalized both by the fact of her color and gender. It is a very self-consciously aware marginalization as it tries hard, a bit too hard, to not exclude. This doesn't seem to be the case with a brown male. They're seldom used as tokens with accord to clothing. Yes, brown males are very much used as markers of racial diversity, in literature and other media generally. However, seldom are they kitted out in Oriental clothing while not playing stereotypically Oriental roles.

Tracing attempts at deliberate inclusion, such kind of representation can also be read as documenting the growth of alternative histories. By the virtue of the presence of representation through such forms as the Indian clothes, the gold bangles on the wrist of the twins and their long dark hair in braids, it is an inclusion and an acknowledgment. It is a making aware of the presence of the "Others." These "very pretty" Indian girls are part of the fabric of the same society and inhabit the same world as the other white characters in *Harry Potter*. However, following the text closely, the narrative premise seems to only partially allow this argument, especially as the Patil twins are quickly sidelined.

From reading them as an attempt at inclusion and documenting alternative histories, they can be viewed neatly ensconced in preexisting categories where nothing radical is happening. Parvati's character can be read as operating within frames of a silly, giggly girl, obsessed with the subject of Divination (which the protagonists consider fraudulent and annoying to the point that the clever and dedicated student Hermione decides to give it up as not worth her efforts and attention). Parvati is easily smitten by teachers that Hermione considers frauds—Professor Trelawney and the "gorgeous centaur" Firenze (who Hermione "coolly" considers an approximation of a horse and, thus, unlikeable because she doesn't like horses (Rowling, 2003)). Guin (2004) posits, "'what sells' or 'doesn't sell' can be a self-fulfilling prophecy." The *Harry Potter* texts have been a commercial success. Is it because they are formulaic? What are the implications of narrating the Patil twins bound within certain frames? It is definitely consequential that texts which are commercial successes narrate Parvati as fulfilling certain prototypes of giggly, silly, smitten by teachers and a subject considered annoying by her white peers. It is a "self-fulfilling prophecy" and a vicious circle because if narratives such as these sell, then the minor characters who may be brown in the overwhelmingly white world fantasies will be perpetually narrated as such. Those narratives that take another route might not sell and might thereby not be able to make any difference to the narration of such characters and alternate histories.

Parvati gets more space within the texts, as she's a Gryffindor, the same house as the protagonist. But she seems to constantly be present as The Other to Hermione. She can be read as all that Hermione isn't and, if the "implied reader" (Cocks, 2004, p.95) is to align themselves with the text and its meaning, it would seem that thankfully Hermione isn't what Parvati is. For instance, her deep admiration of Professor Trelawney on one hand whilst on the other, she is even more enamored by the good-looking centaur teacher of Divination, Firenze. Her narration is thus directed towards her unsure admiration, dubitable loyalty, and love of a subject "despised" by even the deputy Headmaster and Parvati's house head, Minerva McGonagall (Rowling, 2005). On the other hand, Hermione, right in the first movie of the series, is narrated as earning a special 50 points awarded by the Headmaster Dumbledore "for the cool use of intellect, while others were in grave peril" (Columbus, 2001).

During the Yule Ball episode, Parvati is described as "looking very pretty indeed" by the narratorial perspective. Harry's direct speech, which gives access to his perspective, describes her as, "'You—er—look nice,' he said awkwardly" (*GoF*, 412). Parvati's appearance moves from very pretty to nice and its acknowledgment entails an awkwardness. The narratorial perspective then goes on to describe Padma as "looking just as pretty as Parvati" (*GoF*, 412). There is an equivalence in their looking pretty that can be read as a huddling together. Padma is in turquoise robes, unlike Parvati's shocking pink ones. There is no mention of Padma's dark hair being braided with gold or gold bangles "gleaming" on her wrist, unlike Parvati's. Instead, the narration is about her "dark eyes" assessing Ron's frayed robes. However, the degree of looking pretty for both the twins is the same without any room for individuality as it were, irrespective of the lack of mention of the gold on one of them. The association with gold is another stereotypical narration of Indianness. These descriptions can be read juxtaposed to Hermione's. She looks pretty, but not "just as" someone else, unlike Parvati and Padma. She is described as looking pretty to such a degree that Harry's "jaw dropped" (*GoF*, 414). Neither Patil twin is described as pretty enough to do that, even though one of them has the potential of being his romantic partner, but their characters are marked by a lack, as this potential is clearly not fulfilled.

The twins can be discussed as defined by an inherent lack in their characterization: a lack of being Hermione. Despite her being partnered with Ron, the book doesn't give access to his perspective on Padma Patil. "Where is Hermione?" Ron asks "again" (Rowling, 2000). The presence of Padma as his partner for the Ball is marked by the reiteration and importance of his perceived absence and thereby his quest for Hermione. "Hermione came over and sat down in Parvati's empty chair" (*GoF*). The lack of Parvati's presence is filled in by Hermione's. Her coming over to take Parvati's recently emptied seat is proactive and of her own accord. While Ron's full attention is on Hermione in the Yule Ball, Padma's narration can be viewed by a lack of it. Parvati seems to be narrated in a similar way. Despite Harry having asked her to be his partner, her narration can be read as marked by a lack of either being physically present in the narration along with Harry or, when she is physically present, of Harry or the narration taking her presence into account at all.

Her deep interest in Divination as a subject, which entails the art of foretelling by reading tea leaves, for instance, can be read as catering to a certain racial stereotype, when discussed in conjunction with both the twins being named after Indian Hindu Goddesses. It is a statement about catering to the racial stereotype of the Hindu belief in their pantheon of Gods. This is also a claim to knowledge about the cultural stereotype that Indians might be interested in astrology and the workings of the divine forces.

Names are as important as interesting in the *Potter* texts. The forenames and surname of the Patil girls can be discussed as a statement towards ideas of race, especially their etymological derivations. Patil is an Indian surname found widely amongst the people originally from the Maratha region. Padma means "lotus" in Sanskrit. The lotus is important in the Hindu culture, as it stands as a signifier of something holy. Here is a claim to knowledge about how Hindu Indians might be named after their gods and goddesses. This can be juxtaposed to other representations of Indian diasporic children in literature. In *The Namesake* (Lahiri, 2003), for instance, the protagonist is a boy born to Indian parents in America. He is named Gogol, after the Russian writer Nikolai Gogol. Here, nuances of contrast in racial representation and claims to cultural knowledge come forth. The author of *The Namesake*, Jhumpa Lahiri, was born in London to Indian parents. The naming of the characters in her book is a statement, a breakaway from the stereotypically ethnic in one way. It provides a different perspective to the representation of Indian names.

The name Padma is used in Hindu texts to refer to several revered and worshipped characters, including the goddess Lakshmi and the lotus-eyed hero Rama. An inkling to polytheism can be read from the name Padma, which is racially charged. The surname is Hindu and so are the forenames. This directs the idea of the twins' ethnic origin. It can hardly be read as completely innocuous. Especially as the other twin is named Parvati, which means "one who is of the mountains" in Sanskrit. Parvati as a name can be traced to a Hindu goddess. She is the deity with ultimate power in a woman's form. Padma, according to its Hindu origins, has serene connotations, and Parvati more indomitable.

Parvati is mentioned more times in the books than her twin. But the fact that only Padma makes a reappearance in the play *The Cursed Child*

(Thorne, Rowling, & Tiffany, 2016) is significant. Padma is cast as the wife of a white male in an alternate reality. But it is again a case of giving an important role but not following it through, unlike Ginny Weasley, who is Harry's wife and can definitely be read as more than a minor, peripheral character lurking around. Although it might be good to note that Rowling hasn't forgotten her minor characters, Padma's reappearance in the play is in terms of mentions and recalling only. Her presence is, yet again, marked by a lack of actuality, a lack of actually being physically present. It is essentially framed within Albus' question, "Who's Padma?" (*CC*, p.128) Her narration is framed by Ron's perspective, which isn't very flattering. Ron doesn't seem to be happily married to Padma, and describes her to Albus as a woman who "Talks slightly too close to your face, smells a bit minty" (Thorne et. al, 2016, p. 128). His narration of her refers to her strictness and her temper. These events are followed by Ron running into Hermione at Hogwarts, which is marked by a romantically tense moment. Padma and Ron's marriage is only possible in an alternate, parallel universe, one that is apparently undesirable—a universe gone wrong. The Orient continues to be the "...cultural contestant, and one of its deepest and most recurring images of the other..." (Said, 2014) as even in this undesirable, unrealistic parallel universe, even though Padma is Ron's wife, he actually fancies Hermione. Padma's narration is a lack of being Hermione (Trombetta, 2016).

From the books, it is known that the twins are sorted into different houses at Hogwarts. This can be read as an attempt at individuality. Is this then an attempt by the narratorial perspective to not present generic qualities in terms of ethnicity, as different houses represent difference in personalities and character traits? However, there is a shutting up of this attempt at granting individuality when the twins' cinematic depiction is focused upon. They're both placed in the same house in the movies. They have been given the same pink and orange Indian-looking clothes, vis-a-vis the shocking pink or turquoise robes mentioned in the book. The actress Afshan Azad, who plays the role of Padma Patil in the films, talks about how the director Mike Newell decided to put her in Gryffindor, the same as Parvati. She points out that in the book their characters are meant to be identical twins, but in the films, she looks nothing like Shefali Chowdhury, who plays the role of Parvati Patil. Newell made sure that they were in the same house and their hair, makeup and robes were exactly the same; even the two beauty spots that were drawn on their faces (Azad, 2012). This can be read as a shutting up of the attempt to grant individuality to the twins. Even though the twins in the books can be read to be of Hindu British Indian ethnic origin, both the actresses playing the roles in the movies are British Bangladeshis—culturally close to the Indian sub-continent, but not precisely from the same culture. Does this kind of character casting border on the verge of cultural approximation? If so, what are the implications of this? Can this be read as a shutting out of individuality through a shutting down of ethnic specificity?

The Patils in Action

The twins are narrated in the books bound within a framework of either being shut up or shutting someone else up. The imbalance of power in the dynamics of the relationships between the twins and the other characters can be read as a statement of racial representation. According to Sarland,

> In eighteenth- and nineteenth-century didacticism the promotion of values had often taken the overt form of direct preaching, while in the 1970s the specific form of the debate was to do with questions of character representation and character role. The analysis consisted in showing how children's fiction represented some groups at the expense of others, or how some groups were negatively represented in stereotypical terms. The argument was that by representing certain groups in certain ways children's books were promoting certain values—essentially white, male and middle-class, and that the books were thus class biased, racist and sexist. The fact that the protagonists of most children's books tended to be white middle class boys was adduced in evidence.... Girls were only represented in traditional female roles [Sarland 2009].

The narration of the girls doesn't move much beyond "traditionally female roles." Instances of this can be read from the "gold bangles," "long plaits," and "a large ornamental butterfly" in the hair. Even Hermione is not spared from the "traditionally female." To become beautiful and worthy of Ron's fancy, her "bushy hair" becomes "sleek and shiny" and "an elegant knot at the back of her head." Her posture, her body language, and even her smile evoke "unflattering disbelief" in Parvati. To conform to this tradition of being a pretty female, she has to actually not "look like Hermione at all" (*GoF*).

Harry has brought Parvati Patil to the Ball as a "drastic" act, which depicts his complete lack of interest in her. Significantly, the "best-looking girls in the year" hadn't been asked to the Ball by anyone else. They seem to be have been waiting for the famous white male hero, Harry Potter and his best friend, Ron, to come and ask to take them to the Yule Ball (and then show complete lack of interest in them to the point of trying to ruin it for them). Here lies a very strong statement of white male privilege.

Parvati, the brown girl, who is decked in stereotypically traditional Indian attire, is narrated as looking at Hermione, who she says "...looks beautiful" (Newell, 2005). Parvati's look is distanced from Harry on multiple levels in terms of the gaze. Firstly, Harry is quite self-consciously aware that he is not looking at Parvati. Secondly, their respective gazes are in opposition, as she describes Hermione as "beautiful" and Harry acquiesces, saying yes, she does look beautiful (Newell, 2005). But he is saying this about Cho, who is positioned at a lower level, on the ground floor, in the opposite direction to Hermione, who is positioned on an elevated level at the top of the stairs. The beauty of the white girl, Hermione, is thus presented at a level much higher than the Indian girl, who might be beautiful but doesn't catch the eye of the white male hero and is stood below the stairs, admiring the white girl. The white girl's beauty is so overpowering that it makes the white male hero shift his admiring gaze from the other Asian girl, who he does fancy, to the white girl herself, whom he sees as a friend. The white girl's beauty thus wins, hands down, guaranteeing all eyes on her.

The events of the Ball can be viewed in terms of the idea that even though the sequence of events do not favor Parvati, she breaks the potentially stereotypical molds of the traditional, docile Indian girl, and is instead characterized as empowered. She refuses to cut a sorry figure or wallow in self-pity. The twins are not cast in the roles of the classic Penelope figure. They do not sit around waiting for Harry or Ron to return their attention. They wait around only long enough to try and give the boys a chance to redeem themselves. Parvati is proactively empowered despite her gender, her race, her color and her status as a peripheral character. At least the apparent empowerment is in place, albeit a tad desperate. These are how the arguments would appear on the surface.

Scratching the surface a bit reveals these events are detailed from the narrator's perspective. The narratorial perspective in the book seems to be holding a camera that is focusing on the characters turn by turn. The focus seems to be on the gaze. Who is looking? What is being looked at? Who is being shown? The answers to these questions have deep underlying impacts. The gaze and the gazing have rippling effects on the characters. The sequence of events, in this case, highlights disjuncture, as the focus sweeps from one character to the other. The characters are narrated bound within frames of looking. The three female characters, in this case, are presented not in terms of where, who or what they are looking at; instead, whether they are being looked at or not by the male characters. The female characters' identity, in this case, appears to be etched out by being looked at or not by their male romantic dates. The look defines the love interest or the lack of it. The depth of the interest also intensifies the depth of the look, taking it to a deeper degree of "watching."

Harry is concentrating "...on not tripping over his own feet" (*GoF*, 415), so he is clearly not looking at Parvati Patil. This not looking frames the narration of Parvati in this episode; it depicts Harry's lack of interest in her. On the one hand, Parvati's character begins to elicit sympathy, especially when the scene is read from the movie. Parvati, with oodles of racial stereotypicality sprinkled on to depict her character, is not of any interest to Harry, romantic or otherwise. She is juxtaposed to another Asian girl, Cho Chang, whom Harry has the hots for. The racial Othering here is a double stance. The positioning is such that the white boy fancies the other Asian girl who is "not narrated as brown." So, she is Other to the white male Harry and depicts his fleeting, adventurous, adolescent interest in the exotic East. This becomes certainly prominent as Harry's final love interest, whom he also ends up marrying, is the white girl, Ginny Weasley. Said on *Orientalism* is pertinent here,

> So far as a European was concerned.... The Orient was almost a(n) European invention, and had been since antiquity 'a place of romance, exotic beings, haunting memories and landscapes, remarkable experiences. The main thing for the European visitor was a European representation of the Orient [Said, 2014].

Harry feels like a show dog with Parvati. This is a perspective upon perspective. Harry's perspective is being narrated through the narratorial perspective. Harry has no direct speech here and thus there is no direct access to what he feels. This is consequential in terms of the reading of Harry's interaction with Parvati in the episode of the ball. The events here are again narrated as if contained within a frame of the narratorial gaze. Parvati's apparent enjoyment and "beaming around at everybody" (*GoF*, 413) are focused on by the narratorial gaze in an almost critiquing manner. The racial element comes to the foreground when the narratorial perspective details that Parvati's beaming around entails and is firmly interlinked to "steering Harry" (*GoF*, 415). So, the brown girl is trying to appear in control and so happy that she beams by the sheer virtue of accompanying the white male hero, whose lack of looking as a consequence of lack of romantic interest in her makes her appear desperate in more ways than one. This can be read from the narratorial perspective that sees the brown girl not only "steering" the white hero but also "steering … so forcefully that he felt as though he were a show dog she was putting through its paces" (*GoF*, 415). There are multifaceted claims here. The white, heterosexual, male hero is given such an elevated status that he seems to be extortionately expensive and a marker of the owner or walker's high economic/social status. A show dog being put through its paces would merit the aforementioned claims. However, it also appears that the brown girl is desperate enough to show off her status of being the famous Harry Potter's date to the Ball. Despite the fact that she has accompanied the eponymous, white hero to the Ball, she doesn't become the belle of the Ball, and she seems aware that she will not have a Cinderella ending. Thus, she acts in such an inappropriate manner that she transforms the hero from being one of the four champions leading the Ball to a dog that can be showed off or is putting on a show.

How can ideas about the dark hair and dark eyes of the Patil twins be read? All major characters are Caucasian, including the negative ones. But the chief villain Voldemort is often named as the "Dark Lord," and his magic, which is the wrong kind of magic and pure evil, is termed as "dark" magic. Connections can be drawn when reading him, as He Who Must Not be Named, and the Patil twins' introduction, where their forenames are not named during the sorting ceremony in the first book of the series. Here, the Patils are part of the category of people where 'not many people were left now' (SS, 121). This reads similarly to the descriptives used for Voldemort as one who doesn't even have enough human left in him. So, even though the Patil twins are part of the goody gang and Dumbledore's Army, the references to darkness are still as much connected to them as to the ultimate baddie, Voldemort.

The "Hi, Harry Girls"

> Immature people crave and demand moral certainty ... Kids and adolescents struggle to find a sure moral foothold in this bewildering world; they long to feel they're on the winning side...
>
> —Le Guin, 2004.

Given Le Guin's (2004) ideas on fantasy, can the Patils then be read as immature characters through this prism? In this bildungsroman, they are on the hero's side in the battle between good and evil. Their "moral certainty" seems to be in place. They are positioned to fight against evil on the side of the presumed good. However, there is no developmental trajectory to follow on how this certainty has been arrived on. Thus, at no point is a closure readable in the narrative. The silly, giggly girl that Parvati is narrated as in the books and, the "Hi, Harry Girls" (Azad & Chowdhury, 2005), as both the twins are narrated cinematically, can be read to fit within a scheme of the "struggle to find a sure moral foothold in this bewildering world" (Le Guin 2004). They indeed find themselves "on the winning side" (Le Guin 2004). It is not plausible to read either of the twins' narration as fully rounded characters. They are minor characters in the narrative, no doubt; however, their characters can't be discussed in more than the light of merely being present for the idea of ethnic diversity. They fit in conceptually with such stereotypes that diversity seems equivalent to stereotypes within these texts.

Reading the Patils

> Children of color need to be able to imagine themselves having the same adventures as white children.... Children should be able to start fresh and don't need the stereotypicality we hand over to them
>
> —Welch, 2016.

If racial stereotypicality of the Patil twins is to be read as a documenting of the growth of radical alternative histories, is this a well-rounded documentation? Exploring the idea of Hogwarts as a microcosm of the real/ imagined/ perceived world, the Patils can be read as reflective of the kind of parts British Indian girls play within a British school system. If this in itself is a minor, unicellular reflection of society, it is difficult to understand why other children of color would like to identify themselves with these girls, or why other people of similar ethnic origins would associate with this kind of experience. If the fantastical entails a wish fulfillment element, what ideas can be read through the Patil twins? Are they representative of certain people's ideas and ambitions based on either their gender or ethnic origin? Hero worship of the white male with the cape, and aligning themselves with the assumed good, point towards a lack of maturity in the characters who can't see beyond the seeking of the good and the evil.

White characters are narrated with characteristics such as valor, courage, intelligence, and being good in academics, represented through Ron and Hermione, for example. Harry appears to be the supreme white male hero who wears the eternal cape that he has the burden to always act as the savior in general. This can be read when Lucius Malfoy says, "Let us hope Mr. Potter will always be around to save the day." To this Harry retorts, "Don't worry. I will be" (Columbus, 2002). The nobility of his heart seems to be his driving force amongst others. His character can be discussed as more rounded. He is afraid but becomes wiser—he lets courage overrule fear.

In the *Potter* world, changing Padma's schoolhouse to Gryffindor can be viewed as sacrilege. But this has been able to pass, probably because they are minor characters. However, what are the implications of this huddling together? In a CBBC interview, the actresses Afshan Azad and Shefali Choudhury, who played Padma and Parvati Patil's roles in the movies, talk about how they were "the Hi, Harry Girls" on the film sets:

> It was like every time we walked past it was: "Hi, Harry" and he was like 'Gosh.' We were saying that they would make these dolls of us saying, "Hi, Harry" [Azad & Chowdhury, 2005].

No such dolls have been made, or at least they haven't been popular enough to fall within the radar of this research. The Patils, then, are not much more than "the Hi, Harry Girls." They exist for the purpose of providing shadow and relief to highlight the supremacy of the protagonists, Harry and definitely Hermione. They are always the "dark" shadows that highlight the features of the protagonists in relief, with the idea that this is what the twins are like. But the protagonists aren't like that. For instance, Hermione's sheer logic which propels her narration is opposed to Parvati being narrated always as framed by being shut up.

In the book *PS* (Rowling, 2015, P. 121), Parvati's rebuffing of Malfoy entails double degrees. Firstly, a direct and vocal shutting up by the use of the words to that effect. The second level in attempting to shut up Malfoy is non-vocal but it is a snapping nevertheless. This is furthered by Pansy Parkinson's jeering at Parvati, which is a questioning, passing of a judgment of perception, all to the effect of attempting to finally shut up Parvati herself. This process of snubbing involves four characters, but essentially it is Parvati who is narrated as framed within this process. She begins attempting snubbing Malfoy and is jeered at by Pansy Parkinson to shut her up. This involves Neville Longbottom as well, as Pansy's perception has apparently been taken by surprise. This is because she (1) never (2) thought that Parvati would (3) like (4) fat (5) little (6) crybabies. Thus, Parvati is framed within these multiple ideas as well. However, this narration is problematic at quite a few levels. Firstly, this is Pansy Parkinson's direct speech, so it is her perception of Parvati. Whether readers align themselves with the implied meaning of the text is their choice. Also, the narration is quite self-consciously aware that Pansy Parkinson might or might not be aligned with the narratorial perspective. It not only gives access to Pansy Parkinson's perception of Parvati Patil, it also frames Pansy by certain adjectives such as "a hard-faced Slytherin girl." The narration gives readers a choice to align themselves, whether with Pansy or not, by presenting Pansy in this way. The "negotiation" (Cocks, 2004) of meaning going on between the text and the reader is crucial here for the adoption of the implied meaning by the reader. If the choice is to be aligned with Pansy's perception of Parvati, then Parvati can be read along multiple lines. Her snapping and telling Malfoy to shut up can be then read as act of "sticking up." This is functioning on the presumption that this sticking up is "for" Longbottom. Parvati can be read as someone who doesn't like (6) "crybabies" who are (4) "fat" or (5) "little." The problems of narration here are that, if Parvati is read along these lines, then it is based on Pansy's thinking. This is also a question of her perception, as Pansy has "never thought" that Parvati's liking might amount to this, based on her perception of Parvati's likes. This also involves her dislikes, as they are correlated. This reading of Parvati is then also based on the "never"-ness of Pansy's thought. Another problem of narration is that this reading of Parvati, although it stands its ground according to the text, leads to unsure grounds with the narratorial stand. Is the narrator aligned with the "hard faced Slytherin girl('s)" perspective of Parvati or not? Due to these problems of narration, the reading of Parvati Patil within this scope is dubitable.

Another instance where Parvati can be read within the frame of being shut up is when she says to Professor McGonagall, "It wasn't his fault, Professor—" and is told "Be quiet, Miss Patil" (Rowling, 2015, p. 123–124). The "Hi, Harry Girl" has jumped in to defend him, only to be dismissed. The

Patils are not part of the first movie; they are mentioned but do not appear. So, for a child of color, especially for a child of the British Indian or Indian ethnic origin, how does this work? Having read the book first, if there is a desire to see these characters on the cinema screen, a denial of desire can be read here. The desire to see the experience of being sorted, which is rather ceremoniously narrated, is snubbed. This is another frame of shutting up. The adventure of being sorted out is narrated as an experience for white kids only. So, what are the consequences of leaving out such experiences of the Patil twins in terms of race and culture for children's literature specifically? This question arises especially because it is a conscious leaving out of details from the book. There might be arguments about how it is not feasible to concentrate on every detail of the book and narrate it in the movie. So, it is a question of selection in the screenplay and what is worth narrating. What or who is perceived as worthy of narration and screen space and time? This perception chooses to either not narrate events involving the Patil twins in the first two movies, or narrate them despite the twins' absence from these two movies. What are the implications of assumptions that this is acceptable?

Conclusion

The Patils can be read as always part of a group, belonging to some sort of set theory, as it were; always huddled together either with each other or, as in the case of Parvati Patil, with her best friend, Lavender Brown. Right from the commencement, the Patil twins cannot be read for who they are individually. It is a mentioning but within an anonymity. They comprise the shadows to highlight and gradually bring to relief the grandeur of Harry's sorting ceremony, which seems exaggeratedly climactic. In terms of ethnic representation, this seems to be a statement that the Patil girls are present in this world of Harry Potter—an imaginary world of fantasy which appears to be a British boarding school. As at most British schools, students of Indian ethnic origin are present here. However, if this is representative of a cross section of the British society, why aren't there more students or staff of different color? But of course, this is an imaginary world and in the genre of fantasy. Borrowing Le Guin's ideas on fantasy in general ("…Whenever I find a fantasy that is set in a genuinely imagined society and culture instead of this lazy-minded, recycled hokum, I feel like setting off fireworks" [Le Guin 2004]), it is worth arguing that even though the *Potter* books and films have been a commercial success, traces of avant-garde elements are hard to find as far as narratives, specifically, children's literature for characters of color, are concerned.

REFERENCES

Azad, A. (2012). Ascendio 2012—Padma the Gryffindor. Retrieved from https://www.youtube.com/watch?v=GB4oaVDejDI&t=7s.

Azad, A., & Chowdhury, S. (2005). NR chats to GOF's Patil twins. *Newsround*. Retrieved from http://news.bbc.co.uk/cbbcnews/hi/newsid_4440000/newsid_4447400/4447406.stm.

Chambers, A. (Ed.) (1990). *The Reader in the Book*. Abingdon-on-Thames: Routledge.

Cocks, N. (2004). *The Implied Reader. Response and Responsibility: Theories of the Implied Reader in Children's Literature Criticism*. New York: Palgrave Macmillan.

Columbus, C. (Director). (2001). *Harry Potter and the Philosophers Stone*. Warner Bros. Pictures.

Columbus, C. (Director). (2002). *Harry Potter and the Chamber of Secrets*. Warner Bros. Entertainment.

Lahiri, J. (2003). *The Namesake*. London: Fourth Estate.

Le Guin, Ursula K. (4 June 2004). "Some Assumptions about Fantasy." Retrieved from http://www.ursulakleguin.com/SomeAssumptionsAboutFantasy.html.

Le Guin, Ursula K. (2008). "The Scientific Indian." Retrieved from http://scienceblogs.com/thescian/2008/03/25/ursula-k-le-guins-interview/.

Newell, M. (Writer). (2005). *Harry Potter and the Goblet of Fire*. In H. Films & P.I. Productions (Producer): Warner Bros. Pictures.

Rowling, J.K. (2000). *Harry Potter and the Goblet of Fire*. London: Bloomsbury.

Rowling, J.K. (2005). *Harry Potter and the Half Blood Prince*. London: Bloomsbury.

Rowling, J.K. (2003). *Harry Potter and the Order of the Phoenix*. London: Bloomsbury.

Rowling, J.K., and Fry, S. (10/12/2005, 2017). *Living with Harry Potter*. BBC Radio 4 Podcast. (2017). Retrieved 8 September 2017.

Rowling, J.K., and Kay, Jim. (2015). *Harry Potter and the Philosopher's Stone*. London: Bloomsbury Publishing.

Said, E. (2014). *Orientalism*. New York: Knopf Doubleday.

Sarland, C. (Ed.) (1999). *The Impossibility of Innocence: Ideology, Politics, and Children's Literature*. Abingdon-on-Thames: Routledge.

Thorne, J., Rowling, J.K., & Tiffany, J. (2016). *Harry Potter and the Cursed Child*. (Special rehearsal edition ed.). London: Little, Brown.

Trombetta, S. (2016). "Why Are Padma and Ron Married In the Alternate Reality of 'Cursed Child'?" Retrieved from https://www.bustle.com/articles/175979-why-are-padma-and-ron-married-in-the-alternate-reality-of-cursed-child.

Welch, B. (2016). "Missing Adventures: Diversity and Children's Literature | TEDxEHC." Retrieved from https://www.youtube.com/watch?v=Yq2opVinciA.

Time Travel and the *Cursed Child*

Elizabeth Morrow Clark

> There was a young lady of Wight
> Who traveled much faster than light.
> She departed one day,
> In a relative way,
> And arrived on the previous night.
> —Stephen Hawking, *A Briefer History of Time*

> "Time isn't a straight line. It's all ... bumpy-wumpy. There's loads of boring stuff ... and ... big temporal tipping points."
> —Dr. Who, "The Impossible Astronaut"

Harry Potter and the Cursed Child premiered on July 30, 2016, on the eve of Harry Potter's 36th birthday. The night Michael Billington of *The Guardian* got a preview of the show, the audience was handed "Keep the Secrets" badges. Nevertheless, Billington was allowed to characterize the production as a "thrilling theatrical spectacle," while also cautioning the audience that the play was primarily for established fans, referring to "hardened Potterheads" as a "global cult" (Billington).

The book (script) release on July 31, 2016, had the familiar midnight parties and late hours at bookstores attendant. By the end of the quarter in which the script was released, the U.S. publisher, Scholastic, was showing a $70 million jump and a 48 percent jump over the first quarter of the 2016 fiscal year (Publishers). The motivation for the release was described by a publishing representative as responding to "massive public demand" and to a desire to "enable the epic eighth Harry Potter story to be read by those fans globally who may not be able to see the stage version" (Bookseller).

By opening in the West End, it seemed that America was getting a reminder that Harry belongs to the Old Country, and the old ways (like theater). Running six hours at the Palace Theatre in London, the play relied on nineteenth-century sensationalism "stimulating the audience with the latest stage technology" for the "quintessential melodrama for the twenty-first century" (Wilson, 2017, 86). The time-travel effects were especially impressive.

Authorship and the right to canon status were immediately a theme in script reviews. In spite of being described by some as little more than authorized "fan fiction," *Cursed Child* (henceforth *CC*) both benefits and suffers from the insatiable appetites of Harry Potter fans (Coats). The New Zealand online pop culture magazine *Spinoff* went so far as to call *CC* a "delicious hot mess of time travel and popular fanfiction tropes from the mid–2000s" from a review author who admitted she found the epilogue "pure, unrealistic wish fulfillment" (Graham). The self-indulgent use of Time Turners to address "what ifs" in past plots irritated some reviewers, and the appearance of Delphi was described as "utterly terrible" unless one imagined "that Rowling secretly put in a lot of hours on Fanfiction.net over the years, cry-laughing and pouring herself more wine" (Graham). Graham decried Rowling for lending her name to this and other expansions, from *Fantastic Beasts* and expanded theme parks to duvet covers. This might seem specious criticism, if it weren't for the line of Potter-themed items featured in PBTeen for the fall 2017 season (Matthews).

Kelly Link of the *New York Times* freely admitted great trepidation in approaching the text. "What if it was like a high school reunion? Harry Potter and I were both older. What if I didn't recognize him? What if we no longer had anything in common?" (Link). Immediately, Link acknowledged, this was Jack Thorne's elaboration on a story that Rowling, Thorne and director John Tiffany worked on collaboratively. Nevertheless, Link credits Thorne with writing a book "I would previously have assumed only J.K. Rowling could write" (Link).

By exploring time travel in the Wizarding World, this essay will draw comparisons to time travel in literature and popular culture, from H.G. Wells to *Dr. Who* to Madeline L'Engle, with special attention paid to "time slip" youth literature. The essay will also consider how scientific and philosophical conversations about time travel can be understood in and through literature. There is a specific purpose to time travel tales, and this essay will argue that *Cursed Child* fits in this genre.

What Is Cursed Child, *as a Text?*

In order to make an argument that studying the time travel concept used in *CC* offers insight into both children's literature and Harry Potter Studies, one must first accept the play as sufficiently connected to both Harry Potter and its author to merit study. In accepting credit for *CC* as her own original story, and in putting her name on the publication, Rowling has made her position clear: that this story is approved by her and may be entered into the Potterverse.

Rowling has demonstrated herself to be an interfering author (or a generous one, depending on one's position) when it comes to interpretation and revelation about the Wizarding World. A living, producing, engaging, *Pottermore*-designing, script writing, interview-giving author cannot be dead, however vehemently Roland Barthes may demand the liberation of a text from an author. In a world where "reader response" also means "consumer-response," studying paracanon is revealing about both author and text. Harry Potter Studies scholars have striven to establish a common canon-related vocabulary for the Potterverse (Camacci, 2016; Bell, *Fandom*, 2016). I argue for the inclusion of *CC* as a paracanon text clearly linked to Rowling, similar to the theme parks and film scores. The collaborative authorship does not interfere by definition, because other elements of paracanon may be items created by fans or as parodies, such as *AVPM: A Very Potter Musical* and "Potter Puppet Pals." Gérard Genette's explanation of a paratext refers to that which is around the text, outside the text but experienced elements as text, like the cover or the author's name. Since Rowling's name is associated with *CC*, even though not listed as the author, even this simple element means *CC* belongs to the Potterverse since "the addresser is defined by putative attribution and by assumed responsibility" (Genette, 1991, 266). *Pottermore* is considered canon, as it is published, and given as "supplementary material" prepared beforehand by the author (Bell, *Fandom*, 2016, 3). This differs from Rowling's observations about Dumbledore being gay, regrets about the Hermione-Ron pairing, or other claims shared in less controlled environments, which, coming after the fact, can be considered metacanon (Bell, *Fandom*, 2016, 3).

The eight studio-produced films, according to Bell and in the catalogue of artifacts shared by Lauren Rose Camacci, are considered alternative canon, since they form the foundational story for many fans, even though they do not reflect the books exactly and are written and directed and interpreted by others, aside from Rowling, but with her participation. The audio podcast *Pottercast* refers to "book canon" and "film canon" in a similar vein (Pottercast). For the purposes of this essay, the following parameters will be observed: that the text is worth studying as a part of the Potter phenomenon, that its creation is more closely linked to Rowling than, for instance, the theme parks, but further from canon than the original books. It qualifies as paracanon. It is not, whatever the publicity hype might claim, an "8th" Potter book on a par with the original seven. It is not, for instance, equivalent to the relationship and canonical relevance between Madeline L'Engle's *A Wrinkle in Time* (1962) and *An Acceptable Time* (1989).

Summary of Cursed Child

As is often true of backwards-moving time travel narratives, *CC* is deeply nostalgic. The past lives on in the very names of the next generation of Potters: James Sirius, Albus Severus and Lily Luna. Any time a parent names a child after a loved one, they seek to extend life into the future, which is itself a sort of time travel. The trio of Weasley, Granger and Potter all get their happy ending and appropriate pairings in the canon, then, through the meddling of a time-turner in *CC*, lose those happy endings, and in some timelines, their very lives. Battle scenes remind *CC* consumers of past victories and challenges. Time travel to the Triwizard Cup and dream sequences involving Hagrid are also backward-looking.

The story also allows for a peek into the adult lives of the characters. Harry's job as Head of Magical Law Enforcement gratifies fans who knew he wanted to be an Auror. Hermione as Minister of Magic has a certain poetry to it. She kept her maiden name, as well, while her daughter's is hyphenated: Rose Granger-Weasley. Ron Weasley fares less well in terms of ambition, but his character is even more lighthearted than in the books, as he takes on Fred's role as raconteur and joke shop owner. Draco Malfoy is a widower, though it is still unclear what sort of profession a Malfoy might pursue. At one point, he confesses to Harry that he has no interest in politics, unlike his own father, and that his dream of playing professional Quidditch was dashed because he was simply not good enough (*CC*, 2016). In *Pottermore*, Rowling notes that Draco has several hobbies that link him to his past, including the collection of Dark artefacts (Draco Malfoy), one of which becomes an important prop in *CC*. Draco has already suffered through multiple layers of regret and nostalgia, as his family strove to regain the position of power they had enjoyed at Voldemort's height, only to be thrown down at the Battle of Hogwarts. Family loyalty, which is a recurring theme, is a strong Malfoy trait.

Harry has burdens and regrets as well. The central one of the story is the death of Cedric Diggory. This is presented as a kind of "unfinished business." It seems odd, considering how many other people died in Harry's name, but the youth of Cedric, the trauma of the cemetery, and the fact that he was apparently the first death Harry consciously witnessed, all mean this was a watershed moment. "[W]ithin children's time-slip fantasy ... generally, unfolding the secrets of history reveals ... reenactment of a national past" (Balay, 139).

The central relationships in *CC* hinge on Albus Severus Potter. Sorted into Slytherin house, Albus has a best friend, Scorpius Malfoy. It is rumored in the Wizarding World that Scorpius is actually the result of a liaison between Astoria Malfoy (née Greengrass) and Voldemort, facilitated through a surviving Time Turner. This cruel twist alienated Draco from the rest of the world even further. Scorpius knows about the rumors; he gestures to his blond hair as proof he is his father's son, commenting, "I mean—father-son issues, I have them. But, on the whole, I'd rather be a Malfoy than, you know, the son of the Dark Lord" (*CC*, 2016, 17).

Albus does not have it as bad, though he plays the martyr. Albus resents Harry, who, while heroic, displays a strong dose of self-centeredness, which is, again, backward looking. Albus overhears (an uncharacteristically sour) Amos Diggory castigating Harry over Cedric's death and soon afterwards learns that the Ministry has acquired a Time Turner. He encounters Diggory's caregiver, Delphi, who convinces Albus and Scorpius they should go back and save Cedric. It is evident that Albus desires more than to correct a past injustice, but is suffering from a deep father-son division. His decision is a criticism of Harry's choices, and of his status as The Boy Who Lived. It also reveals that, as the second son, Albus identifies with Cedric being called "the spare." Albus drags Scorpius, who is a sincere, sensitive bookworm, into the plot. In the end, Albus and Scorpius expose Delphi as a villain and learn more about time travel. Nevertheless, it is the Trio, plus Draco, who arrive to rescue Albus and Scorpius from a time crisis, and, with help from the boys, to defeat the Dark, once again gaining redemption, improving their parenting skills, and bonding with their children. Thus, having attempted to abuse time travel to change history, in the end, time travel functions to restore the present order.

Time Travel and the Time Turner in Cursed Child

Time travel in *CC* allows fans to pursue alternate storylines, much as fan fiction does, by addressing several "what-ifs." Many of these are plot-driven. What if Cedric had not been at the graveyard? What if Hermione had gone to the Yule Ball with Ron instead of Viktor? What if Neville died during the Battle of Hogwarts? Others seem more philosophical. Could a Hufflepuff be a Death Eater? Does torturing and killing during a pregnancy affect the unborn child? Why is the original timeline the only way to defeat Voldemort? Time-travel fiction that relies on backwards-moving time often addresses these sorts of "what ifs." World War II is a popular era for such stories, as is evidenced in the classic *The Man in the High Castle*, by Philip K. Dick, which depicts the United States partitioned between victorious Axis Powers Nazi Germany and Japan. Thus, it is not surprising that alternate endings in *CC* lead to a dystopia featuring the fascistic Death Eaters in a totalitarian system ruled by Voldemort.

In the first use of the Time Turner, the awkward two-boys-and-one-female trio plans to prevent Cedric from winning the Triwizard Tournament and thus prevent his death. They opt to try to keep him from completing the first task. The boys convince Delphi to stay behind, but she offers them this advice, "Today you get an opportunity few are given—today you get to change history—to change time itself" (Thorne, 2016, 100). The first time the play introduces the use of the Time Turner, the stage directions read "And time stops. And then it turns over, thinks a bit, and begins spooling backward, slow at first…" (Thorne, 2016, 105). The insouciant tone reminds one of Douglas Adams more than Rowling. Unfortunately, this anthropomorphizing of time is an underused element in the script. Each time the Time Turner is used, this phrase appears, but no other personality traits emerge. The realization of an explosion of movement, or how time "thinks a bit" is left to the play's director, and lost on the reader. The Time Turner being used by Albus and Scorpius, though described as shining "alluringly" and as "entirely different" as well as more advanced than the one Hermione had used (which had only been for hour-reversals), is revealed to have been a prototype, leaving one to wonder if a more complete version also exists (Thorne, 2016, 30, 260). It does not work for more than five minutes at a time, and using it risks incurring great pain. After they return, Albus' travel injury seems "like it was broken twenty years ago and allowed to set in the 'most contrary' of directions" (Thorne, 2016, 111).

This first shift in the timeline reveals several changes: Albus is a Gryffindor, rather than in Slytherin (where he sorted in the original timeline), Ron married Padma Patil and has a problematic child at Hogwarts, and Harry is an interfering parent, pressuring McGonagall into spying on Albus with the Marauder's Map. Hermione teaches Defense Against the Dark Arts and is single. Ron and Hermione never married because Hermione did not attend the Yule Ball with Viktor Krum, being suspicious that the Triwizard Cup had in some way been corrupted (true, due to Albus and Severus' time travel). This means Albus has participated in the elimination of his cousins Rose (on whom Scorpius has a crush) and Hugo. Many things remain the same, such as Cedric's death, and Harry's eventual victory over Voldemort. When Albus frets over his father's harsh punishments, Scorpius admonishes him:

> Have you heard me, Albus? This is bigger than you and your dad. Professor Croaker's law—the furthest someone can go back in time without the possibility of serious harm to the traveler or time itself is five hours. And we went back years. The smallest moment, the smallest change, it creates ripples. And we—we've created really bad ripples. Rose was never born because of what we did [Thorne, 2016, 139].

The next use of the Time Turner has much more dire consequences. Instead of simply trying to knock Cedric out of the running for the Triwizard cup, the duo decides to try to humiliate him during the second task, with help from Moaning Myrtle. They do, but when Scorpius is thrown back into his own time, he is dragged back to school by Dolores Umbridge, on Voldemort Day. This alternate timeline shows Scorpius what life for him could have been like, had his family been at the center of power, instead of outcasts. This is Part Two of the play. Instead of seeming more like bookish Hermione, Scorpius is like Harry, or like a more complete version of Draco. He is athletic, a successful Slytherin Seeker, Head Boy material, liked by the most popular girls, and nicknamed "Scorpion King." Other students do his homework for him, freeing him up to torture Muggles. Hogwarts seems to be a combination of books five and seven. Scorpius' change is a reflection of the change in the world. Draco is in Harry's job, as Head of Magical Law Enforcement. Voldemort is back in power and at his side is someone called the "Augurey" whose motto is "the future is ours to make" (Thorne, 2016, 170). Snape is still a double agent, and Hermione is the leader of the underground DA, which includes Ron. Harry, however, is dead (explaining Albus' absence), because losing the Triwizard tournament caused Cedric to turn into a Death Eater, fight for Voldemort, and kill Neville Longbottom, leaving a Horcrux unkilled by Neville and thus Voldemort undefeatable. The "grandfather paradox" of time travel had come home to roost. Hermione, Ron, and Snape all sacrifice themselves in this timeline to get Scorpius back in place so he can counteract the effects of the first changes in the timeline. Already a reluctant time traveler, Scorpius observes, "It feels like we were all tested and we all—failed" (Thorne, 2016, 170). The moralizing tone seems directed at both the characters and the observer. How dare one wish for an alternate ending, or a different scenario. The consequences are always dire. People die.

Returning to a readjusted normal timeline and just at the moment when Albus and Scorpius decide they have had enough of playing with time, the true identity of the character Delphi is discovered, and completes the father-child circle by giving truth to the claim that Voldemort had a child (by Bellatrix, in this case). Though this is the sort of "reveal" that has led critics to compare *CC* to fan fiction run amok, it balances the generational element of the story with the science-fiction fantasy themes. Delphi steals the Time Turner, calling herself the new past, and the new future, and proclaiming the prophecy she learned from Rodolphus Lestrange when he returned from Azkaban, "When spares are spared, when time is turned, when unseen children murder their fathers: Then will the Dark Lord return" (Thorne, 2016, 287). While unfortunately phrased and lacking any context, at least part of Delphi's plot seems clearer in this moment—that the "spare" would be Cedric and that the most eloquent murder of a father would be that of Harry, by one of his children (Thorne, 2016, 220). In a continuation of re-balancing the original canon, Draco provides an illegal object, a Time Turner built just for his father. He had kept it, wishing for a way out of his widower's grief. "It is exceptionally lonely, being Draco Malfoy. I will always be suspected. There is no escaping the past." Harry agrees, and admits that, as a parent, he also was guilty of trying to rewrite his own past, and damaging his present in the meantime (Thorne, 2016, 261). This is something the Potter Generation, many now parenting or soon to parent, can recognize: that living one's past over again, through one's children, is harmful. It is also a heavy-handed and didactic use of time travel as a literary device.

Harry Potter and the Time Slip Traditions

Cursed Child is not quite a time-slip story. The British style time-slip fantasy depends on time travel as an accident, outside the control of the traveler, much like the world-changing experiences of the Pevensie children in the C.S. Lewis Narnia stories. It has been argued that time-slip stories and time travel tales in general are conservative, disappointing, and anti–Marxist, because they reinforce the moral value of a set timeline, and often glorify the past "in response to a disappointing present" (Balay, 131; Rosenthal, 103). By expanding the timeline of the story and adding a second epilogue to the book series, *CC* functions as an act of completion, rather than closure. Cadden posits that epilogues often exist because authors do not trust children to comprehend a story. When adding an epilogue that reinforces a happily-ever-after, authors limit a child's imagination and offer an unhealthy reassurance that life will not change. *Cursed Child* often falls into this trap.

American children often are introduced to time travel and time-slip style narratives in the "Magic Tree House" series. In Lloyd Alexander's *Time Cat*, Gareth the cat takes his owner, Jason, across his nine lifelines, and Jason learns "what you have to know to be a grown up" (Alexander, 203). Like *Star Trek*'s Prime Directive, *CC* implies that there are regulations to limit the damage done by intervention in another's experience. Like *Dr. Who*, the story considers whether certain events are fixed, and if unhinged, what damage might prevail. Like Connie Willis' short novel *Firewatch*, moral decisions and participation in history transform a character. While other elements of *CC* are static, the transformation of Albus is active and the revealed goodness in Scorpius bodes well for the future of the Wizarding World.

A more sophisticated example of time slip is Madeline L'Engle's *A Wrinkle in Time* in which characters traverse time and space, using a *tesseract*, to right a wrong, relying on physics and spiritual strength, which definitely comes across as magic. While *Wrinkle* is the most familiar of the series, it belongs to the "Time Quintet." All of the books feature time travel at some level, and the last two can be considered time-slip, that is, hinging on accidental time travel. In *Many Waters*, two characters are sent back in time by computer, and in *An Acceptable Time*, a character is sent back in time. Only in *A Swiftly Tilting Planet* does a character, Charles Wallace, intentionally traverse through time in order to alter history. This is the most similar example to Albus and Scorpius' travel, with the exception that Charles Wallace is cast more in the line of Harry Potter-savior, supervised by wiser and more powerful beings, whereas Albus and Scorpius' journey is unauthorized and unsupervised. The character of Delphi is the reverse of Dumbledore in this instance, though not quite Voldemort. Albus and Scorpius are not Draco, being sent in as a proxy in a larger ideological war, but agents of chaos, tampering with time and history. Thus *CC* breaks with the Harry Potter tradition of launching protagonists into dangerous but worthy adventures. In doing so it also violates the comforting characteristics of a completed Epilogue. Clearly *CC* adheres to the form of children's science fiction fantasy literature, while also aiming for the adult Harry Potter Generation audiences able to afford tickets to West End, and now Broadway, theaters.

Rather than positing theories of time travel, as does L'Engle, exploring the past, as does Alexander, or foretelling the future of humanity through science fiction, as Isaac Asimov or H.G. Wells have done, *CC* reflects primarily on the changes to the Wizarding World that might have taken place if several plot changes often favored by fans had been corrected or altered. In this way, it considers the moral and ethical choices made by characters who might change the past. For canon-watchers, it is also relevant that Rowling's comments about regretting the Ron-Hermione "ship" are called into question. Ron and Hermione are in love and are better people and more productive citizens when the timeline puts them together. Ginny and Harry, when they continue to exist, are a given, and so are Scorpius' parents. The role of time travel, therefore, is to reinforce the truth of the past in the Wizarding World. This is an important characteristic of time-travel and time-slip literature, that it reinforces the reality of the fantasy story, by giving it a past that is set in time, and that, if changed, affects the future chronology of a known narrative (Balay, 133).

The Science of Time Travel

Time travel entered into the literary imagination with H.G. Wells' *The Time Machine* in 1895, a modern mode of fantasy (Gleick, 5). Wells' Time Traveller character introduced his circle to the idea of four dimensions, a concept Charles Howard Hinton had already proposed as a *tesseracti*, a four dimensional model. The Time Traveller proposed that just thinking about the past, being "lost" in thought about the past, was a primitive sort of time travel compared to his invention, analogous to a person jumping up and down versus using a balloon to leave the earth (Wells, 7). When Wells wrote his story, the time machine called to mind the phenomenon of the bicycle, a modern object that now seems quaint. Similarly, the technology of the Time-Turner in *Harry Potter* is a quaint hourglass, made of metal, glass and sand, but still in the category of steampunk design that characterizes other magical machines depicted in the stories. It is more modern than, say, a wand, or a bowl of magical Pensieve fog, or a fireplace. While critics of Harry Potter consider the relatively pre-industrial Wizarding World to be positively Luddite, the Time Turner comes straight out of a modern science fiction and fantasy tradition (Teare, 2002, 339).

In Victorian England, time travel fell into the same category as other mysterious and unexplainable aspects to existence, like the occult, or telepathy. The temporal dissonance brought on by the speed of modern life and dominated by trains and the telegraph, required a sociocultural adjustment. This modern idea looked forward, as modernity does. Time travel in *CC* is, however, backward looking, about regret, whether personal or inherited.

Time travel as a device to observe or change the past demonstrates that historical knowledge has value. Early critics of Wells' time machine noted that there were profound ethical and logical flaws with a machine that could move backward, though the Time Traveller never uses this function. "A past that included a Time Traveller would be a different past, a new past" (Gleick, 49). Professor Walter Pitkin of Columbia University responded to Wells in 1914, saying "real time is history: and history is the course of physical events. It is the sequence…" (Gleick, 52). *Cursed Child* confronts multiple crises in chronology, including the "grandfather paradox," as introduced by Hugo Gernsback, the Luxembourgish émigré and pulp magazine publisher extraordinaire, who had to his credit multiple science magazines, and famously, *Amazing Stories*. The "grandfather paradox" posits that one cannot go back in time and kill one's grandfather before the conception of one's parents, because then one could never exist to travel back in time in the first place.

From fiction to physics, conceptualizing time travel has become a part of contemporary life in the arts and sciences. Historians posit as a given that "multiple observers experience their own present moments," and, thus like Einstein, must argue against simultaneity, and perhaps, hold a space for reconsidering time (Gleick, 79). The moment we observe an event, it is in the past. The debate between Einstein and Henri Bergson plays out in philosophy and science and history and Harry Potter. Moving through time is about process, and human existence and consciousness depends on time, not space, for its essence. "What really *exists* is not things made but things in the making…. Time is action" (Gleick, 51, 81). Einstein's own response to death and time offers much to the Harry Potter philosopher with the words, "the distinction between past, present and future is only a stubbornly persistent illusion" (Gleick, 84).

Stephen Hawking and Leonard Mlodinow have acknowledged that any presumption of time travel is inextricably linked to the ability to travel faster than light (Hawking, 2005, 107). They note that one flaw in science fiction is that, though traveling faster than the speed of light solves plot problems with intergalactic exploration or warfare, it does not take into account that "if you can travel faster than light, the theory of relativity implies you can also travel back in time" (Hawking, 2005, 108). Using particle accelerators, scientists have gotten particles to 99.99 percent of the speed of light, but no further. Hawking explains that "what is needed in order to warp space-time in a way that will allow travel into the past is matter with negative energy density." Quantum laws, based on the uncertainty principle, might allow for such negative energy (Hawking, 2005, 110). If an advanced civilization could keep a wormhole open long enough to get a spaceship through it, travel into the past might result. Magic replaces technology in the Wizarding World, but whether this magic is evidence of a more advanced civilization is doubtful. The Wizarding World has many of the same things as the Muggle World, and inhabits the same space. There is no indication that there is a separate dimension or time travel in order to reach the Wizarding World. Nevertheless, one wonders if Stephen Hawking would allow for wizards as an advanced civilization and a Time Turner as a wormhole in space.

Certainly, in the imaginations of the directors of Potter films, bending around space has been depicted in connection with travel. In *PoA*, Rowling's description of time travel is limited to "the sensation that he was flying very fast, backward" (Rowling, *Azkaban*, 394). In *PoA*, Harry and Hermione do not have to use the Time Turner again, since they used up the 3 hours they were gone, and returned at the moment they had departed, replacing themselves. One presumes Hermione has been doing this all semester, as part of her double-course schedule. No wonder she was tired, since she was living longer than 24-hour days.

Roger Highfield wonders if the magic of Tom Riddle's diary or reaching Platform 9¾ might, in fact, be wormhole portals (Highfield, 2002). Apparition and Floo powder, in Highfield's view, also present experiences much like those wormhole experiences depicted in Carl Sagan's *Contact*, but the science of that experience has been criticized. Highfield expounds on Stephen Hawking's wormhole theories, reminding Harry Potter fans that inserting a particle into a wormhole, according to Hawking, will destabilize it. This is called a chronology projection conjecture. According to Hawking, it disproves the possibility of time travel, making "the universe safe for historians" (Woodward, 1995, 3).

Time travel along one's own timeline is problematic. If a character is placed in a distant past, they may affect a long timeline, or they may simply observe society and bring wisdom back to the present. When a character is placed in the recent past, either in their own generation or the generation before, there is often a desire to change or correct mistakes, in addition to gaining pure knowledge. "Characters may also be faced with the choice of staying in an idealized past, thus remaining children, or returning to their own time, to continue maturing into adulthood" (Balay, 134). This combination of gaining historical understanding and maturity can also be seen in the core *Harry Potter* books, when Harry is magically exposed to the past through the Pensieve and through Riddle's diary, via a form of temporary time-travel (but one in which he can only serve as observer) and he returns with a more complete understanding of the present context. He also encounters events which compromise an idealized past, such as his father's ruthless teasing of Snape, and the conditions of Hagrid's expulsion from Hogwarts. Lavoie argues that the Mirror of Erised also functions as a sort of time-vision, seeing "through or past death" and calls to mind the Biblical reference from Corinthians 13:10, "For now we see through a glass darkly; but then face to face." (This apt reference also reminds readers of C. S. Lewis' adult story of two sisters *Till We Have Faces: A Myth Retold*.) The themes of death and forgiveness in *Till We Have Faces* are also evident in the glimpses of the past evidenced in the spell "Priori Incantatem" (GF) and in the use of the Resurrection Stone (DH). Thus, Harry himself is constantly linked, through his own past and the prophecies that touch his future, to a timeline. His ability to "accept traces as connections to the past" are "indications that the past has passed" (Zimmerman, 194).

Tangentially, the role of prophecy in the seven books represents time travel into the future. Acceptance of or rebellion against prophecy allows characters some mode of control *vis a vis* time, destiny, and linear expectations. During an interview about *Deathly Hallows*, Rowling invoked Shakespeare saying, "like Macbeth, Voldemort sealed his fate by believing it was decided in the first place" ("Rowling"). By tampering with future time, Voldemort created his own nemesis. Harry's visions may also be a type of foresight, while Horcruxes are a perversion of time and humanity (Lavoie, 48, Zimmerman 199).

Reviewers used words like "post–Freudian" and "Oedipal" to describe *Cursed Child*, which has its share of teen angst and frustration. This dovetails with time-travel narratives in which "[c]hildren who are isolated or damaged by culture and consequently resistant to maturity are, by virtue of their liminality, well positioned to see and understand the disturbing, hidden pasts layered in these locations" (Balay, 139). Damaged children like Harry, Draco, Scorpius and Albus have an especially profound relationship to the past, to hidden histories, and to place. In *CC*, one can go back in time with a Time Turner, but one does not change physical place, so that a hidden past is both a chronological and geographical given. The history element of time travel present in *CC* also dovetails with Richard Feynman's "way of expressing quantum theory as a sum over histories" (Pössel). In this idea, a universe does not just have one history, but every possible history, with its own probability. Alternative history writers presume that there are different planes of histories, as described by Hugh Everett III, parallel universes. In this case, rather than having all possible outcomes of an experience collapse into one real measurement, because the universe is expanding and splitting, there is no collapse, and every outcome of a measurement exists in its own universe, displaying a multiverse. This concept is played out in the 1990s television series *Sliders* and in more recent television programs like *The Flash, Supergirl,* and *Arrow*. Nevertheless, both Feynman and Rowling consider a history to be timeline-consistent. Thus, McGonagall is right; meddling with time is dangerous and the consequences can be grim.

The (Changeable?) History of Harry Potter

The themes of time presented by CC, for all that it is set in "the future" (the present?), is also about the past, about consequences, about turning points, and most especially, about Time Turners. It is shocking that the Ministry's entire supply of Time Turners was destroyed by random misfires of magic during the battle in the Department of Mysteries during Harry's fifth year, a battle between half a dozen teenagers and some seemingly incompetent Death Eaters. It seems even more improbable that Time Turners would be so closely monitored as to be hidden in the depths of the Department of Mysteries, but one was given to Dumbledore to help eighth-grader Hermione (for all that she was the brightest witch of her age) just to go to classes. And who believes that at some point in the next two years, Dumbledore, who was searching for Horcurxes, just blithely returned it to the Ministry? Thus, the premise in *CC* that only a beta-version edition and one Malfoy commission would really still exist within a generation seems improbable, but that improbability is not just Jack Thorne's responsibility. Rowling set up a less-than-credible scenario from the start.

Reviewer Kelly Link observed that the questions posed and answered in *CC* are those "you can ask only after a series has been wrapped up successfully and everyone has had their just deserts" (Link). At the core is the question—what if we could see our loved ones, whether people or characters, just one more time? This is the question the *CC* indulges, while it also explores the nature of time and history, the simultaneous immutability of the timeline of the plot with the flexibility of the text once it leaves the hands of its author.

The question of time travel and alternative history in the *Harry Potter* series begins by begging the question of free will and fate. If not all prophecies have been fulfilled, but the prophecies relating to Voldemort will inevitably involve Harry, can he be the master of his fate, or can he only manipulate his fate in a narrow window? Correspondingly, if Albus and Scorpius can use the Time Turner to alter history, does this negate the power of prophecy in general? Since the prophecies and Time Turners exist in the same Wizarding World, one must reconsider how exploding the canon can liberate the story line from some of its fairy-tale conventions (Pond). Scientists and philosophers also find the free will aspect of time travel a puzzlement. "If time travel is possible, then the past has a real objective existence, as does the future, and 'free will' is irrelevant" (Woodward, 1995). In a multiverse or transactional model, time travel might be possible, because many worlds could exist.

While the dangers of using a Time Turner, whether a demo model or the real thing, are discussed in *Prisoner of Azkaban* (risk of madness) and these dangers are a theme in popular culture and in science, what better way to bridge the temporal gap between the stories we love and a new timeline? Like the Pensieve, the Time Turners offer a glimpse of a future reality, but this time, with the opportunity to make a change. Readers can get a glimpse, or in *CC*, several glimpses, of alternative histories. If one can get past the technical aspects—time travel can be a physically harmful magical task, with consequences, like splinching in apparating, or that one can exist in two places in the same five-minute span without tearing apart the time-space continuum, *CC* explores the consequences of the past on the present through familial relationships with big-picture consequences. Whereas in *PoA*, the primary concern is that one not see oneself, or be seen by others, moving contrary to the timeline, *CC* directly addresses the corruption of the past. In *PoA*, "some interference from the present may be a predestined part of the past" (Zimmerman, 202). Since it is implied that Buckbeak could die, but he is not depicted as actually being killed, and since Harry sees himself conjure the Patronus, violating Dumbledore's injunction, but in his ignorance, avoiding the consequence, Rowling seems to be leaning more towards a prophecy-and-predestination theme than a time-travel tale. Dumbledore suggests to the pair that two innocent lives could be saved, meaning Buckbeak and Sirius. Hawking and Mlodinow suggest that this resolution of a possible paradox can be explained by the premise that:

> what happens in space-time must be a consistent solution of the laws of physics. In other words, according to this viewpoint, you could not go back in time unless history already showed that you had gone back and, while there, had not killed your great-great-grandfather or committed any other acts that would conflict with the history of how you got to your current situation in the present. Moreover, when you did go back, you wouldn't be able to change recorded history; you would merely be following it. In this view the past and future are preordained: you would not have free will to do what you wanted [Hawking, 2005, 115].

Harry's experience, seeing himself conjure a Patronus, offers several layers to the time-travel imagery in Rowling's works. First, the reader knows that Harry looks like his father, that he has seen pictures of his father, and that he thinks he sees his father conjure the Patronus, "it looked like him.... I've got photos of him..." (Rowling, 1999, *Prisoner*, 407). Next, his father's Patronus was a stag, as was the animal "Prongs" that he transfigured into. This was the corporeal Patronus Harry witnessed. Kj Swanson has noted that "When Harry shouts 'Expecto Patronum,' he acts on the expectation of seeing his father (*expect pater*), but at the same time sends his own protector (*expecto patronus*)" (Bell, *Legilimens*, 108). Expecting someone from the past to re-appear, Harry, himself living in the past, rescued himself. "I knew I could do it this time," he says, "because I'd already done it" (Rowling, 1999, *Prisoner*, 412). Scorpius notes a similar lesson learned from the Time Turner, when he changed himself back, "because I knew what I should be." He was able to fend off dementors, lured by those who have suffered past hurts, by thinking of his friend, again echoing Harry's experiences (Thorne, 2016, 211, 212).

While this is a critical moment of realization in the series, it is possible that re-introducing the Time Turner in *CC* is a recognition of the incomplete use of this magical object in past narratives, as well as an opportunity to address basic time travel questions about why bad things might be left unaddressed, in a world blessed with Time Turners. The Wizarding World seems to have few rules about time, unlike the Timelords' Laws of Time in *Dr. Who*, which posit that there are fixed points in time which cannot be changed. In the episode *Father's Day*, the Ninth Doctor warned Rose Tyler not to encounter her former self, and create a paradox. Rose Tyler saved her father's life on the day he should have died, held herself as an infant, and created a paradox-driven time rift, allowing creatures called "Reapers" to enter and a catastrophe to ensue. In order to set things right, her father had to allow himself to die on that day.

In the end, *Cursed Child*, by playing with time travel, reinforces historical narratives and story. By answering "what ifs" that have certainly dogged fan culture, Rowling, through Thorne, has the last word. Fans can linger again in the Wizarding World, reassured by this epilogue to the Epilogue: that the happy ending of marriage-family persists (even if a mother dies, the fairy tale of the family structure remains). This is both gratifying and stifling, as nostalgia often is. Nostalgia extends past wishing for a romanticized past by evoking "the pangs of longing for another time, another place, another self," and that these longings "can also be the refracting lenses of constructive critique" (Balay, 140). Fandoms themselves are rife with nostalgia, and the positive audience responses to the "firsts" that characterize most people's experiences of *Harry Potter* occur multiple times in *CC*. The story may also leave audiences wishing, like Harry as he approaches middle age, to reify youth. There are dangers in the middle phase of life.

The elements of fan fiction at work in Thorne's script—the following through of a few ideas, the occasional stylistic slip, and the exploration of new characters—take on the weight of canon when published, heralded, produced, and rewarded. The result is a *Man in the High Castle* style moral warning, an apocalyptic H.G. Wells scenario, the shattering of history as in *Slaughterhouse Five*, and a *Dr. Who*-like historical confection. Doors open for fans in some cases. If a reader interprets Hermione as black, this is now permitted, and co-exists with the white Hermione of film and illustrated editions. If a reader rehabilitates Slytherin as a house that can produce heroes, Scorpius is a charming and brave example. But *Cursed Child*, like Pottermore and *Fantastic Beasts* and other glimpses into the back-story and past of the Wizarding World, also serves as a slammed door in the face of any other fan theories about what might have happened "if." It is a time travel fantasy of the conservative backward-looking genre.

REFERENCES

Alexander, L. (1963). *Time Cat: The Remarkable Journeys of Jason and Gareth.* New York: Puffin.
Anelli, M. Franco, F., Luay, Z., and Noe, J. (2016, May 31). *Cursed Child Party at GeekyCon.* [audio podcast]. Retrieved from www.pottercast.com.
Balay, A. (2010). "Zilpha Keatley Snyder's *The Truth About Stone Hollow* and the Genre of Time-Slip Fantasy." *Children's Literature Association Quarterly*, 35(2), 131–143.
Bell, C.E. (2016). *From Here to Hogwarts: Essays on Harry Potter Fandom and Fiction.* Jefferson, NC: McFarland.
_____. (2012) *Hermione Granger Saves the World: Essays on the Feminist Heroine of Hogwarts.* Jefferson, NC: McFarland.
_____. (2013). *Legilimens! Perspectives in Harry Potter Studies.* Newcastle upon Tyne: Cambridge Scholars.
_____. (2016). *Wizards vs. Muggles: Essays on Identity and the Harry Potter Universe.* Jefferson, NC: McFarland.
Billington, M. (2016, July 26). "Harry Potter and the Cursed Child Review—Duel of Dark and Light Carried Off with Dazzling Assurance." *The Guardian.* Retrieved from www.theguardian.com/stage/2016/jul/26/harry-potter-cursed-child-review-palace-theatre-london.
Cadden, M. (2012). "All is Well: The Epilogue in Children's Fantasy Fiction." *Narrative*, 20(3), 343–356.
Camacci, L. (2016). "What Counts as Harry Potter Canon?" *In Media res.* Retrieved from www.mediacommons.futureofthebook.org/imr/2016/11/10/what-counts-harry-potter-canon.
Coats, K. (2016, November 10). "Review, *Harry Potter and the Cursed Child.*" In *Bulletin of the Center for Children's Books*, 70 (3).
Dick, P.K. (1962). *The Man in the High Castle.* New York: G.P. Putnam's Sons.
Genette, G. and M. Maclean. (1991). "Introduction to the Paratext." *New Literary History* 22 (2), 261–272.
"Harry Potter and the Cursed Child: Emma Watson Praises Noma Dumezweni's Hermione." (2016, July 8). *The Guardian.* Retrieved from www.theguardian.com.
Highfield, R. (2002). *The Science of Harry Potter.* New York: Penguin.
"J.K. Rowling's answers questions about 'Hallows.'" (2007, July 10). *Daily Press.* Retrieved from http://www.dailypress.com/news/dp-now-harrypotter-authorinterview-story.html.
Kerbarle, K. (2009). "'If Rowling Says Dumbledore Is Gay, Is He Gay?' Harry Potter and the Role of Authorial Intention." *Hogshead Conversations: Essays on Harry Potter, Vol I.* edited by Travis Prinzi. Allentown, PA: Zossima.

Lavoie, C. (2014). "Rebelling Against Prophecy in *Harry Potter* and *The Underland Chronicles.*" *The Lion and the Unicorn* 38 (1), 45–65.
L'Engle, Madeleine. (1962). *A Wrinkle in Time*. New York: Farrar, Straus and Giroux.
_____. (1989). *An Acceptable Time*. New York: Farrar, Straus and Giroux.
Link, K. (2016, September 4). "Letting All the 'What Ifs' Out to Play." *The New York Times Book Review*, 8.
"Little, Brown, Bags Potter Play Script." (2016, February 12). *The Bookseller* (5702), 8.
Matthews, L. (2017, September 14). "This Harry Potter Décor Collection is Magical AF." *Cosmopolitan*. Retrieved from www.cosmopolitan.com.
Millot, J. (2016, September 26). "'Cursed Child' Drives Big Gains at Scholastic's Trade Group." *Publishers Weekly*. Retrieved from https://www.publishersweekly.com/pw/by-topic/industry-news/financial-reporting/article/71538-cursed-child-drives-big-gains-in-scholastic-s-trade-group.html.
Moffat, S. (Writer). Hurran, N. (Director). (2013, November 23). "Day of the Doctor" (television series episode). In S. Moffat, and Faith Penhale (Producers) *Doctor Who*. London: BBC One.
Pond, J. (2010). "A Story of the Exceptional: Fate and Free Will in the Harry Potter Series." *Children's Literature* 38, 181–206.
Pösell, Markus. (2006). "The Sum Over All Possibilities: The Path Integral Formulation of Quantum Theory." *Einstein Online*, 2, 1020.
Rosenthal, J. (2016). "Some Thoughts on Time Travel." *Victorian Studies* 59 (1), 102–104.
Rowling, J.K. (1999). *Harry Potter and the Prisoner of Azkaban*. New York: Scholastic.
_____. (ND) "Writing by J.K. Rowling: Draco Malfoy." *Pottermore*. Retrieved from https://www.pottermore.com/writing-by-jk-rowling/draco-malfoy.
Teare, E. (2002). "Harry Potter and the Technology of Magic." *The Ivory Tower and Harry Potter: Perspectives on a Literary Phenomenon*. Edited by Lana A. Whited. Columbia: University of Missouri Press.
Wells, H.G. (1895). *The Time Machine*. Retrieved from https://www.fourmilab.ch/etexts/www/wells/timemach/timemach.pdf.
Wilson, J. (2017, March). "Review, *Harry Potter And the Cursed Child, Parts 1 And 2.*" *Theatre Journal* 69 (1), 86–88.
Woodward, J.F. (1995). "Making the Universe Safe for Historians: Time Travel and the Laws of Physics." *Foundations of Physics Letters* 8, 1–39.
Zimmerman, V. (2009). "Harry Potter and the Gift of Time." *Children's Literature*, 37, 194–215.

Frisky, Risky Firewhisky
The Rhetorical Function of Alcohol
Lauren Camacci

"'You know what?' Ron murmured, looking over at the bar with enthusiasm. 'We could order anything we liked in here, I bet that bloke would sell us anything, he wouldn't care. I've always wanted to try firewhisky—'You—are—a—*prefect*,' snarled Hermione" (*OotP*, p. 337). In this entertaining moment in *Order of the Phoenix*, Ron once again struggles to conduct himself as a prefect. Wandering off the beaten path and entering The Hog's Head pub, he is tempted to try hard liquor, before Hermione (as usual) reminds him to behave himself. Although there might be a lot of distance from here to Hogwarts, past scholarship and popular observation have noted the valuable life lessons muggles can learn from *Harry Potter*. Many behaviors are common to wizards and muggles alike, straddling the boundary between adolescence and adulthood, such as romance, loyalty in friendships, work ethic, balancing academics and extracurricular activities, and the use of alcohol.

There is no shortage of scholarship on the different life lessons to be gained from reading *Harry Potter*. Vezzali et al. (2015), for example, conducted social science research that showed that children exposed to Rowling's series and who identify with heroic characters like Harry or Hermione tend to be more tolerant of differences in sexuality and immigration status than those who have not read or identified with *Harry Potter*. Similarly, authors throughout the many volumes of scholarship on the series—including the other Bell volumes—highlight life lessons from *Potter*. Bell's 2012 *Hermione Granger Saves the World*, for example, contains 11 essays on feminism and the power of women in the series, meeting a decade-long need for more involved scholarship in this area. As with the message of friendship and tolerance, one will have missed an important point in Rowling's series if one walks away from the series without an increased respect for intelligent women. The combination of life lessons and massive readership make *Harry Potter* ripe for scholarly inquiry.

As Hermione tells us in *Sorcerer's Stone*, *Harry Potter* teaches readers about "friendship and bravery," among many other life lessons. But what of those life lessons the books do not overtly teach? Many book series geared towards young adults take on weighty themes like friends' betrayal, sex, death, and substance use. These series allow young people to tackle symbolically some of the inevitable conflicts of growing up. The lessons of *Harry Potter*, by contrast, seem to have more in common with the lessons one expects to find in children's literature, those broader lessons about friendship, perseverance, bravery, and loyalty. Bridging the gap between a children's series and YA novels, the *Harry Potter* series navigated the space that exists between the types of lessons such series offer. The role of alcohol, I believe, illustrates this duality exceptionally.

Why is such a study necessary? I see three main rationales for scholarly investigation into the role of alcohol in *Harry Potter*. First, as stated above, *Harry Potter* is one of the most universally consumed stories in the world. Scholastic's author page on J.K. Rowling estimates that around 400 million copies of the books have sold over the two decades of *Potter*'s existence—and this does not even consider the wide range of the films and other paracanon.[1] As any public speaking teacher (like myself) should be able to tell you, the "bandwagon" is a logical fallacy for a reason; just because something is popular does not mean that it is good or should be followed. Arguing something's worth based on its popularity brings to mind the high school "popularity contest" and its attendant shallowness. But when a decidedly not-shallow text like *Harry Potter* reaches such a massive level of popularity, the lessons it imparts are worth our attention.

Second, studying alcohol in the series can teach us about the plot of the novels. The series is not *about* alcohol, but hard beverages play a central role in forwarding the plot of the books. Drinks that decrease one's ability to make good choices and behave admirably feature centrally in a series where a main lesson is the importance of good choices and actions. This dissonance, I suggest, offers insight both into the plot of the series and into the rhetorical choices that Rowling made in transitioning her story from children's to young adult (YA) novels.

The final rationale is a matter of application. Universities around the United States have been dealing with an increasing alcohol problem on their campuses; young people in the U.S. are engaging in dangerous drinking that has led to serious injuries and deaths (e.g., Flanagan, 2017). Fisher (1989) asserted that humans are storytelling animals, and that storytelling can change minds better than "traditional persuasion." The popularity of the Rowling story may provide a useful means to understand more than just the role of alcohol in the series, perhaps offering real-life advice. Indeed, Welsh (2007) notes the surprising amount of alcohol provision to minors present in *Half-Blood Prince*. In this article, he points to concerning moments of alcohol use in the text and posits the many routes educators could take to integrate conversations about adolescent alcohol use into their classrooms using this touchstone text. He asks many of the same questions about the purpose of alcohol in the books as I ask in this essay, but he offers educational interventions rather than seeking textual answers for such questions. In this climate of dangerous drinking among a generation that grew up reading *Harry Potter*, Welsh's suggestion that interventions occur is timely advice. I have been contemplating the role of alcohol in *Harry Potter* for about ten years, but investigating it seems even more socially salient at this time when youth and alcohol are clashing with deadly consequences.

To provide a concise but thorough assessment of the role of alcohol in *Harry Potter*, I made several strategic choices about scope. The films took several liberties when adapting the novels for the screen, including some moments of increased alcohol consumption. Indeed, popular press articles have noticed with concern the boozier aspects of the films (e.g., Parker-Pope, 2009), and Daniel Radcliffe's revelations of his struggle with alcoholism brought conversations about *Potter* and alcohol into many households (see Hough, 2012). While these rhetorical choices are worthy of inquiry, to treat both films and novels responsibly would require a much lengthier project. I see similar merit in studying the *Potter*-themed cocktails that have sprung up over the years, as well as the drinking games that accompany some viewers' screenings of the *Potter* movie marathons. That a drinking culture could evolve from a series of children's novels is a fascinating phenomenon worthy of study in another project.

In this essay, I argue that alcohol has a unique place in the *Harry Potter* series, both within the individual book plots and the overall story-arc. Both unremarkable and indispensable, both transparent and substantive, Rowling's series in many cases relies on booze while neither glorifying it nor condemning it. Indeed, I will suggest that alcohol is one means by which Rowling engages the choice/fate dichotomy so vital to the series. In the pages to follow, I will first situate *Harry Potter* within a long tradition of children's/YA novels that feature alcohol to show that this is not a Rowling innovation. I will then explore the many, varied, and often-paradoxical roles of alcohol in the *Potter* series before drawing conclusions.

Alcohol in Children's/YA Literature

While it may seem unintuitive, alcohol has long been a feature in children's/YA literature. Whether it is the central plot point, entirely banal, or peripheral to the plot, alcohol is a common part in children's/YA fiction. Before the publication and proliferation of the *Harry Potter* series, Swan (1992) differentiated between books with alcohol as a "major theme" and those with "incidental" alcohol references. Both have a role in the wide selection of reading material for children and young adults; alcohol is a literary theme to varying extents.

As a major theme in children's/YA literature, alcohol teaches life lessons. Many authors have written books to try to explain alcoholism to young readers. For example, Hastings and Typpo (1994) wrote *An Elephant in the Living Room* explicitly to help children comprehend and get through a family member's alcoholism. These books focus on the interpersonal and medical realities of alcohol in an attempt to mediate the sociological difficulties of addiction. *Elephant* is a type of self-help book to help young people work through the complicated reality of living with an addicted person. These stories fill an important need. As Burke (1967) asserted, literature is "equipment for living"; reading stories about alcoholism can teach young people lessons about coping with alcoholism in their own lives.

A similar life-lessons approach appears in young adult fiction. Many coming-of-age stories show their teen characters consuming alcohol and dealing with the attendant consequences or complications. The main characters in *The Sisterhood of the Traveling Pants* series, for example, grapple with the responsible use of alcohol—sometimes turning to drink in times of crisis, other times consuming wine and beer casually with family on special occasions (Brashares, 2001, 2003, 2005, 2007, 2011). Many other books follow teens' struggles with growing up, often including alcohol in some measure. In stories like *Go Ask Alice* (Sparks, 1971) and *Inexcusable* (Lynch, 2016), alcohol/drugs teach lessons about the intersection of growing up, learning to deal with conflict, and the consequences of substance use.

Many older children's/YA novels focus far less on alcohol as a major theme; alcohol is instead incidental, often banal. Just as adults casually smoke cigarettes in children's/young adult stories from as late as the 1990s, standards for casual alcohol consumption may have been more lax than they are now. For example, the young protagonists in *Anne of Green Gables*, Anne and Diana, get drunk on currant wine in one memorable episode (Montgomery, 1908). *Gables* is not a fantasy story, but fantasy tales like *Alice in Wonderland* also feature food and drink that have some profound effect on the body (Carroll, 1865). In these stories, substances create moments for important plot development.

Many other children's/YA fantasy stories from the past include alcohol in passing, as just another part of life. *The Chronicles of Narnia* and *The Hobbit/The Lord of the Rings* feature alcohol in this way. Especially when the heroic characters have won a victory, celebrations include wine, beer, and mead. In his *Companion to Narnia*, Ford lists at least nine instances in the series where characters imbibe, usually through toasts or drinking wine at celebrations (1980, pp. 309–310). Wine and beer are an expected part of revelry, but they are not central to these celebrations and only rarely are they consumed to such excess that they drive the plot. The barrel scene in *The Hobbit* is one such rare instance, when the Dwarves and Bilbo Baggins ride empty wine barrels out of captivity after the Elf guards pass out from too much drink. Although it was a short scene, it was very important to the plot that the guards acted immorally and got drunk, thereby allowing the heroes' escape.

Indeed, banal references to alcohol in these older fantasy texts are often moralized. In the *Narnia* books, for example, heroic characters consume "softer" alcoholic drinks like beer and wine, and usually do so at celebrations. The evil or bad characters, on the other hand, consume hard liquors or perverted versions of wine and beer and display drunkenness. C.S. Lewis associates an evil wine with the Lady of the Green Kirtle from *The Silver Chair,* for example, and the Orc draught in *The Lord of the Rings* is a hard liquor drunk regularly by evil characters and which burns the throats of the good characters. Other series, such as *Redwall*, moralize alcohol in a similar way. As another essay in this book explains of fatness in *Harry Potter*, Manichean frameworks in children's/YA series and implicit biases of writers make it easy to associate a socially acceptable trait, behavior, or object with "good" people and something less-accepted or unacceptable with "bad" people (Henderson, 2018). *Harry Potter*'s treatment of alcohol both resists and affirms this black-and-white dynamic and intersects banality and centrality.

Alcohol in Harry Potter

Harry Potter is rarely a story that casually mentions alcohol as an ordinary part of daily life, nor is it an obvious case study that parents and educators could use to begin conversations about alcoholism/alcohol use with young readers. The Rowling novels present a paradox: alcohol is a major plot-mover, but Rowling does not present obvious opportunities to discuss the damaging health and emotional effects of booze or the nefarious purposes to which alcohol can be used, but neither does she appear endorse the consumption of alcohol. To understand these paradoxes better, I examine the moments in which alcohol appears in the seven novels and its function when it does.

Just a Part of Life

Sometimes alcohol appears in just a linguistic capacity, providing a simple analogy for other, more abstract emotions that Harry experiences. The phrase "like firewhisky" appears at least four times to describe sensations like intense romantic passion, deeply felt loss, intense shock, or the bright flame of courage (*DH*, pp. 79, 84, 116, 620). This turn of phrase would make sense in an adult novel, presumably because adults know the physiological feeling of swallowing liquor that they could then use to concretize complex emotions. They may seem out of place in a YA series, as its main audience has presumably never consumed alcohol. This linguistic inclusion is perhaps even concerning: if a young reader reads that the experience of intense emotion and the consumption of alcohol are similar, they might be tempted to imbibe to experience a sensation like emotion. This is not likely, in my estimation, but it does seem possible. The metaphorical use of alcohol may raise concerns, as does the actual consumption of drink in the novels.

Usually actual alcohol in the series is moralized to varying degrees, spanning the range of acceptable to unacceptable. When used in moderation and at important moments, it is moral (or else not moralized), but it becomes immoral when used in excess. Moments of "traditional" alcohol use at celebrations occur in *Harry Potter*, though they are not common. George mentions in passing that his Great Uncle Bilius used to overindulge during celebrations and make a scene at family weddings (*DH*, p. 142). The excess here, however, is merely a passing joke. At two other points in the final book, the heroic characters solemnly raise a glass to toast Mad-Eye Moody's passing as well as to welcome Remus's son, Teddy Lupin, into the world (*DH*, pp. 79–84, 513–518). The characters share one, maybe two glasses of firewhisky at the news of the death, but imbibe many bottles of wine to celebrate the birth. Reserved use of spirits marks a loss, but wine flows freely on the joyful occasion. In these cases, the situation dictates the proper (or improper) use of alcohol, and Rowling saved these "appropriate" occasions for alcohol consumption until the Trio (Harry, Ron, and Hermione) are of adult age in the Wizarding world.

Sometimes, however, underage characters imbibe or plot to do so. Sneaking drinks of alcohol is a common caper in teenage life and literature, one occasionally present in *Harry Potter*. The opening quote of this essay shows Ron plotting to get some firewhisky, which Seamus and Dean also attempt in *Order of the Phoenix* (p. 738). The protagonist, Harry, is on the periphery in most of these cases; it is not Harry trying to sneak an illegal drink. Given that an author usually expects her reader to identify with the protagonist, we can surmise that Rowling is not endorsing Ron, Seamus, and Dean's attempts to get a drink when they are underage. However, Harry does sometimes casually use alcohol when underage. As I will discuss below, butterbeer likely has a small amount of alcohol in it, and Harry begins drinking that at age 13. Later, throughout *Half-Blood Prince*, professors offer the 16-year-old Potter alcohol on at least four different occasions, and he accepts the alcohol offered to him on three of those occasions—with Dumbledore at the Dursley house, at Slughorn's Christmas party, and after Slughorn cures Ron of the love potion (*HBP* pp. 48–51, 314–320, 395–398). These instances of underage drinking are not consistently moralized, and it seems that underage alcohol use with an adult's permission and supervision is more acceptable in Rowling's fictional world than teenagers attempting to lay hands on forbidden drinks. Regardless of this inconsistent moralizing, the series never features casual liquor consumption among youths, though young people consistently drink mildly alcoholic butterbeer with no concern or objection from adults. Indeed, underage students use butterbeer so often and without becoming obviously intoxicated that it is easy to forget that butterbeer does contain some small amount of alcohol.[2]

Though infrequent, older adults—specifically Hogwarts teachers—occasionally consume alcohol in a casual, non-moralized way. In *Sorcerer's Stone*, for example, Rowling mentions in passing that the teachers consumed enough wine with Christmas dinner that Professor McGonagall only giggled when Hagrid kissed her on the cheek (p. 204). The passage is mildly silly, and seems to make no other, larger point. In another Christmas party scene, Slughorn's guests in *Half-Blood Prince* may partake in a variety of alcoholic drinks to celebrate the holidays (pp. 314–320). Alcohol among these adults often appears as "just something adults do," where alcohol is an accessory to a party or to important conversations between adults, poured out more for tradition and politeness than out of a desire to become drunk. For example, Fudge offers the muggle Prime Minister a glass of (the Prime Minister's own) whiskey while they discuss Voldemort's return to power (*HBP*, p. 8). At another time, Dumbledore shows Harry a memory in which Dumbledore offered Tom Riddle/Voldemort wine as they discussed his possible employment at Hogwarts (*HBP*, pp. 440–446). Whether at parties or important meetings, the presence of alcohol in these scenes appears merely to be one of many markers of adulthood; its lack may seem more out-of-place than its inclusion.[3]

Besides holiday revelry and intense discussions among adults, the second most common, casual, and non-moralized use of alcohol is the administration of brandy or other hard liquor after some shock. Although sometimes characters are served tea to soothe the nerves (e.g., *SS*, p. 28; *PoA*, p. 219; *GoF*, p. 452), alcohol appears with similar frequency in this calmative capacity. In the first book, for example, Aunt Petunia rushes Uncle Vernon a brandy after Harry accidentally performs magic at the zoo (*SS*, p. 29). Hagrid also requests brandy after the distressing flying motorcycle ride in *Deathly Hallows* (p. 68), and Mr. Weasley puts a shot of firewhisky in his wife's tea after her hysterical reunion with her family after the Quidditch World Cup in book four. To calm her as she begs for him to help Draco, Snape plies Narcissa Malfoy with wine early in *Half-Blood Prince* (*HBP,* pp. 23–37). As I discuss later of alcoholism, these instances portray alcohol as a medicine, as a means by which to cure one's problems. Alcohol is curative and calmative here, perhaps numbing a shock. While medicating with alcohol may seem a poor, even dangerous choice, Rowling rarely moralizes it as such.

The most significant casual, non-moralized use of alcohol appears in *Prisoner of Azkaban*, when the teachers, the barmaid Rosmerta, and Minister of Magic Fudge sit down at The Three Broomsticks and discuss Sirius Black and the death of the Potters. Some of the adults order ostensibly non-alcoholic drinks ("a large gillywater" and "a cherry soda with umbrella" for McGonagall and Flitwick respectively), but the others order some type of alcohol, which they drink during a serious conversation on the final day of the term (*PoA,* pp. 201–209). The facts revealed to the Trio during this conversation are central to the story, but the alcohol is not related to the exposition of these facts. The hard beverages are, again, merely the expected accessories of an adult conversation that takes place in a pub.

Many parts of *Harry Potter* that may seem odd to an American reader result from genre, and I suggest that genre partially explains the portrayal of banal alcohol use. In large part, Rowling was writing a "British school story" when she wrote *Harry Potter*, and thus the novels will necessarily include conventions from this genre. Serving someone a liquor drink after a shock, for example, seems to be a very traditional, very British thing to do. Similarly, with a drinking age tied to coming-of-age in Britain, it should be unsurprising that 17-year-old wizards may imbibe without question in the series. Additionally, not uncommon for parents to give their young teens alcohol in Britain, with one study reporting 34 percent of parents serving children under 14 (Press Association, 2016). Britain and other European countries model the argument that gradually introducing drink to young people often leads to safer alcohol use in later years (see Davey, 2017). *Harry Potter* exemplifies this: the "normal" drinking among adults and older teens appears without fanfare, while use in excess stands out as abnormal.

Alcohol Indicating Immorality or Illness

The *Harry Potter* series often features alcohol in a mostly benign manner, but at other times, use of alcohol reflects some sort of immorality of the drinker or indicates some deeper concern with the character. The series sometimes follows the generic conventions of fantasy stories using alcohol as an indication of a character's immorality. In book three, Harry's terrible anger caused him to inflate his Aunt Marge after she drunkenly bullied him about his parents' reputations (*PoA,* pp. 26–30). Marge drank a lot of wine with dinner, and then consumed copious amounts of brandy with dessert, causing the already cruel woman to verbally attack Harry so viciously that he performed accidental magic. In this scene, Marge's alcohol use has ties to her sinful behavior: she exhibited wrath, sloth, and gluttony. Though more good-natured than Aunt Marge, Horace Slughorn similarly exhibits sins like sloth, greed, and gluttony, which are often represented by or accompanied by alcohol. In *Half-Blood Prince*, the book that features Slughorn most centrally, Rowling often portrays the man surrounded by admirers, clutching crystalized pineapple in one hand and an alcoholic beverage in the other (e.g., pp. 369, 494). While holding these trappings of luxury and excess, Slughorn reveals vital information about horcruxes to a young Tom Riddle, and later when wine-sodden, he reveals similar information to Harry. Such moments are moralized and are also vital to moving the story's plot.

Indeed, this immoral use of alcohol sometimes is tied very closely to plot development. In *Half-Blood Prince*, in addition to the aforementioned Slughorn conversations, the reader joins Harry and Dumbledore in the pensieve, where a young Tom Riddle learns vital information about his mother from his incredibly drunk and mentally disturbed Uncle Morfin (pp. 363–365). In that same book, Ron is poisoned by drinking tainted mead, which he only drinks because he accidentally ingested firewhisky- and love-potion-spiked candies (*HBP*, pp. 395–398). The poisoned mead is part of the larger plot of the book, one in a series of attempts Draco Malfoy makes on Dumbledore's life. An early scene in *Deathly Hallows* also relies on alcohol to reveal important plot information: Ron's champagne-drunk Auntie Muriel reveals disturbing information about the Dumbledore family to Elphias Doge and Harry "Barney Weasley" Potter (*DH*, pp. 153–159). In these cases, alcohol is directly responsible for central plot exposition—and sometimes for dangerous breaches in wizarding law.

Although the traditional conflation of alcohol overuse and a bad personality often appears in the novels, Rowling seems to portray alcoholism as a misguided solution to deep unhappiness. In other words, the characters are not immoral and therefore abuse alcohol; their alcoholism affects these otherwise morally neutral characters. The two outright alcoholics in *Harry Potter* are Winky the house-elf and Professor Sybill Trelawney. After Mr. Crouch Sr., sacks her, Winky and Dobby reunite and find employment at Hogwarts, and while Dobby thrives, Winky falls into deep despair, eventually succumbing to alcoholism. Although commonly consumed by underage students, butterbeer must contain a small amount of alcohol, which we can extrapolate from an exchange between Harry and Dobby: "'Well, it's not strong, that stuff,' Harry said. But Dobby shook his head. 'Tis strong for a house-elf, sir'" (*GoF*, p. 536). Rather than helping her, though, the other elves consider her a disgrace, and Dobby even tells Harry that he has hidden Winky in the Room of Requirement to sober up in private (*OotP*, p. 387). Mourning the loss of her position with the Crouch family and facing the "stiff upper lip" of a British culture that hushes up unpleasantness, Winky turns to alcohol to numb her painful emotions. The only real support she has is the bottle.

Divination teacher Sybill Trelawney similarly begins her alcoholism after a major trauma, but the moral lesson gained from her alcoholism is quite different from Winky. Dolores Umbridge's reign at Hogwarts had many casualties, including the sacking of Professor Trelawney. Although readers were undoubtedly glad that Hagrid had temporarily avoided the pink slip, Trelawney's dismissal was both public and cruel. Terrified of her precarious position at Hogwarts, she begins to smell routinely of cooking sherry even before being fired, becoming increasingly unwell as her addiction grows. It is possible that Trelawney was in her cups before Umbridge's time at Hogwarts, but the reader only knows of her alcoholism from this point forward in the story. Once put on probation, Trelawney's lessons become more erratic, as does her behavior and composure. Even after Umbridge leaves Hogwarts, Trelawney is unable to break free of her addiction (*HBP* pp. 195, 317–318, 322, 426–427, 540–546). Like Winky, she is traumatized and drowning in her emotions and self-medicates with alcohol. Unlike Winky, though, Trelawney's alcoholism becomes vital to the plot development in *Half-Blood Prince*.

Some of the climax of the sixth book relied closely on Professor Trelawney having the "loose lips" associated with drunkenness. Had she been sober, she may never have revealed to Harry that Snape overheard her prophecy about Voldemort's downfall, which ultimately led to the Lily and James Potter's deaths (*HBP*, p. 545). Indeed, this same tipsy state also confirmed that Draco successfully completed his secret work in the Room of Requirement (*HBP*, pp. 540–542). Yet another, seemingly incidental moment in this same segment of the book has important stakes for the plot. Harry hides from Trelawney as she meanders down a corridor reading the tarot cards distractedly, and we hear Trelawney appear to predict the invasion of Hogwarts and death of Dumbledore that would occur later that night (*HBP*, pp. 195, 543). Harry pays this no mind, and Trelawney herself thinks she may be reading the cards wrong, but like a Shakespearian fool, her seeming lack of sanity masks her wisdom.

Rowling appears to cast her alcoholic characters as depressed and depressing, sad and worthy of pity, and in some ways, darkly comical. A broad reading of texts yields the conclusion that Rowling does not condone drinking—and definitely not alcoholism—and yet alcohol is central to many moments of exposition vital to the plot of not only each novel but also of the entire, seven-novel story arc. Both Winky and Professor Trelawney self-medicate their despair with alcohol; they are neutrally sympathetic characters who seem pathetic and in need of help when their alcoholism deepens.[4] While Trelawney and Winky use alcohol to a much greater degree, they are peripheral characters when compared with Rubeus Hagrid, whose alcohol use is truly central to the *Harry Potter* plot.

Alcohol as a Plot-Mover

By now, it is clear that alcohol is a common feature in the *Harry Potter* series, coming in many varieties that span from the mundane to the moralizing. Sometimes alcohol is as banal as having wine at Christmas dinner, while other times Rowling appears to use alcohol as one of many ways to demonstrate the (im)morality of a given character. Sometimes, however, alcohol is the sole means by which the plot moves forward, within each story or throughout the series' arc. As I mentioned in recounting Slughorn and Trelawney revealing important secrets, alcohol consumption loosens lips enough in the *Harry Potter* series to share indispensable information with the protagonists. In this section, I consider the three prime examples of this phenomenon in the books—Slughorn, Mrs. Cole, and Hagrid—to explore the role of alcohol in these watershed moments. Understanding how/in what manner they occur can help us answer to the most important question: why does alcohol have such a central role in a children's series?

In Rowling's series, characters are so frightened of Lord Voldemort that they will not even say his name, so of course these characters usually refuse to discuss him. As Dumbledore emphasized to Harry, however, knowledge of the enemy provides the tools to defeat him. How to solve this dilemma? How does one get people to disclose that which they would rather keep private? In two important moments in *Half-Blood Prince*, the protagonists solve this conundrum with booze: they gain this vital information by getting another character extremely drunk.

Albus Dumbledore requests that Harry take private lessons with him during Harry's sixth year at Hogwarts, during which Dumbledore teaches Harry about Voldemort's background so they might learn how to defeat him. One of the early memories Dumbledore shares with Harry is his own recollection of meeting 11-year-old Tom Riddle for the first time. Before doing so, Dumbledore had to persuade Mrs. Cole, Tom's orphanage director, to allow the meeting and to consent to Tom attending Hogwarts. Early in the meeting, Dumbledore appears to modify Mrs. Cole's memory to get her to stop asking questions about Hogwarts before the gin drinking begins (*HBP*, p. 265). Dumbledore conjures a bottle of gin, and Mrs. Cole begins to consume the liquor (Rowling states that Mrs. Cole poured them both a glass, but never states whether he drank any), and Dumbledore "didn't hesitate to press his advantage" as Mrs. Cole became increasingly inebriated (*HBP*, p. 265). Dumbledore uses Mrs. Cole's intoxication to coax information about Tom's mother and Tom's magical misdeeds from the matron (*HBP*, pp. 265–268). During this conversation, Mrs. Cole provides important information about Merope Gaunt Riddle and about the dark magic experimentation Tom apparently used on his fellow orphans—all information that she seemed hesitant to reveal while sober.

Note also the phrase Rowling selected to describe this extraction process: Dumbledore "didn't hesitate to press his advantage." Most American adults in the current socio-political climate would see the constellation of "press his advantage," hard liquor, and a sober male/drunk female dyad as a possible breeding-ground for sexual assault. Rowling most certainly does not take this scene in such a dark direction, but the choice of phrase does connote a sense of forcibly taking that which belongs to another. Dumbledore uses alcohol to obtain something he wants that the other person would likely not give under sober conditions.

Alcohol provides the means by which to remove another memory against the owner's will. In the course of their private lessons, Dumbledore and Harry realize that they require a memory from Horace Slughorn that they suspect contains essential information about defeating Voldemort. Humiliated by his role in Voldemort's rise, however, Slughorn had altered the memory, and Dumbledore charges Harry with getting the real one from Slughorn. Harry tries flattery and trickery, but he is unable to get it. In the end, however, Harry is successful. As Welsh (2007) notes with alarm, not only does Harry get Slughorn and Hagrid extremely drunk to extract the horcrux memory from Slughorn, Harry does so while under the influence of Felix Felicis (p. 124). Only these two behavior-altering substances—wine and lucky potion—handed Harry the key to learning how to defeat Voldemort.

The sheer amount of alcohol used in both the Slughorn and Mrs. Cole scenes is perhaps more alarming than its use as a coercive tool. Dumbledore and Harry get Mrs. Cole and Slughorn extremely, as the popular phrase goes, "trashed." Indeed, Slughorn becomes so intoxicated that "Felix was telling [Harry] that Slughorn would remember nothing of this in the morning" (i.e., he had blacked out) and Mrs. Cole consumed two-thirds of a bottle of gin according to the text, though she was somehow still steady on her feet (*HBP*, pp. 268, 489). By practically all medical accounts, blacking out and binge drinking are exceptionally dangerous to one's health. While the worst result we see from these episodes in *Harry Potter* is passing out and having a hangover, binge drinking and blacking out in the muggle world often have deadly consequences.

In these scenes, the text models a Machiavellianism much more in line with Dumbledore's philosophy than with Harry's: the means justify the "greater good" ends regardless of possible cost to a single human. Dumbledore, and later Harry, engage others in dangerous drinking behaviors for the sole purpose of taking something from them, risking the health and well-being of the target. Yet within the text, no character criticizes Harry or Dumbledore for this method; indeed, Dumbledore expresses pride and delight that Harry got the memory, never asking *how* he got it (*HBP*, p. 494). This message seems counter to the positive themes that dominate the novels, yet the plots could not unfold without booze.

The centrality of alcohol to plot development is, in fact, present in the texts from the earliest book through the character of Rubeus Hagrid. In *Sorcerer's Stone*, Hagrid hands Quirrell/Voldemort the final piece to the puzzle of accessing the Stone when he drunkenly reveals how to deal with Fluffy the three-headed dog (*SS*, pp. 265–266). In my estimation, Hagrid best exemplifies the complex role of alcohol in the *Harry Potter* series. Few characters are as consistently loveable and good as Hagrid, yet his overuse of alcohol is very much a part of his character; these two elements sometimes move the plot and are always in tension.

In addition to revealing how to handle Fluffy, Hagrid's reputation as a drunkard has other stakes for the plot. In the Slughorn scene, Hagrid drinks with Slughorn, also blacking out and passing out from too much drink; he is a casualty of Harry needing the memory. In *Prisoner of Azkaban*, Hagrid drowns his sorrows of losing Buckbeak's trial in a tankard, and Harry and Hermione later have to hide from the happy, drunken gamekeeper weaving his way towards the school after Buckbeak's escape (*PoA*, pp. 120, 405). Hagrid is well known for becoming boisterous when drinking, so much so that Malfoy shares a rumor with Harry before his first term that Hagrid "gets drunk, tries to do magic, and ends up setting fire to his bed" (*SS*, p. 78; *PoA*, pp. 202, 206). Eleven-year-old Harry then has to decide whether to trust a fellow student or his magical guide. Hagrid's reputation for having loose lips when drunk is so pervasive indeed that the Order of the Phoenix members surreptitiously suspect that he may have leaked the information about the seven Potters escape plan in *Deathly Hallows* (p. 80). As at the crossroads in Madam Malkin's shop with Malfoy in book one, Harry must decide whether to trust his friend regardless of his drink-fueled garrulousness. Hagrid's alcohol use moves the plot in many different ways, sometimes directly and other times through its effect on Harry.

Hagrid embodies the paradoxical role of alcohol in Rowling's series. Hagrid is a good, loving, brave person and a sympathetic protagonist who has many obvious flaws that are an important part of his personality and his role in the book. Similarly, alcohol serves more positive purposes in the series (e.g., to soothe, to socialize, etc.) but also has great flaws (e.g., dependence, coercion, etc.). Rowling's Hagrid teaches us to think beyond the virtuous/evil dichotomy of alcohol and to understand moderation more clearly.

Drink Up, Witches

Alcohol has quite a presence in *Harry Potter*. Yet the essential question remains unanswered: *why* does alcohol have such a central role in a children's/YA series? I see two explanations one can derive from the portrayal of drink in the seven novels: (1) complicating the Manichean dynamics of the characterization and (2) enriching the tension between choice and fate so fundamental to the story.

First, a great weakness of the *Harry Potter* series is Rowling's Manichean portrayal of good and evil. For example, Harry never makes friends with a Slytherin throughout his six years at Hogwarts, and there is not a single Slytherin in the Hogwarts student resistance group, nor is there any who fights against Voldemort and the Death Eaters during the Battle for Hogwarts (save former Slytherin and Head of Slytherin House Slughorn). Although Sirius might assert that "the world isn't split into good people and Death Eaters" (*OotP*, p. 302), Rowling seems to organize her magical world mostly along those lines.

I suggest that Hagrid's alcohol use in particular challenges this black-and-white outlook. Many of the protagonists have some type of major personality flaw (e.g., Harry's temper, Ron's lack of tact, Hermione's constant need to be the best/brightest, Sirius's recklessness, etc.). Hagrid's flaw, however, is the only substance-related one, which in some ways makes it the hardest to redeem, given the stigma associated with alcohol overuse. However, Hagrid never appears to need redeeming; he is an unquestionably good character. The alcohol overuse is a part of a whole character that is ultimately moral and good. That such a major, unhealthy flaw exists in a supporting lead character can perhaps present a challenge to the otherwise Manichean world of *Harry Potter*. Other characters' casual use of alcohol within the texts helps add some familiarity and realism to this fantastic world and sends a mild message of moderation and good choices to readers. By contrast, Hagrid's and other's poorer choices about drink are often central to plot development.

Second, a very important part of the *Harry Potter* series is the tension between choice and fate. Although characters—Harry especially—have to make good and noble choices to finally defeat Voldemort, not all outcomes are left to choice. The Deathly Hallows themselves are instructive: finding and uniting the Hallows in an ethical way is an act of choice, but the power they then bestow upon the holder—to defeat Death—is beyond human choice or control. We see a similar tension when considering the role of Trelawney's prophecy about Voldemort and Harry. Alcohol helps keep these factors in tension. Drinking alcohol may be a choice, but most describe the sensation of being drunk as being "out of control." Harry's choices must sometimes overcome and are sometimes possible only because of things beyond his control and beyond the control of the drinker. Harry (a child) chooses to follow Quirrell down into the Forbidden Corridor, after an act of boozy fate (i.e., Hagrid's drunken, loose lips) shows Quirrell the way in. Later in the series, Slughorn's protectiveness outmatches Harry's wiles, and Harry can only overcome this with a lucky potion and lots and lots of wine. Responsibility and choice exist alongside fate and inevitability, and alcohol helps this complicated dance.

The alcohol *Harry Potter* readers are expected to swallow in this children's/YA series is surprising in both function and amount. A lot more drinking goes on at Hogwarts than may be immediately apparent, by both the adults and the teens and both responsibly and irresponsibly. Alcohol also lubricates the plot, presenting challenges and opportunities to the characters, who must make choices to avoid or encourage actions outside their control. Alcohol in the plot of *Harry Potter* is simultaneously banal and important, an act of choice and a vehicle of fate. It adds another layer of complexity to this story so many around the world share. Potter scholars may hotly debate aspects of the Potterverse, including the complicated role of alcohol in the series, but wizards and muggles alike can raise a glass to toast The Boy Who Lived and his story that changed our worlds.

NOTES

1. After years of scholarly discussion and collaboration, the core leadership group of Scholarly Studies of Harry Potter has created a five-part division of "canon" to help understand and embrace the diversity of the Potterverse. These five parts are canon, altcanon, paracanon, metacanon, and fanon. For more, see Camacci (2016).
2. The films take a liberty with the representation of butterbeer as alcohol (among many other liberties!). The films omit the alcoholic characters (or their alcoholism), Trelawney and Winky, and instead include a scene in *Half-Blood Prince* where Hermione appears very tipsy on her walk back to Hogwarts from Hogsmeade.
3. I am thinking here of Stephenie Meyer's *Twilight* series. Meyer is Mormon, and church doctrine discourages alcohol use. Her characters do not often drink in her four novels.
4. That both alcoholics in the book are female is, I think, quite worthy of attention. It would be beyond the scope of this essay to engage that question, however.

REFERENCES

Bell, C.E. (2012). *Hermione Granger Saves the World: Essays on the Feminist Heroine of Hogwarts*. Jefferson, NC: McFarland.
Brasheres, A. (2001). *The Sisterhood of the Traveling Pants*. New York: Random House.
Brasheres, A. (2003). *The Second Summer of the Sisterhood*. New York: Random House.
Brasheres, A. (2005). *Girls in Pants*. New York: Random House.
Brasheres, A. (2007). *Forever in Blue*. New York: Random House.
Brasheres, A. (2011). *Sisterhood Everlasting*. New York: Random House.
Burke, K. (1967). "Literature as Equipment for Living." In *The Philosophy of Literary Form: Studies in Symbolic Action* (2nd ed.). Baton Rouge: Louisiana State University Press.
Carroll, L. (1865). *Alice in Wonderland*. London: Macmillan.
Davey, M. (2017, January 5). "Children Whose Parents Give Them Sips of Alcohol 'More Likely' to Drink as Teens." *The Guardian*. Retrieved October 5, 2017, from https://www.

theguardian.com/society/2017/jan/05/children-whose-parents-give-them-sips-of-alcohol-more-likely-to-drink-as-teens.
Fisher, W. (1989). *Human Communication as Narration: Toward a Philosophy of Reason, Value, and Action.* Columbia: University of South Carolina Press.
Flanagan, C. (2017, November). "Death at a Penn State Fraternity." *The Atlantic.* Retrieved October 5, 2017, from https://www.theatlantic.com/magazine/archive/2017/11/a-death-at-penn-state/540657/.
Ford, P.F. (1980). *Companion to Narnia.* New York: HarperCollins.
Hastings, J.M., & Typpo, M.H. (1994). *An Elephant in the Living Room: The Children's Book.* Center City, MN: Hazelden Publishing.
Henderson, T. (2018). "I don't think you're a waste of space": Redemption, Activity, and the Social Construction of Fatness. In C.E. Bell (Ed.), *Inside the World of Harry Potter.* Jefferson, NC: McFarland.
Hough, A. (2012, February 3). "Daniel Radcliffe: 'I was drunk during Harry Potter filming.'" *The Telegraph.* Retrieved October 5, 2017, from http://www.telegraph.co.uk/culture/harry-potter/9060794/Daniel-Radcliffe-I-was-drunk-during-Harry-Potter-filming.html.
Lynch, C. (2005). *Inexcusable.* San Francisco: Ginee Seo Books.
Montgomery, L.M. (1908). *Anne of Green Gables.* Boston: L.C. Page and Co.
Parker-Pope, T. (2009, July 27). "The Role of Alcohol in Harry Potter." *The New York Times.* Retrieved October 5, 2017, from https://well.blogs.nytimes.com/2009/07/27/the-role-of-alcohol-in-harry-potter/.
Press Association. (2016, August 18). "Half of UK Parents Allow Children to Drink Alcohol at Home, Says Survey." *The Guardian.* Retrieved October 5, 2017, from https://www.theguardian.com/society/2016/aug/19/half-of-uk-parents-allow-children-to-drink-alcohol-at-home-says-survey.
Rowling, J.K. (1998). *Harry Potter and the Chamber of Secrets.* New York: Scholastic.
Rowling, J.K. (2007). *Harry Potter and the Deathly Hallows.* New York: Scholastic.
Rowling, J.K. (2000). *Harry Potter and the Goblet of Fire.* New York: Scholastic.
Rowling, J.K. (2005). *Harry Potter and the Half-Blood Prince.* New York: Scholastic.
Rowling, J.K. (2003). *Harry Potter and the Order of the Phoenix.* New York: Scholastic.
Rowling, J.K. (1999). *Harry Potter and the Prisoner of Azkaban.* New York: Scholastic.
Rowling, J.K. (1997). *Harry Potter and the Sorcerer's Stone.* New York: Scholastic.
Sparks, B. (1971). *Go Ask Alice.* Upper Saddle River, NJ: Prentice Hall.
Swan, A.M. (1992). "Children's Literature and Alcohol: Being Aware." *Childhood Education,* 69(1), 10–14.
Vezzali, L., Stathi, S., Giovannini, D., Capozza, D., & Trifiletti, E. (2015). "The Greatest Magic of Harry Potter: Reducing Prejudice." *Journal of Applied Social Psychology, 45,* 105–121.
Welsh, C. (2007). "Harry Potter and the Underage Drinkers: Can We Use This to Talk About Teens About Alcohol?" *Journal of Child & Adolescent Substance Abuse, 16*(4), 119–126.

Pure-Bloods, Half-Bloods and Mudbloods

Camilla Schroeder

The status of a character's blood is of constant relevance throughout *Harry Potter*: it is a reason for prejudice, insults and—in the later books—violence. There are three categories depicted: pure-blood, half-blood, and muggle-born. Pure-blood wizards have no Muggle in their family and often prize themselves because of it. Half-bloods are those with at least one Muggle relative. Some of the most powerful wizards within the series are half-bloods, including the main protagonist and antagonist. Muggle-borns are—as the name suggests—born by two muggles with no (or no known) magic blood. They are generally unaware of magic and only realize that they are wizards once they receive their Hogwarts letter. Consequently, they do not know much about the wizarding world—unless they read a lot of books. This essay discusses the significance of blood in *Harry Potter* by examining the links to blood in the seven books and the *Cursed Child* script. The essay is divided into three parts, each discussing one category: pure-bloods, half-bloods, and muggle-borns.

Pure-Blood Wizards

Pure-blood are those wizards who have never had a Muggle in their family. There are three dominant pure-blood families within the novels: the Malfoys, the Blacks, and the Weasleys. All of them belong to the so-called "Sacred Twenty-Eight" (Rowling, "Pure-Blood," 2017), which is a compilation of "truly pure-blood families" (Ibid.) published in an anonymous "Pure-Blood Directory" (Ibid.) in the 1930s. From the beginning, the Malfoys present the prime example of pure-blood wizards and their attitude towards others, as they revel in their pride of their pure-blood status.

Harry is first introduced to Draco Malfoy when trying on robes at Madam Malkin's Robes for All Occasions, where Harry is immediately reminded of his bullying cousin Dudley. After hearing that Harry's parents are dead, Malfoy's first question is, "But they were our kind, weren't they?"; elaborating that in his opinion Hogwarts should not "let the other sort in" (Rowling, 1997, p. 78). The inquiry about Harry's family's blood status display the importance Draco and his family place on being pure-blood wizards. His pride in being a pure-blood puts an early emphasis on pure-bloods being depicted as the evil characters. This impression is further enhanced after the encounter on the train when Draco threatens Harry and Ron tells him that he "heard of [Draco's] family […] They were some of the first to come back to our side after You-Know-Who disappeared. Said they'd been bewitched. My dad doesn't believe it. He says Malfoy's father didn't need an excuse to go over to the Dark Side" (Rowling, 1997, p. 110). Again, their pride and snobbishness depicts them as evil. Furthermore, it is suggested that they are changing sides according to which one they can profit from the most.

Arthur Weasley's claim is proven right in *Goblet of Fire*, when Lucius approaches Voldemort saying that he "was constantly on the alert […] Had there been any sign from you, any whisper of your whereabouts, I would have been at your side immediately, nothing could have prevented me" (Rowling, 2000, p. 650). Despite his insistence on his allegiance to Voldemort, Lucius is guided by a desire to improve his own status—no matter under which leadership. Lucius does prize himself with his pure-blood status and, as Suman Gupta claims, shares Voldemort's ideological perspective (Gupta, 2003, p. 101). Nevertheless, his loyalty is first and foremost with his own family. Thus, he is not portrayed as entirely loyal to either side, as Voldemort points out: "And yet you ran from my Mark, when a faithful Death Eater sent it into the sky last summer?" (Rowling, 2000, p. 650).

This view on the purity of one's blood is not only reflected in the Malfoys, but the house they, for the first volumes, seem to represent: Slytherin. The house is first mentioned by Draco, who declares that he will be in Slytherin as "all our family have been" (Rowling, 1997, p. 77). The different houses are then explained by Hagrid, who tells Harry that "[t]here's not a single witch or wizard who went bad who wasn't in Slytherin. You-Know-Who was one" (Rowling, 1997, p. 80). Thus, Harry is already biased against Slytherin before going to Hogwarts, since the only character from Slytherin he has encountered is a snobbish bully.

However, throughout the series, Harry encounters good wizards from Slytherin. There is the later potions master and head of Slytherin house, Horace Slughorn, who might not be the most sympathetic character, but who fights against the Death Eaters in the Battle of Hogwarts. Most known as a supposedly bad character turning good is Severus Snape, who, after many twists and turns, turns out to be working against Voldemort. Even in the Epilogue, when Harry's son, Albus Severus, is scared of being sorted into Slytherin, Harry comforts him by saying that one of the men he is named after "was a Slytherin and he was probably the bravest man I ever knew" (Rowling, 2007, p. 758).

Nevertheless, the majority of the characters from Slytherin do display a favoritism towards pure-bloods and a resentment towards muggle-borns and are, therefore, generally portrayed as evil. One example of the favoritism is the password for the Slytherin common room in *Chamber of Secrets*, which is "pure-blood" (Rowling, 1999, p. 221). Although there are half-bloods sorted into Slytherin, such as Severus Snape, Horace Slughorn, and Dolores Umbridge, there are never any muggle-borns, as it would be against Salazar Slytherin's intentions (Rowling, "Horace Slughorn fact file" and "Dolores Umbridge," 2017).

This tendency for pure-bloods in Slytherin is established when Professor Binns recounts the history of Hogwarts and the legend of the Chamber of Secrets. It is Salazar Slytherin who created a disagreement between the founders on being "more *selective* about the students admitted to Hogwarts [since] he believed that magical learning should be kept within all-magic families" and that Muggle-born students cannot be trusted (Rowling, 1999, p. 150). Thus, Slytherin left the castle after creating his monster in the secret chamber.

Another prominent family is the Blacks, with their family motto *"Toujours pur"* (Rowling, 2003, p.111). The most present characters are Sirius and his mother, who present two different sides. Although the majority of the Blacks value the status of their blood above everything else, Sirius rejects this view from the beginning and is thus disowned by his mother, whose portrait refers to him as "[b]*lood traitor, abomination, shame of my flesh!*" (Rowling, 2003, p. 78).

The first information Harry receives about Sirius is that he is a mass murderer and loyal servant to Voldemort in *Prisoner of Azkaban*. Yet this image is overturned during the course of the book, and Sirius becomes a close ally. However, only in *Order of the Phoenix* does Harry discover the Black family and its insistence on the purity of their blood. The first of the family members Harry encounters is Sirius' mother, in the form of her portrait. The portrait itself is described in a rather comical way: "The old woman was drooling, her eyes were rolling, the yellowing skin of her face stretched taut as she screamed" (Rowling, 2003, p. 77). Even her screams are rather one-sided and mainly consists of colorful insults, such as *"Filth! Scum! By-products of dirt and vileness! Half-breeds, mutants, freaks, begone from this place!"* (Rowling, 2003, p. 78). According to Rowling, portraits are only "representations of the living subjects as seen by the artist" and are "able to use some of the subject's favorite phrases and imitate their general demeanor" ("Hogwarts Portraits," 2017). Therefore, the portrait depicts her most distinct features: being a proud pure-blood and hating muggles.

The ancestor tapestry across which Harry comes in the house proudly states: "The Noble and Most Ancient House of Black *'Toujours Pur'*" (Rowling, 2003, p. 111). Not only does their family motto *"Toujours Pur"* depict their assertion of being pure-blood, but the adjectives "noble" and "most ancient" implies their state as royalty among wizards. Although only Sirius' brother joined Voldemort's Death Eaters, Sirius claims that his parents' "thought Voldemort had the right idea, they were all for the purification of the Wizarding race, getting rid of muggle-borns and having purebloods in charge" (Rowling, 2003, p. 112). According to him, they were not the only ones, but apparently many "got cold feet when they saw what he was prepared to do to get power, though" (Ibid.). When looking at the tapestry, Harry realizes that all the pure-blood families are interrelated, owing to their insistence of only marrying pure-bloods. Even Sirius and the Weasleys are related over certain corners (Rowling, 2003, p.113).

Contrary to the view of the Malfoys and the Blacks, the Weasleys are pure-blood wizards who associate with muggles and muggle-borns. Despite belonging to the "Sacred Twenty-Eight" and being related to "almost every old Wizarding family in Britain" (Rowling, "Pure-blood," 2017), the Weasleys often declared that they have muggle ancestors, which results in them being labelled "blood traitors" by other pure-blood families. The first description we get of the Weasleys is the haughty remark by Draco to Ron: "No need to ask who you are. My father told me all the Weasleys have red hair, freckles, and more children than they can afford" (Rowling, 1997, p. 108). Thus, not only Arthur Weasley's job in The Misuse of Muggle Artifacts Office and his affinity for all things muggle, but also their lack of wealth plays a part in their status.

In contrast to the Malfoys, the Weasleys do not have much wealth, which is one of the areas Draco often makes fun of. For instance, after Ron admires Harry's new Nimbus 2000, Draco comments "you couldn't afford half the handle […] I suppose you and your brothers have to save up twig by twig" (Rowling, 1997, p. 165). In this way, Draco is copying his father. Throughout the book, there is a certain hatred between Lucius Malfoy and Arthur Weasley. Lucius looks down on Arthur for associating with Muggles and also his low income. He describes Arthur as a "flea-bitten, Muggle-loving fool" and "a disgrace to the name of wizard" (Rowling, 1999, p. 51). The Malfoys' contempt for the Weasleys only increases Harry's fondness for them. They are welcoming, interesting and kind right from the beginning, when Molly Weasley helps him finding his way to Platform 9¾.

Despite Arthur's love for all things Muggle, he lacks a general understanding of how the Muggle world works. Therefore, he provides many humorous moments, including his mispronunciation of certain words—"eckeltricity" (Rowling, 1999, p. 47), "escapators" (Rowling, 2000, p. 46), and "fellytone" (Rowling, 2003, p. 869), and his joy and inability to light a fire with matches at the World Cup (Rowling, 2000, p. 85). Thus, even the most muggle-friendly pure-blood is still unaware of the day-to-day life muggles live.

Although pure-bloods are perceived as the most powerful wizards, the main antagonist, Voldemort, is a half-blood. Thus, the question arises what caused his obsession with the purity of a wizard's blood. The first mention of his blood status comes from the manifestation of a horcrux: Tom Riddle's diary. After Tom Riddle reveals himself to Harry as Lord Voldemort, he remarks: "You think I was going to use my filthy muggle father's name forever?" (Rowling, 1999, p. 314). This and the graveyard incident are the only times Voldemort (or at least a part of him) recognizes his status as a half-blood.

Even when it comes to his followers, they seem to be unaware of it. When Harry says Voldemort's name in front of Bellatrix Lestrange, she shrieks: "You dare speak his name with your unworthy lips, you dare besmirch it with your half-blood's tongue, you dare" (Rowling, 2003, p. 784) to which Harry replies: "Did you know he's a half-blood too? [...] Yeah, his mother was a witch but his dad was a muggle—or has he been telling you lot he's pure-blood?" (Ibid.). Due to Lestrange's obsession with the purity of someone's blood, it is unlikely that she was aware of Voldemort's past as Tom Riddle. It is likely that only a small number of Death Eaters are aware of his status as a half-blood: those who knew him in Hogwarts and Wormtail, who helped to resurrect him with the bone of his father.

Voldemort's obsession with his own heritage—as the last living descendent of Salazar Slytherin—and his loathing of his Muggle father who abandoned him and his mother might be the reasons for his fixation on pure-bloods. Dumbledore tells Harry that Voldemort had an obsession with his parentage, which, to an extent, is natural since he grew up in an orphanage. According to his sources, Voldemort first looked for any traces of Tom Riddle, Sr., in Hogwarts—"on the shields in the trophy room, on the lists of prefects in the old school records, even in the books of Wizarding history" (Rowling, 2005, p. 362). Dumbledore believes that when Voldemort realized that his father was never in Hogwarts, he dropped the name Riddle forever and "assumed the identity of Lord Voldemort" (Ibid.). Subsequently, he began researching his mother's heritage, which he had previously ignored because of her "shameful human weakness of death" (Rowling, 2005, p. 363). On his search, Voldemort confronts Morfin, who mistakes him for the muggle Tom Riddle, which is how Voldemort confirms that he is a half-blood (Rowling, 2005, p. 365). Afterwards, he murders his father and grandfather, thereby "obliterating the last of the unworthy Riddle line and revenging himself upon the father who never wanted him" and also takes Slytherin's ring from Morfin to take on his new role as heir of Slytherin (Rowling, 2005, p. 367).

During one of Harry's lessons with Dumbledore, he is confronted with Voldemort's ancestors the Gaunts, which is another family of the "Sacred Twenty-Eight." The family only consists of Marvolo Gaunt and his children, Morfin and Merope, who had been driven into poverty due to generations of Gaunts living in splendor (Rowling, 2005, p. 212). Nevertheless, Marvolo Gaunt prides himself on his ancestry and personifies the old perception of pure-bloods: That they are above muggles and can treat muggles how they want. The scene Harry witnesses in Dumbledore's Pensieve, when Bob Ogden visited the Gaunts' home, depicts their muggle loathing and pride in their ancestry. Odgen informs Marvolo that his son Morfin has broken wizard law by performing magic in front of a muggle, yet Gaunt simply mimics him and states that Morfin "taught a filthy muggle a lesson" (Rowling, 2005, p. 206). When Ogden presses further, Gaunt attacks him verbally by calling him a "filthy little Mudblood" (Rowling, 2005, p. 207) who thinks that he and his family are scum because he is unaware of their connection to Salazar Slytherin. The insult might not necessarily be based on Odgen's blood status, but based on Gaunt's view that anyone who does not belong to one the ancient bloodlines is beneath him. He proceeds by flaunting his family heirlooms: the ring on his finger, which has been in his family for centuries and shows that they are "pure-blood all the way," and Slytherin's locket around Merope's neck to underline that they are "his last living descendants" (Rowling, 2005, pp. 207–208).

Half-Blood Wizards

Despite Voldemort's belief that only pure-blood wizards are worthy, he chooses the half-blood Harry and not the pure-blood Neville Longbottom as his enemy. Sybill Trewlawney's prophecy about Voldemort states that: "The one with the power to vanquish the Dark Lord will be born as the seventh month dies" and "born to those who have thrice defied him" (Rowling, 2003, p. 841). Yet, this could have been either Harry or Neville. According to Dumbledore, Voldemort "chose the boy he thought most likely to be a danger to him" (Rowling, 2003, p. 842) and a half-blood, just like himself. Thus, the series' main protagonist is also a half-blood. In contrast to Voldemort, both of Harry's parents were wizard; his father was a pure-blood and his mother was muggle-born.

Two other significant half-bloods are Albus Dumbledore and Severus Snape. It is revealed in *DH*, Dumbledore's mother Kendra was muggle-born and his father Percival was either a half- or a pure-blood (Rowling, 2007, p. 115). In his youth, Dumbledore had some dangerous ideas concerning the status of wizards. One surprising fact the Trio stumbles upon is Dumbledore's letter to Gellert Grindelwald, discussing Grindelwald's idea about *"Wizard dominance being FOR THE MUGGLES' OWN GOOD"* (Rowling, 2007, p. 357). In it, he mentions how although the wizards' power gives them *"the right to rule [...] it also gives* [them] *responsibilities over the ruled"* (Ibid). Therefore, he proposes that they should *"seize control FOR THE GREATER GOOD"* (Ibid.) and if they meet resistance, they should only use *"the force that is necessary and no more"* (Ibid.). His early views do alienate the Trio, because until then Dumbledore has been a shining hero. However, he did deviate from these views, defeated Grindelwald, and focused on the education of young wizards and witches.

When the 'Half-blood Prince' is revealed as Severus Snape, Hermione mentions that his mother's name was Eileen Prince. Hermione points out that Snape "must have been proud of being 'half a Prince'"—half a pure-blood wizard. Harry theorizes that Snape played up "the pure-blood side so he could get in with Lucius Malfoy and the rest of them" (Rowling, 2005, p. 637). He also notices the similarities between Snape and Voldemort; that Snape also has a muggle father and pure-blood wizard mother, and is "ashamed of his parentage, trying to make himself feared using the Dark Arts, [and] gave himself an impressive new name—the Half-Blood *Prince*" (Ibid.). The similarities are eerie. By equating the two, Snape is depicted as just as cruel as Voldemort. Yet, they do not know his stance on muggle-borns. Although it is shown that Snape sees wizards above muggles, he does not care about purity of blood—at least not with Lily Potter.

Muggle-Born Wizards

Muggle-borns are wizards who come from muggle parents. Although muggle-borns are wizards just like everyone else, there are certain prejudices set against them. As Draco articulates other wizards' point of view: "They're just not the same, they've never been brought up to know our ways. Some of them have never even heard of Hogwarts until they get the letter, imagine" (Rowling, 1997, p. 78). Since Harry grew up in the Muggle household of the Dursleys, he has hardly any advantage over muggle-borns, since he was unaware of his heritage before Hagrid revealed it to him. Despite this apparent disadvantage, the most prominent Muggle-born in the series, Hermione Granger, is constantly the best in (almost) every class. This fact is even highlighted early on in *Chamber of Secrets* when Draco's father calls his son out for not being "ashamed that a girl of no wizard family beat [him] in every exam" (Rowling, 1999, p. 52). Additionally, Ron points out that the majority of wizards know that it does not make it difference whether someone is Muggle-born. As an example, he mentions Neville Longbottom, who is a pure-blood "can hardly stand a cauldron the right way up" and Hagrid adds that "they haven't invented a spell our Hermione can' do" (Rowling, 1999, pp. 116 and 52).

From *CoS* onwards, another term is introduced: Mudblood. Draco Malfoy is the first one to insult Hermione this way, after she remarked that no one in the Gryffindor Quidditch team had to bribe their way in (Rowling, 1999, p. 112). Although the other students' reactions make it obvious that "Mudblood" is a serious insult, neither Harry not Hermione, who have both grown up with muggles, know the full meaning of the insult. The term is then explained by Ron who says that "mudblood's a really foul name for someone who is Muggle-born" (Rowling, 1999, pp. 115–116) and is mainly used by the likes of the Malfoys who prize their pure-blood status.

Subsequently, the person who mostly uses the term is Draco, in reference to Hermione. He uses it as a threat towards her and other muggle-borns in *CoS*, threatening that "You'll be next, Mudbloods!" (Rowling, 1999, p. 139), showing his skepticism that "the long-molared Mudblood" (Rowling, 2000, p. 404) got a date in *GoF*, or even when deducting points as a member of the inquisitorial squad in *OotP*: "You're a Mudblood, Granger, so ten for that" (Rowling, 2003, p. 626). After six books of being referred to as a "Mudblood" in *DH*, Hermione stands up and declares that she is a "Mudblood, and proud of it!" (Rowling, 2007, p. 489). This moment shows an important stage for her, as she is owning the insult, rather than letting it affect her.

Another victim of the insult "Mudblood" is Harry's mother, Lily Evans. Lily Evans is also muggle-born and, similar to Hermione, is also one of the best students. This surprises Horace Slughorn, her potions teacher, who tells Harry that he "[t]hought she must have been pure-blood, she was so good" (Rowling, 2005, p. 70), adding that he isn't prejudiced against muggle-borns, since Lily was one of his favorite students. Although the reader gets only a glimpse into her character, one instance that stands out is the quarrel between Snape and Lily, when he dismisses her as a "filthy little Mudblood" (Rowling, 2003, p. 648). He later tries to apologize by saying that he never meant to call her that. However, Lily is aware of his links to the Death Eaters and questions why, when he calls every muggle-born a Mudblood, she should be the exception. Since there is no answer, apart from his love for her, their friendship is over. This incident appears to haunt Snape later. When Phineas Nigellus' portrait calls Hermione "Mudblood," Snape immediately interferes: "Do not use that word!" (Rowling, 2007, p. 689).

Although the term is often mentioned, especially by Voldemort supporters, there are no direct consequences for muggle-borns attached to it.

However, the treatment of muggle-borns worsens in *DH* once Voldemort is in power. While the Trio is hunting the Horcruxes, Lupin informs them that there is a muggle-born registration, in which muggle-born wizards and witches are stripped of their wands and often imprisoned. The opening for a "Muggle-born Register!" in the *Daily Prophet* reads as follows: "*The Ministry of Magic is undertaking a survey of so-called 'muggle-borns' the better to understand how they came to possess magical secrets*" (Rowling, 2007, p. 209). This opening is followed by a claim that the Department of Mysteries has revealed that people without a wizard or witch in their family cannot possess magic, and therefore must have acquired it by theft (Ibid). Thus, they invite muggle-born witches and wizards to come to the Ministry for an interview (Ibid).

After reading the article, Ron mentions how "mental" the allegations are, because "if you could steal magic there wouldn't be any Squibs, would there?" (Rowling, 2007, p. 209) His question lays bare the Ministry's seemingly illogical approach. However, since their intent is to eradicate all muggle-borns, they needed a pretense for wizards, who might object. Therefore, claiming that muggle-borns "steal" magic gives the Ministry a valid excuse to imprison them. And there are muggle-borns showing up for the registration, partly because of the element of fear, but also because of the unawareness of what will happen to them, since the article simply states that they are invited to "present themselves for interview" (Rowling, 2007, p. 209). Additionally, muggle-borns are sought out and brought in, if they do not show up voluntarily. Similarly, the compulsory attendance requirements for the children at Hogwarts is problematic. Not only does Voldemort have access to a whole new wizarding generation, but because students are given a blood status, "it's also another way of weeding out muggle-borns" (Rowling, 2007, p. 210).

Although Harry, Ron and Hermione are aware of the implications of what the muggle-born register would do, they are faced with the reality when they enter the Ministry of Magic, where the golden fountain is replaced by a giant statue depicting a witch and a wizard on a throne overlooking the witches and wizards with the words, "MAGIC IS MIGHT" (Rowling, 1999, p. 221) engraved on a plate the bottom. The statue appears disempowering, looking down on the workers and reminding them of their place, and also intimidating them to behave correctly. Yet, this is not the worst part of the statue. Hermione points out to Harry that the wizards' thrones are made of hundreds of naked human bodies. Furthermore, Hermione remarks how this positioning represents the wizards' view of Muggles, as they are positioned "in their rightful place" (Rowling, 2007, p. 242).

It is interesting to note the difference in their perception. Whereas Harry's focus is on the whole impact of the statue, Hermione focuses on the detail—the muggles. The underlying tone of displaying the elegantly dressed wizards above naked muggles is to display why wizards should rule over muggles and muggle-borns. The wizards appear more cultivated and powerful and therefore made to lead. In search of Umbridge's office, Harry sees another element of the ministry's brainwashing: a pamphlet entitled *Mudbloods and the Dangers They Pose to a Peaceful Pure-Blood Society* (Rowling, 2007, p. 249).

In the waiting- and the investigation room, Harry experiences how the Muggle-borns are treated. First, they have to wait for the interrogation in a small room with dementors floating around between them, spreading cold, hopelessness, and despair (Rowling, 2007, p. 257). Then, during the interrogation of Mary Cattermole, the wife of the man Ron had transformed into, Harry witnesses how the interrogations work. Mrs. Cattermole is asked for her name, marriage, and children, which she answers in tears. Every emotion she shows is ignored. When she mentions how her children are frightened, because they think that she "might not come home," she is met with an unsympathetic sneer: "The brats of Mudbloods do not stir our sympathies" (Rowling, 2007, p. 259). The most dramatic demeanor towards muggle-borns is Umbridge's assertion during the interview that muggle-borns cannot possess a wand. Umbridge asks Mrs. Cattermole if she recognizes the wand and from which witch or wizard she took it. When Mrs. Cattermole replies that the wand chose her, Umbridge accuses her of lying because: "wands only choose witches or wizards. You are not a witch" (Rowling, 2007, pp. 260–261).

Again, muggle-borns are depicted as less than wizards because they do not have a connection to wizard blood and thus should not possess magical powers. Claiming Mrs. Cattermole had stolen a wand and used it provides Umbridge with a purpose to detain and question muggle-borns. Thus, asserting the muggle-borns stole wands demonstrates a need for them to be imprisoned and their wands given to "real" wizards and witches.

A more extreme Wizarding World is presented in the alternate reality in *Cursed Child*; the imprisonment, torture, and killing of muggles and muggle-borns is actively celebrated. When Scorpius Malfoy lands in the alternative universe where Harry Potter has been killed by Voldemort, he discovers that there are muggle-borns screaming in the dungeons and that people openly celebrate to go and "spill some proper Mudblood guts" (Throne, 2016, p. 182 and 181). There is also an eerie similarity to the Third Reich with the added salute "for Voldemort and Valor" (Thorne, 2016, p. 180).

Not only the Wizarding World is focused on blood. Even in Harry's experience in the muggle world, there are connections drawn to a person's blood and their demeanor. For instance, in *PoA*, Aunt Marge compares Harry's apparent "mean, runty look" with one of her dogs she had to put down (Rowling, 1999, p. 26). According to Marge, "[i]t all comes down to blood [...] Bad blood will out [...] your sister was a bad egg. They turn up in the best families. Then she ran off with a wastrel and here's the result right in front of us" (Rowling, 1999, p. 28).

Although the blood status of a character plays a part in the series, it is only of importance to those characters who place importance on it. In the F.A.Q. section of her website, Rowling mentions that the expressions regarding someone's blood status—pure-blood, half-blood, and muggle-born—were created by wizards to whom the distinction matters. Thus, if there is a single muggle-born present in someone's parentage, they would only be considered a "'half' wizard" ("F.A.Q.," 2017). Rowling equates that logic with those of the Nazi ideology regarding "Aryan" and "Jewish" blood, where "a single Jewish grandparent 'polluted' the blood, according to their propaganda" (Ibid).

The compilation of the Trio—Harry, Ron, and Hermione—connects all aspects of a wizard's origin and therefore offers an insight to understand and sympathize with each perspective. Ron comes from an ancient pure-blood family, Hermione is muggle-born and Harry is a half-blood. However, none of the characters conform to any of the stereotypes associated with their respective blood status. Ron does not pride himself on being a pure-blood, Harry with two wizards as parents grew up as a muggle, and Hermione is the best witch in her class and stands out because of her intelligence and diligence. Thus, although it might appear that characters are defined by their blood, they are not. Pure bloods can be both noble and treacherous; the most prominent villain is even a half blood. Even muggles—the Dursleys—are depicted as being unsympathetic. Ultimately, it is about the inner qualities of a character that defines them.

REFERENCES

Gupta, Suman. (2003). *Re-Reading Harry Potter*. Basingstoke: Palgrave Macmillan.
Rowling, J.K. (2017). "Dolores Umbridge," *Pottermore*, https://www.pottermore.com/writing-by-jk-rowling/dolores-umbridge. [accessed 17 August 2017].
Rowling, J.K. (2017). "F.A.Q.," *Webarchive of J.K. Rowling Official Site*, https://web.archive.org/web/20060316221500/https://www.jkrowling.com/textonly/en/faq_view.cfm?id=58. [accessed 15 October 2017].
Rowling, J.K. (1999). *Harry Potter and the Chamber of Secrets*. New York: Scholastic.
Thorne, Jack. (2016). *Harry Potter and the Cursed Child*. London: Little Brown.
Rowling, J.K. (2007). *Harry Potter and the Deathly Hallows*. New York: Scholastic.
Rowling, J.K. (2000). *Harry Potter and the Goblet of Fire*. New York: Scholastic.
Rowling, J.K. (2005). *Harry Potter and the Half-Blood Prince*. New York: Scholastic.
Rowling, J.K. (2003) *Harry Potter and the Order of the Phoenix*. New York: Scholastic.
Rowling, J.K. (1999). *Harry Potter and the Prisoner of Azkaban*. New York: Scholastic.
Rowling, J.K. (1997). *Harry Potter and the Sorcerer's Stone*. New York: Scholastic.
Rowling, J.K. (2017). "Hogwarts Portraits," *Pottermore*, https://www.pottermore.com/writing-by-jk-rowling/hogwarts-portraits. [accessed 14 July 2017].
Rowling, J.K. (2017). "Horace Slughorn fact file," *Pottermore*, https://www.pottermore.com/explore-the-story/horace-slughorn. [accessed 17 August 2017].
Rowling, J.K. (2017). "Pure-Blood," *Pottermore*, https://www.pottermore.com/writing-by-jk-rowling/pure-blood. [accessed 05 April 2017].

"You have your mother's eyes"
Inheritance and Social Class

Alison Baker

In the first chapter of her book *Fantasy and the Real World in British Children's Literature* (Webb, 2015), Caroline Webb notes that Harry Potter's origin story has long been compared to a fairy tale: abandoned on a doorstep, he turns out to be a hero. Webb quotes Alison Lurie, M. Katherine Grimes and Julia Eccleshare (Webb, 2015, pp. 24-25) all referencing Cinderella when describing Harry's living conditions in 4, Privet Drive at the start of *Harry Potter and the Philosopher's Stone* (Rowling, 1997) However, while Harry is neglected, poorly treated and dressed in cast-offs, like Cinderella, and forced to serve his cousin (Rowling, 1997, pp. 20-21), like the Brothers Grimm's telling of Cinderella (Grimm, 2007), Harry is the child of a wealthy man. In the wizarding world, Harry is, through his inheritance, a lost prince.

This essay seeks to discuss social class in the wizarding world described by J.K. Rowling. I use both the classifications used by the Office of National Statistics (ONS) and Bourdieuian taxonomy of class, which includes consumption of cultural goods and practices as markers of social class. I discuss the relative social positions of wizards who are pureblood, half-blood and muggle-born, and the social capital accrued by each. I also discuss inheritance, both material and social, and what that means in the wizarding world. Finally, I discuss attitudes to non-wizard magical beings and the extent to which social class applies to them.

Rowling outlines different kinds of inheritance: material goods and monetary wealth; power structures, particularly those used to oppress; and physical characteristics that indicate kinship. The Weasley family is all red-haired and freckled (Rowling, 1997, p. 69; 2000, p. 49): Draco Malfoy recognizes Ron on the Hogwarts Express by his red hair. He passes on his father's disparaging opinion of the Weasleys' appearance: red hair and freckles; and of their financial status: having "more children than they can afford" (Rowling, 1997, p. 81). Despite their shortage of money, the Weasleys have considerable class privilege, something that Park does not address in her chapter, "Class and Socioeconomic Identity in Harry Potter's England" (Park, 2003, p. 186)), where she describes them as "dirt poor" and suggests Irish heritage for the family. Arthur Weasley at the beginning of the series works in an obscure department of the Ministry of Magic; the Misuse of Muggle Artifacts. Arthur is a civil servant, and manages one member of staff, Perkins (Rowling, 1998, p. 29) meaning that his socio-economic classification according to ONS is L3: Higher Professional Occupations (Office of National Statistics, 2010, p. 9) or Established Middle Class (Savage, et al., 2013, p. 231). The Weasleys live in a large house in the village of Ottery St. Catchpole (Rowling, 1998, p. 29) (possibly a reference to Ottery St. Mary in Devon), which they expanded by magic to accommodate the needs of their growing family. The family has land for chickens (Rowling, 1998, p. 30), a large garden (Rowling, 1998, p. 32), a paddock (Rowling, 1998, p. 39), and an orchard (Rowling, 2007, p. 115). We do not know whether the family inherited this house or bought it, but ownership of a large house like this in the southwest of England would confer a high level of capital to a family; a search of the property-finding website Zoopla.co.uk for a detached house with five bedrooms and an orchard in Devon shows prices of between £950,000 and £1,195,000. Mendlesohn (Mendlesohn, 2002, p. 173) suggests that the Weasleys' financial situation might be to indicate their virtue, and this is an interesting point. Perhaps it is also to indicate Harry's virtue; he is not picking his friends because of their social position; in fact, Draco's mockery of Ron's family draws defense from Harry and rejection of Draco's offer of friendship.

Siisiäinen (2000) succinctly summarizes Bourdieu's approach to the concept of capital. Bourdieu uses a Marxist characterization of economic capital; that is, the financial ability to buy goods and sell them at a profit, but also economic possessions that "increase an actor's capacities in society" (Siisiäinen 2000 p. 11). Siisiäinen outlines Bourdieu's three approaches to cultural capital: early childhood upbringing and experiences (pedagogy), access to cultural artifacts, and "it also exists institutionalized in cultural institutions and is expressed in terms of certificates, diplomas and examinations" (Siisiäinen, 2000 p. 11). Finally, Bourdieu's conceptualization of social capital is summarized; firstly, as access to social networks and group membership, and secondly from the "mutual cognition and recognition" that such membership confers; the social capital is symbolic, since it comes with the ability to recognize the "objective" differences that comes with belonging to networks and groups (Siisiäinen, 2000, pp. 11-12).

Ron's advantage over muggle-born Hermione and half-blood Harry, brought up by his muggle aunt, is his social and cultural capital from his Pureblood status and upbringing. Siisiäinen (2000) summarizes Bourdieu's conceptualization of capital as firstly, economic capital in the Marxist sense, but also in other "economic possessions that increase an actor's capacities in society" (Siisiäinen, 2000, p. 11). The Weasleys have some similarities to the Marlow family in Antonia Forest's Kingscote boarding school series; the inheritors of a large farmhouse and land in the South of England, the father of the family a naval captain and the oldest son a naval lieutenant. There are eight children in the family including a set of twins. Because they are such a big family, the twins, Nicola and Lawrie, frequently have their older sisters' castoffs because their parents are often short of money, a theme of Forest's book *Cricket Term* (Forest, 1974). Large upper-class families with little money, like the Weasleys, are a familiar type to readers of British boarding school stories.

Hermione's parents are dentists, categorized as "Traditional Professionals" by Savage et al. (2013, p. 224). Savage et al. (2013, p. 232) give dentists as an example of the "elite" in the *Great British Class Experiment,* and they are categorized as L2 by ONS (2010), so in the muggle world, she is likely to have access to economic and social capital. However, in the Wizarding World, she has very little. She relies heavily on research and reading to navigate the Wizarding World and to prepare herself for its unfamiliarity. The first time Harry and Ron meet Hermione on the train to Hogwarts, she tells them that she has learned the set books off by heart, and has already read beyond (Rowling, 1997, p. 79). The extent to which Hermione's sense of her need to succeed academically and to "learn" a world that she has not encountered through due to her lack of cultural capital in the Wizarding World; after the Defense Against the Dark Arts practical examination in *PoA,* Hermione reveals that the Boggart took the form of Professor McGonagall telling her that she had failed everything (Rowling, 1999, p. 234). Hermione's "self-made" status in the wizarding world is further demonstrated by Crookshanks, her cat. While Ron inherits Scabbers, and is later given Pigwidgeon, his little owl, by Sirius Black, another scion of an old wizarding family (Rowling, 1999, p. 316), and Harry is given Hedwig, his owl, by Hagrid, who guides him back to the wizarding world (Rowling, 1997, pp. 62-63). However, Hermione chooses Crookshanks for herself, and pays for him (Rowling, 1999, pp. 49-50). As Miss Tick in Terry Pratchett's *The Wee Free Men* explains, having a witch ancestor helps, because inheriting a pointy hat saves a "great deal of expense" (Pratchett, 2003, p. 42).

Brown (Brown, 2008, p. 36) maps the hierarchy of the Wizarding World, with squibs, the non-magical members of wizarding families, placed fourth, below muggle-borns and above muggles. There are three representations of non-magical magical people in the Harry Potter series, and all of them are in positions subservient to wizarding people. Firstly, Hagrid, who has both wizard and giant ancestry, and a half-brother who is a giant, Grawp (Rowling, 2003, p. 610). Hagrid is trusted by Dumbledore to deliver Harry to the Dursleys (Rowling, 1997, p. 16), and is Harry's, and the reader's, introduction to the Wizarding World. At the same time, he is also presented as a naïve, buffoonish character, endangering the school and students several times through his weakness for dragons (Rowling, 1997), giant spiders (Rowling, 1998) and Blast-Ended Skrewts (Rowling, 2000). Hagrid's service role, as Keeper of the Keys and Grounds at Hogwarts, is indicated by his rural accent. He is reminiscent of Dickon in Frances Hodgson Burnett's *The Secret Garden,* whom Mary Lennox calls "like an angel" (Hodson Burnett, 2005, p. 213) in his natural affinity for animals, but without Dickon's competence and wisdom. As Mendlesohn indicates, it is strange that Hagrid's years of study and employment at the school have not changed Hagrid's accent (Mendlesohn, 2002, p. 163), and he is either excluded from, or excludes himself from, Hogwarts castle (Rana, 2009, p. 50). He and Firenze the centaur are the only teachers who do not live in the castle. Hagrid lives in a cottage on the grounds, which seems to be tied to his role as grounds keeper, rather than as a teacher. Harry, Ron and Hermione are constantly having to rescue Hagrid from scrapes, such as over Norbert the dragon (Rowling, 1997). Draco Malfoy's classist, wizard supremacist attitude is evident firstly in classifying Hagrid as a servant (Rowling, 1997, p. 60) and by his lack of respect for Hagrid as the professor of Care for Magical Creatures (Rowling, 1999, p. 87). Hermione, who must take her education as witch seriously since she lacks the social and cultural capital to gain essential knowledge of the wizarding world elsewhere, becomes frustrated by Hagrid's teaching despite her fondness for him. As Rana states (Rana, 2009, p. 52), Hagrid's attempts to move out of his social class are doomed to failure, due to his lack of education, including his magical education after his expulsion from Hogwarts (Rowling, 1997. P. 48) and are treated as humorous, such as his use of flobberworms to teach the students after the disastrous lesson with Buckbeak (Rowling, 1999).

Secondly, the school caretaker, Filch, is a Squib (Rowling, 1998). Squibs are non-magical members of magical families (Rowling, 1998 p. 110–111); both Squibs introduced in the books are in service positions. Filch cleans the castle and elderly Arabella Figg babysat Harry as a young child (Rowling, 1997, p. 22) and continues to look after him undercover as he gets older (Rowling, 2003, p. 23–27). Brown (2008, p. 36) places Squibs as fourth in the wizarding hierarchy, below muggle-borns but above muggles. They are above muggles since they have knowledge of the Wizarding World, but are subservient to wizards and witches since they cannot do magic. It appears to be shameful to have a squib in the family; Neville's family try to force magic out of him as discussed below; Ron's first reaction to discovering Filch's status is to snigger, and Filch appears to be trying to learn magic by correspondence course (Rowling, 1998, p. 97–98). The term is used as a slur by Lord Voldemort's grandfather and uncle against his mother, Merope (Rowling, 2005, p. 195), who is from a family that lives in squalor, and whose obsession with their pure blood status has led to inbreeding and destitution (Rowling, 2005, Ch 10).

It is evident that the harmonious representation of the wizarding world in the Fountain of Magical Brotherhood does not tell the whole story of wizarding world hierarchies. Harry and his fellow Gryffindor first years discuss their families openly (Rowling, 1997, p. 93). Seamus Finnigan states that he is "half and half," but Neville, brought up by his witch grandmother, states that his family feared that he was a muggle (Rowling, 1997, p. 93). However, we learn in later books firstly that Neville Longbottom's parents were aurors, tortured by Voldemort's followers and living in St Mungo's hospital (Rowling, 2003, p. 453–455). Therefore, Neville's grandmother and great-uncle Algie must have thought that Neville was a squib, not a muggle.

The third non-magical creature is banned from using wands. They are not considered human, but are humanoid, and can speak. House elves are owned by old wizarding families, have magical powers of their own but are not allowed to use them without their masters' permission (Rowling, 1998, p. 27). They are in a service position, but as Winky explains to Harry, house elves are not supposed to be paid (Rowling, 2000, p. 89). They are in accommodation tied to their employment and cannot leave of their own will, though they can be given clothes and released from their bonds. Savage et al. refer to a class replacing the traditional working class as "precariat," a group of service workers who are "characterized by very low levels of capital" (Savage et al. 2013, p. 220). The power balance between the elf and the master is purely on the side of the master; the elf's role is simply to serve, with no material return. However, by the terms of the 2015 United Kingdom Modern Slavery Act, house elves are not slaves:

(1) A person commits an offence if—
    (a) the person holds another person in slavery or servitude and the circumstances are such that the person knows or ought to know that the other person is held in slavery or servitude, or
    (b) the person requires another person to perform forced or compulsory labour and the circumstances are such that the person knows or ought to know that the other person is being required to perform forced or compulsory labour [The Stationery Office, 2015, Part 1].

Hagrid reminds Hermione that the house elves do not want to be paid and her attempts to liberate them without working with them is unkind and inappropriate (Rowling, 2000, p. 233). Since the elves do not feel that they are in slavery or forced to work, they are not willing to be liberated. In fact, the difficulties that Dobby and Winky find themselves in through their liberation (Rowling, 2000, p. 329–331) mean that Hermione's attempts to trick the elves into accepting clothes and forcing them out of Hogwarts is uncharacteristically cruel of her (Rowling, 2003, p. 230–231) and is unlikely to work, since Hermione is not the house elves' master. Yeğenoğlu (Yeğenoğlu, 1998) discusses the Western feminist assumptions about Muslim women's lives in the early 20th Century, seeing polygamy, the harem and the veil as symbols of women's oppression (Yeğenoğlu, 1998, p. 100). This Orientalist attitude towards non-Western ways of life led to misunderstandings and misinterpretation, since Western feminists were ascribing false meaning to Muslim traditions. To Western feminists, it was more important that Muslim women adopted "the illusion of agency" (Yeğenoğlu, 1998, p. 101) than Westerners came to understand the meaning of Muslim culture and traditions. Thus, Dobby has sought freedom and has found liberation and contentment in his new life because he has chosen to do so; but Hermione must not generalize for all house elves from his experience (Rowling, 2000, p. 330).

Harry's experience of employment in the wizarding community outside of Hogwarts is necessarily limited in the first book to the shopkeepers of Diagon Alley and the barman of the Leaky Cauldron (Rowling, 1997). However, as he grows, Harry encounters a wider group of magical people and their employment, and it is through the limited third person narration that we see Harry's experience of the world. I will consider three categories of employment: retail, public transport and health services.

The retail workers that are depicted in the books are not those that Jones described in *Chavs* (Jones, 2011), with a lack of autonomy over their working lives (Jones, 2011, p. 144), whose precarious working lives were documented by Ehrenreich in *Nickled and Dimed* (Ehrenreich, 2002). These shops are not part of chains, but the owners are artisans or craftspeople, such as Madam Malkin or Mr Ollivander, or selling desirable goods linked to culture, such as the bookshop Flourish and Blotts. Thus, they do not entirely fit with the categorisation of Savage et al. with retail workers in the Newly Affluent category; they do not "shun" the traditional culture of the wizarding world (Savage et al., 2013, p. 238). However, as Savage et al. describe, they do have extensive social contacts; Mr Ollivander recognises all wizards and witches through their wands (Rowling, 2000, p. 270–272), and Mr Borgin knows enough about the Malfoy family to suspect that there are Death Eater artefacts in Malfoy Manor (Rowling, 1998, p. 44). Notably, Lucius Malfoy, whose wizarding supremacist views are known to the reader, addresses Mr Borgin as "Borgin." The lack of honorific demonstrates his lack of respect; the reader knows that this is not the attitude of the wizarding community that we are supposed to view positively.

Secondly, Stan Shunpike, the conductor of the Knight Bus, like Hagrid, still speaks with a working-class accent; in this case, the dropped H and "nuffink" for nothing suggesting a London accent like London Transport employees (Rowling, 1999, p. 32). Ernie Prang, the Knight Bus driver, is classified in the Standard Occupational Classification data as Routine Manual Service Occupation (Office of National Statistics, 2010, p. 28); that is, traditional working class in Savage et al. London Transport no longer employs bus conductors, so it is not possible to classify Stan Stunpike in current occupational terms. However, his name has associations with Steerpike from Mervyn Peake's 1946–1959 *Gormenghast* Trilogy, (Peake, 1995) and with the old English term "turnpike," a highway that led from town to town. These names suggest Stan's role travelling from town to town, but also perhaps that he untrustworthy. Steerpike is young, but ruthless. Stan, on the other hand, is arrested after boasting about Death Eater activity and later joins the Death Eaters under an Imperious curse.

Finally, Healers are equated with Hogwarts staff; Dilys Derwent was a healer before taking over the role of headmistress (sic) of Hogwarts (Rowling, 2003, p. 428). Savage et al. describe the Elite as the group with the highest level of all kinds of capital (Savage et al., 2013, p. 233); Dumbledore's public roles in the Wizarding World, aside from his duties as headmaster of Hogwarts, demonstrate his social and cultural capital. Therefore, if being a healer is an appropriate role before taking charge of such a socially and culturally important role, it must also be classed as socially and culturally significant.

Despite Ron's shock at Harry asking whether the wizards and witches at St Mungo's are doctors (Rowling, 2003, p. 428), the description of what the wizards and witches are doing in the hospital mainly correlates to the role of what the reader would expect a health services professional to do. Rowling is explicit that the role of Healer is not gender specific, although it should be noted that the role of receptionist seems to have been taken by a Welcome-Witch, not WelcomeWizard (Rowling, 2003, p. 428–429), and the nurturing and slightly indiscreet healer looking after Gilderoy Lockhart on the closed ward is a witch (Rowling, 2003, p. 451).

As Groves points out (Groves, 2017), Rowling uses the "third person limited omniscient view" (Groves, 2017, p. 100) as a narrative voice; that is, the action is told in the third person, where the plot is described through the voice of a narrator external to the plot. At the same time, most of the action is from Harry's viewpoint. His thoughts and emotions are the ones that the reader has access to; for example, in *PoA* (Rowling, 1999), the secret of Hermione's packed timetable is not explained until the end of the book. The experience of using the Time-Turner is only described when Hermione uses it with Harry. His keen sense of loss of his parents is expressed many times throughout the series. For example, in chapter twelve of *PS* (Rowling, 1997),

"The Mirror of Erised," the mirror, which shows the viewers' hearts' desire, shows Harry with his parents by his side. In *GoF* (Rowling, 2000), the Weasleys are described as "Harry's favorite family" (Rowling, 2000, p. 25); Harry longs to confide in a parent about the pain in his scar (ibid). Thus, the focus on family, position and kinship could be Harry's focus. His need to find his place in the Wizarding World, to find a family, and to understand the structure of the society, could be why it is described in such detail.

Harry Potter inherits a considerable amount of wizard money (Rowling, 1997, p. 58), as well as the cloak of invisibility (Rowling, 1997, p. 148) and the Marauders' Map (Rowling, 1999, p. 142). Harry has the economic capital of his deceased father; Hagrid states that the gold is from his parents (Rowling, 1997, p. 58), but since Lily Potter was a muggle-born witch, and Petunia Dursley does not appear to be independently wealthy, it can be assumed that the money is from James Potter's family. As well as economic capital, Harry has social and cultural capital at Hogwarts from his family's position in the wizarding world, and because he is the Boy Who Lived. Dumbledore anonymously gives Harry the Cloak of Invisibility, passed down from his father—originally Death's own cloak ("The Three Brothers" in Rowling, *The Tales of Beedle the Bard*, 2008). Because he was brought up by muggles, Harry has never heard the tale; Hermione has inherited the book of the *Tales* from Dumbledore and has read them (Rowling, 2007, p. 330). However, neither Hermione nor Harry have the cultural capital from their early childhood experiences to interpret the story, or to link it with other wizarding proverbs, while Ron does (Rowling, 2007, p. 336). Ron's value in the Trio in their quest is his access to cultural and social capital from his upbringing.

Ron's brothers, Fred and George, give Harry the Marauder's Map (Rowling, 1999, p. 142); they explain to Harry that they stole it from Hogwarts' caretaker Argus Filch (Rowling, 1999. p. 143), but that since they know it by heart, Harry can make use of it to get to Hogsmeade, which he does not have permission to visit. Once Harry activates the map, he reads that it was created by "Messrs Moony, Wormtail, Padfoot and Prongs" (Rowling, 1999, p. 144), nicknames of James Potter (Prongs) and his friends Remus Lupin (Moony), Peter Pettigrew (Wormtail) and Sirius Black (Padfoot) (Rowling, 1999, p. 260). Again, we can see that Harry has social capital but not cultural capital: Fred and George must teach him how to use it.

Sirius Black, Harry's godfather, is from an old pure-blood wizarding family. The portrait of Sirius Black's mother continues to hold the supremacist views that the Black family held in her lifetime (Rowling, 2003, p. 74); from the tapestry family tree at 12 Grimmauld Place, Harry learns from Sirius about the intertwined nature of the old wizarding families. The tapestry at 12 Grimmauld Place bears the Black family motto, "*Toujours pur*" (Rowing, 2003, p. 103); that is, "Always pure." As Sirius explains, there are very few pure-blood families left, so the choice of marriage partners is limited; indeed, Tonks' mother Andromeda has been removed from the family tree after marrying a muggle, and the Weasleys are missing as they are "blood traitors" for their opposition to wizard supremacist attitudes (Rowling, 2003, p. 105).

As Biressi and Nunn write in their chapter "The Upper Classes" (Biressi & Nunn, 2016), the contemporary upper class is no longer confined to the aristocracy and the "landed gentry"—that is, those who live off the proceeds of their estates (Biressi and Nunn, 2016, p. 118). The upper classes now include the very wealthy and the famous; Biressi and Nunn provide the examples of the very wealthy such as entrepreneurs Sir Richard Branson and Sir Alan Sugar, and star Sir Paul McCartney and his designer daughter, Stella. Diana, Princess of Wales, was "an important transitional figure in the refashioning of upper-class elites" (Biressi and Nunn, 2016, p. 121). Diana served to make the upper class "Sloane Ranger" lifestyle more visible; after her marriage to Prince Charles, *Harpers and Queen* columnist Peter York and Ann Barr published the humorous *Sloane Ranger Handbook* (Barr & York, 1982), marking the lifestyle, praxis and their methods of exclusion of those "Sloane Rangers" considered undesirable. Draco's comments on muggle-born wizards not being brought up to know wizarding ways and his belief that Hogwarts should only allow students from old wizarding families (Rowling, 1997, p. 61) demonstrate his membership of the elite, but also the extent to which he seeks to exclude others, as the upper classes in Barr and York are described doing.

As Rowling has stated in interviews (for example, De Volkskrant, 2007), the rise of the Death Eaters in the Harry Potter universe can be seen to have parallels of the rise of European fascism in the 1930s. Not just Hitler but also Franco and Mussolini were influential upon Oswald Mosley, leader of the British Union of Fascists (BUF) (Mosley, 1968). British Fascism in the 1920s was supported by many in the aristocracy and upper classes; not only the well-known, such as the newspaper publisher Lord Rothermere, whose titles included the *Daily Mail* and the *Daily Mirror*, and *Unity*, and Diana Mitford—the latter, married to Oswald Mosley, interned in Holloway Prison during the Second World War (Mosley D., 1977), Reginald Hugh Dorman Smith, Minister for Agriculture 1939–1940 (Stone, 2003, p. 342), but also former Suffragettes Mary Richardson and Norah Elam (Gottlieb, 2003, p. 295).

The wizarding supremacy enacted by the Death Eaters at the Quidditch World Cup very explicitly humiliates muggles, with undertones of sexual violence against the woman (Rowling, 2000, p. 108), a threat that is later repeated by Draco to Hermione (Rowling, 2000, p. 110). Tilles (Tilles, 2011) outlines how the antifascist action that came to be known as the Battle of Cable Street, preventing a BUF Blackshirt march on 4th October 1936 through Whitechapel, East London, the home of many Jewish residents of London, led to an increased membership of the British Union of Fascists, and to physical attacks on Jews. Like the appearance of the Dark Mark and the march of the Death Eaters, the show of force in the East End and the increasing antisemitism in the *Blackshirt* BUF newssheet seems to have acted as an impetus to direct violent action. The statuary of the Ministry of Magic after the rise of Rufus Scrimgeour is reminiscent of the neo-classicist architecture of Nazi Germany. The Fountain of Magical Brethren that Harry first sees on his way to his hearing on Misuse of Magic (Rowling, 2003, p. 117) depicting harmony between wizards, witches, centaurs, goblins, and house-elves (though not dementors, werewolves or giants) is replaced during the wizard supremacist Death Eaters with the Magic is Might statue: a witch and wizard carved in black stone, sitting on thrones made of the naked bodies of muggles, their faces carved to look stupid and ugly (Rowling, 2007, p. 198–199). The black stone is reminiscent of the black shirts of the British Union of Fascists, the dehumanized representations of humans of Nazi propaganda, and the comparisons of so-called "Aryans" with Jews, people of color, Gypsies and Slavs. The Muggle-Born Registration Committee (Rowling, 2007) is the benign title of legislation removing the rights of muggle-born wizards and witches, baselessly accusing them of obtaining magical skill by theft or destruction. Some muggle-born wizards seek to hide their identities; Ted Tonks refuses (Rowling, 2007, p. 242) and Dean Thomas is forced to leave Hogwarts, as he cannot prove his father's wizard status. This can be compared with the laws restricting the rights of Jews (and by extension other non–Aryans), such as the Nuremberg Race Laws of 1935 (United States Holocaust Memorial Museum, n.d.).

From the time that Harry meets Hagrid, Harry's physical resemblance to his parents is emphasized (Rowling, 1997, p. 39). It is clear that Harry also inherits more than money from his father; he has inherited his Quidditch skills from his father (Rowling, 1997, p. 113), and on seeing his family in the Mirror of Erised, Harry's heart's desire is to know where he has come from. He recognizes that his eyes are the same color and shape as his mother's, but he also has inherited some physical features from his father: his untidy hair and the need for glasses to correct his eyesight. He inherited his appearance from his extended family; he sees the same eyes, nose and knobbly knees reflected through generations. The need to know where he comes from and to recognize his family inheritance is very strong in Harry (Rowling, 1997, p. 153).

While it is clear that the authorial voice disapproves of the attitudes of the aristocratic wizard supremacist Malfoy, Black and Lestrange families and their wish to keep the Wizarding World closed to half-blood and muggle-born witches and wizards, the concept of blood heredity is not confined to them. Mr. Borgin, the owner of the sinister Borgin and Burke's shop on Knockturn Alley, complains to Lucius Malfoy that "Wizard blood" is becoming less important as time goes on (Rowling, 1998, p. 44). Readers of *PS* (Rowling, 1997) know that the Malfoys' attitudes are classist and "racist" within the terms of the novel. Draco does not use racial slurs towards characters of color, but as Horne states, Death Eaters' attitudes to muggle born "Mudbloods" are clearly intended to stand as a proxy for racism as well as classism (Horne, 2010, pp. 76-77). As Blake comments, "the magic racists are always consistently represented as evil" (Blake, 2002, p. 103).

However, a little later in the same chapter of *CoS* (Rowling, 1998), Hagrid uses the term "bad blood" in connection with the Malfoys (Rowling 1998, p. 5). The concept of "bad blood" is explored more explicitly in the play *Harry Potter and the Cursed Child* (2016), where Delphi, the daughter of Lord Voldemort and Bellatrix Lestrange, is the Augurey, whose destiny is to bring back the Dark Lord (Harry Potter Theatrical Productions Ltd, 2016, p. 260). Bellatrix's husband, Rodolphus Lestrange, told Delphi of her heritage and the prophecy she was to fulfill on his return from Azkaban; Delphi states that she has tried to follow her father's example (Harry Potter Theatrical Productions Ltd, 2016, p. 307). However, Harry, disguised as Voldemort, talks of Delphi as "his blood" (Harry Potter Theatrical Productions Ltd, 2016, p. 308). Within the world of Harry Potter, evil is an inherited trait. This is seen very clearly in the ceremony of the Sorting Hat, where children aged eleven are categorized as brave (Gryffindor), clever (Ravenclaw), hard working (Hufflepuff), or power-hungry (Slytherin) (Rowling, 2000, p. 157). Not all children are in the same house as their parents or siblings, for example Parvati and Padma Patil, sorted into Gryffindor and Ravenclaw, and Albus Potter, sorted into Slytherin (Harry Potter Theatrical Productions Ltd, 2016, p. 21). Albus's sense of disconnection from his family comes from his sorting, and much of the plot of *Harry Potter and the Cursed Child* is redeeming Slytherin.

The scholar writing about a universe that the author has not finished exploring is always going to be on shaky ground, especially when there is a dynamic, mutable resource such as *Pottermore* constantly expanding and explaining the existing printed material. However, studies in the *Harry Potter* series now are in a more knowledgeable position than those in 2002 and 2003, when the series was ongoing.

Rowling was publishing in the neo-liberal world after the United Kingdom General Election of 1997, won by the New Labour government of Tony Blair. New Labour ostensibly rejected the nostalgic, so-called Back to Basics politics of the John Major Conservatives, but the social change the party aspired to did not lead to a meritocracy. Rowling's depiction of elitism in education and the functions of government continue to be relevant in contemporary Britain precisely because the supremacist ideology of the wizarding world continues to be the ideology in our world.

References

Barr, A., & York, P. (1982). *The Official Sloane Ranger Handbook: The First Guide to What Really Matters in Life.* London: Ebury Press.
Biressi, A., & Nunn, H. (2016). *Class and Contemporary British Culture.* Basingstoke: Palgrave Macmillan.
Blake, A. (2002). *The Irresistible Rise of Harry Potter.* London: Verso.
Brown, K.A. (2008). *Prejudice in Harry Potter's World.* College Station: Virtualbookworm.com.
De Volkskrant. (2007, 11 19). "New Interview with J.K. Rowling for Release of *The Deathly Hallows*." Retrieved August 25, 2017, from The Leaky Cauldron: http://www.the-leaky-cauldron.org/2007/11/19/new-interview-with-j-k-rowling-for-release-of-dutch-edition-of-deathly-hallows/.
Ehrenreich, B. (2002). *Nickled and Dimed: Undercover in Low-Wage USA.* London: Granta.
Forest, A. (1974). *Cricket Term.* London: Puffin.
Gottlieb, J.V. (2003). *Feminine Fascism: Women in Britain's Fascist Movement.* London: I.B. Tauris.
Grimm, B. (2007). *The Complete Fairy Tales.* (J. Zipes, Ed., & J. Zipes, Trans.) London: Vintage Classics.
Groves, B. (2017). *Literary Allusion in Harry Potter.* Abingdon-on-Thames: Routledge.
Harry Potter Theatrical Productions Ltd. (2016). *Harry Potter and the Cursed Child.* New York: Little, Brown.
Hodson Burnett, F. (2005). *The Secret Garden.* Project Gutenberg.
Horne, J.C. (2010). "Harry Potter and the Other: Answering the Race Question in J.K. Rowling's Harry Potter." *The Lion and the Unicorn, 34*(1), 76–104. doi:https://doi.org/10.1353/uni.0.0488
Jones, O. (2011). *Chavs: The Demonisation of the Working Class.* London: Verso.
Mendlesohn, F. (2002). "Crowning the King: Harry Potter and the Construction of Authority." In L. Whited, *The Ivory Tower and Harry Potter: Perspectives on a Literary Phenomenon* (pp. 159–181). Missouri: University of Missouri Press.
Mosley, D. (1977). *A Life of Contrasts: The Autobiography of Diana Mosley.* London: Hamish Hamilton.
Mosley, O. (1968). *My Life.* London: Nelson.
Office of National Statistics. (2010). *Standard Occupational Classification 2010.* London: Palgrave Macmillan.
Park, J. (2003). "Class and Socioeconomic Identity in Harry Potter's England." In G. Anatol, *Reading Harry Potter: Critical Essays* (pp. 179–190). Westport, CT: Praeger Press.
Peake, M. (1995). *Titus Groan (The Gormenghast Trilogy).* London: Bloomsbury.
Pratchett, T. (2003). *The Wee Free Men.* London: Doubleday.
Rana, M. (2009). *Creating Magical Worlds: Otherness and Othering in Harry Potter.* New York: Peter Lang.
Rowling, J.K. (1998). *Harry Potter and the Chamber of Secrets.* London: Bloomsbury.
Rowling, J.K. (2007). *Harry Potter and the Deathly Hallows.* London: Bloomsbury.
Rowling, J.K. (2000). *Harry Potter and the Goblet of Fire.* London: Bloomsbury.
Rowling, J.K. (2005). *Harry Potter and the Half-Blood Prince.* London: Bloomsbury.
Rowling, J.K. (2003). *Harry Potter and the Order of the Phoenix.* London: Bloomsbury.
Rowling, J.K. (1997). *Harry Potter and the Philosopher's Stone.* London: Bloomsbury.
Rowling, J.K. (1999). *Harry Potter and the Prisoner of Azkaban.* London: Bloomsbury.
Rowling, J.K. (2008). *The Tales of Beedle the Bard.* London: Bloomsbury.
Savage, M., Devine, F., Cunningham, N., Taylor, M., Li, Y., Hjellbrekke, J., and Miles, A. (2013). Friedman, S., and Miles, A. (2013) "A New Model of Social Class? Findings from the BBC's Great British Class Experiment." *Sociology* 47(2), 219–250.
Siisiäinen, M. (2000, July 5–8). "Two Concepts of Social Capital: Bourdieu vs Puttnam." Retrieved August 25, 2017, from Indiana University Digital Library of Commons: https://dlc.dlib.indiana.edu/dlc/handle/10535/7661.
The Stationery Office. (2015). *Modern Slavery Act 2015.* Norwich: The Stationery Office.

Stone, D. (2003). "The English Mistery, the BUF and the Dilemmas of British Fascism." *The Journal of Modern History*, 75(2), 336–358. doi:http://www.jstor.org/stable/10.1086/380138.
Tilles, D. (2011, October 10). "The Myth of Cable Street." *History Today*, 61(10), not numbered. Retrieved August 25, 2017, from http://www.historytoday.com/daniel-tilles/myth-cable-street.
United States Holocaust Memorial Museum. (n.d.). "Nuremburg Laws." Retrieved from United States Holocaust Memorial Museum: https://www.ushmm.org/wlc/en/article.php?ModuleId=10007902.
Webb, C. (2015). *Fantasy and the Real World in British Children's Literature: The Power of Story*. Abingdon-on-Thames: Routledge.
Yeğenoğlu, M. (1998). *Colonial Fantasies: Towards a Feminist Reading of Orientalism*. Cambridge: Cambridge University Press.

The First Gift
Owls as Paragons of the Non-Human
Keri Stevenson

Introduction

The humans of the *Harry Potter* universe have a domineering attitude toward most non-humans—sometimes subtly so, sometimes openly sneering and contemptuous. This is particularly pronounced among wizards, for all that they also share their world with intelligent and powerful beings who could be a threat to them. These possible threats include house-elves, who can fling their former masters down a staircase if provoked (*CoS*, p. 337); centaurs, who express anger at the thought of one of their own even willingly giving a ride to a human (*SS*, p. 256); and Dementors, whose mere presence is enough to make Harry faint, which Voldemort's presence cannot do (*PoA*). But still, house-elves are mistreated, Hagrid thinks little of the way centaurs communicate and their emphasis on stargazing, and Dementors remain as the guards of Azkaban with license to eat the souls of escaped prisoners. Human-like or part-human forms plus enormous powers are not enough to earn them respect.

How much more so, then, is the lack of respect afforded to most animals or creatures that wear an animal shape? Hagrid is the only secondary or tertiary character who is enthusiastic about most of them, and given his poor judgment when it comes to things like the breeding of Blast-Ended Skrewts, the narrative casts doubt on whether other characters should mimic his attitude. The majority of the close companions and pets of the protagonists fare little better. Scabbers, although he turns out to be a villain and one of the major reasons Harry does not have parents, is introduced with Ron's gloomy take that he is merely a hand-me-down rat, undifferentiated from Ron's other possessions bequeathed by family (*SS*, p. 99). Hermione's cat, Crookshanks, earns disapprobation from Ron for attacking Scabbers and dislike from Harry for his looks (*PoA*, p. 50). Even when Crookshanks turns out to be pivotal to the plot of *PoA* by sneaking out to help Sirius and partially responsible for revealing Scabbers as an Animagus, he receives little notice or thanks.

And if heroic animals are forgotten, other animals are actively evil or at least dreaded. Nagini, Voldemort's horcrux serpent, is in the end more important as an instrument of terror and an object to be destroyed than as an animal in and of her own right. Likewise, the basilisk in *CoS* represents itself in Parseltongue as mindlessly hungry (*CoS*, p. 119), and becomes an instrument also, although in this case for the show-down between Harry and Tom Riddle's shade and as the means of destruction for horcruxes. Harry and Voldemort's ability to communicate with serpents is what Tolkien, a very different fantasy author with respect to animals from Rowling, could represent as "one of the primal "desires" that lie near the heart of Faerie: the desire of men to hold communion with other living things…. The magical understanding by men of the proper languages of birds and beasts and trees, that is much nearer to the true purposes of Faerie—a deep desire of the soul" (1966, p. 43). But in the *Harry Potter* series, it is almost purely used by Voldemort, horcruxes, or as a sign of the horcrux accidentally placed in Harry, all of them evil. Harry does not rejoice in his ability to understand snakes, get a pet snake, or use them as spies on Voldemort, all feasible courses of action if he saw the ability as neutral instead of evil. Instead, he rarely uses the ability, and does not have it as a "deep desire of the soul."

On the whole, then, the Wizarding World is neither a good world in which to be an animal nor a "creature," which may be human-shaped at least some of the time. However, there is one broad exception to this human exceptionalism, the belief that humans are the center of the universe and should be used as the measure of all other-than-human creatures (Waldau, 2013). That exception is owls. Even though they do serve a useful purpose to the wizarding world in their delivery of messages, they are also beloved pets, mentioned approvingly by the narrative and human characters, and the animals with the most screen time. This essay aims to show why, drawing on human perceptions of owls in general as among the most "human-like" birds as well as analysis of Rowling's portrayals of the birds. This liminal space in which owls are able to exist as more than instruments for wizards' power and control or symbols of fear could also, possibly, expand to encompass other animals; in the last part of this essay, I analyze how likely this actually is.

Owls as Companions of the Human

Calvez, in her memoir of visiting and studying owls around North America, notes that, despite some cultures' association of owls with death and fear, we have a biological connection to them that predisposes us to approve of these raptors. These features center on their faces. While the owls, of course, have evolved such features in order to increase their hunting success, they happen incidentally to increase our feeling of seeing the human in the owl as well. Calvez notes that "Nature, it seems, has prepared us biologically to be attracted to owls by giving them such big eyes…. Perhaps in the face of an owl we recognize ourselves" (2016, p. 1). To relate to another creature because it resembles us can seem like merely seeking out our own reflection, not actually reaching across boundaries to establish a kinship. But compared to the completely self-focused gaze that human exceptionalism resembles, the gaze directed to the owl's face is a revelation. Berger makes a point in his famous essay "Why Look at Animals?," which meditates on the exchange of human and animal gazes, that humans "are always looking across ignorance and fear" (1992, p. 5) when meeting the eyes of an animal. Yet that fear does not prevent us from believing that there is "a power ascribed to the animal, comparable with human power but never coinciding with it. The animal has secrets which, unlike the secrets of caves, mountains, seas, are specifically addressed to man" (Berger, 1992, p. 5). That power is particularly acute with owls. If we return their gazes and acknowledge their power, that is not pure and disinterested appreciation of the owl for its own sake, but at least we know their eyes are not exactly like our own, and they have a knowledge of life that we do not.

It is much better than the attitude of dismissal that surrounds so many animals in the wizarding world. Even the fear that some cultures have associated with the owl is better than that dismissal, because it at least places owls within the bounds of human thoughts, not within thoughtlessness. Windrow, who shared his own life with a tame tawny owl for fifteen years while a resident of London and Surrey, says that at first, "the idea that [his ownership of his owl Mumble] might lead to any kind of real two-way relationship had seemed remote" (2013, p. 101). But Mumble soon created a place for herself within his thoughts, and inspired him not only to treasure her as a valuable companion and friend, but to learn more about owls and especially the tawny species, become devoted to her care and feeding, and eventually write the memoir of his life with her (after going into such deep mourning from her loss that it took him twenty years to distance himself from the emotions enough to do so). A large magnitude of difference from seeing her merely as a "distraction from my glum introspection" (Windrow, 2013, p. 101). Owls have also earned a better place in the larger culture than as mere distractions; Windrow notes that for a time, owls in Britain "were routinely massacred as "vermin" by the gamekeepers of shooting estates, in the belief that this was necessary to protect the chicks ("poults") of the game birds that they were rearing in huge numbers for the guns" (2013, p. 126), but this attitude had changed to a much more positive one and the killing had lessened years before Rowling began to publish her books. This does not mean either the wizards of the story or the audience reading that story knows everything about owls, but it ensures a more cordial reception to them.

That cordial reception can involve almost forgetting that owls are predators. Windrow says with a touch of slyness that "The owls in the *Harry Potter* films are seen benignly carrying messages to the dining tables of Hogwarts—audiences are unlikely to give a thought to what they get up to at their own mealtimes" (2013, p. 63). Likewise, owls in the books tend to be "fed" with either coins, like the owl that comes to deliver the *Daily Prophet* to Hagrid in *SS* (p. 62), or bits of toast and other food on the humans' plates (*SS*, p. 134). Harry does see owls in the Hogwarts Owlery returning with mice after an evening's hunt (*GoF*, p. 491), but this is also one of the very few instances where we, the book audience, see the predatory nature of owls even mentioned, and we do not actually get to see the birds devour the mice. Owls are rendered tame and human-like not only by their faces but by the very civilized nature of their dinners.

The question might arise, then: given how civilized and how tamed they are, do the owls of the books count as "real" owls at all?

Owls and the Nature of Nature

McKibben, author of *The End of Nature,* believes that nothing on the planet anymore can truly be called natural, for nothing has escaped human influence. "This buzzing, blooming, mysterious, cruel, lovely globe of mountain, sea, city, forest; of fish and wolf and bug and man; of carbon and hydrogen and nitrogen—it has come unbalanced in our short moment on it. It's mostly us now" (2003, p. xx). This, to McKibben, is a cause for great sadness. Implicitly, the only way something can be "natural" is for it to have escaped human influence entirely, for it to be something not only non-human but also utterly alien to our species. This would cut out any domesticated animal, any animal affected by hunting and fishing, even animals like crows, pigeons, and rats, who live alongside humans and benefit from the way we are simplifying and urbanizing their environment. It would, in fact, leave almost no animals in nature at all. And since the taint of human presence would presumably include thinking about animals in symbolic and literary ways, filling their wild worlds with another reminder of us, it would render even the "purest" of environmental literature problematic. There is no place left for animals in a view like this, and no possibility for authenticity. If the only real nature left is nature untouched or unaffected by humans, we cannot even communicate about it without spoiling it, at least via the initial visit or research that would enable us to discuss it.

Luckily, McKibben's view is one end of a spectrum (and perhaps a necessary counterbalance to the relentless "disnification" of animals that makes their representation "generally denigrated as 'childish,' thereby associating a dispassionate, even alienated perspective with maturity. Disnification exacerbates this existing association ... to describe something as trivial or worthless" (Garrard, 2004, p. 142)). It is not a vital precondition for viewing all literary animals, even ones as potentially unrealistic as Rowling's owls. Within a certain fictional world, animals still possess a place, perhaps even agency, and may influence audiences for the better. Rowling's world, while relentlessly human-exceptionalist, may seem worse than ours partially because it is so small and contained, easy to view and survey. And owls occupy a substantially better position in it than other animals, making it obvious that different levels of humane treatment and human consideration *can* exist. This raises the possibility that other animals might join owls on their level.

What besides their features and cultural significance makes the owls different from other animals? In part, while they fulfill a useful function, that is not all they do. Post-owls regularly bring letters and packages to Hogwarts students and professors in the morning, but they may also visit, as Hedwig does with Harry, simply to see their human friends (*SS*, p. 134). They are beloved pets and companions, as Harry's stunned and horrified reaction to Hedwig's death makes clear (*DH*, p. 52), but not often confined to a cage or even a bedroom or common room as Scabbers and Crookshanks largely are. *Harry Potter* owls have the freedom to come and go, spending time in an Owlery at Hogwarts when not actually in the process of delivering the post, and flying easily through the air when fulfilling their function. While in practice they may be compared to carrier pigeons, owls are portrayed as considerably more intelligent than most humans think of pigeons as. Hedwig knows and understands Harry's emotions and empathizes with them (*CoS* p. 25); she even displays her own complex emotions when showing jealousy of Ron's owl Pigwidgeon (*GoF*, p. 37). Researchers working with domestic animals have shown that jealousy is suspected, although it cannot be conclusively proven in dogs, mainly because of the emotion's complexity; Bradshaw notes that "To feel jealous, an animal would have to be capable of recognizing others as individuals and to possess some concept of the quality of the relationships between those individuals" (2011, p. 214). Hedwig understands her own relationship with Harry and the fact that Pigwidgeon is, in her eyes, not a trustworthy letter carrier. Harry, while a pet owner instead of a scientist and so not as skeptical about Hedwig's emotions as Bradshaw would be, is generally a trustworthy narrator, with the things he is mistaken about, such as Severus Snape's true allegiance, being conclusively stated in the text. His relationship with Hedwig sets her free of scientific objectivity, which, while valuable in many studies of animals, is in other ways a trap. Haraway explains in her studies of primates that objectivity often does not exist, especially when speaking about or studying animals closely connected to humans (1989). And Harry does not relate to Hedwig as study subject or even pet; he relates to her as beloved friend and near-family.

Hedwig

Hedwig is Harry's first friend other than Hagrid; his initial description of her is of her physical beauty (*SS*, p. 80), but he quickly becomes involved in choosing a name for her and picks one that reflects his own life, as Saint Hedwig is the patron of orphans (*SS*, p. 88). Hedwig's first role in the series, in fact, outside of birthday gift, is that of companion to Harry as he waits in Privet Drive for his first year of school to begin; he does not have anyone in the wizarding world to write to at first, so she is not delivering his post. In fact, she regularly brings back her own dead prey to the room, but there is no sign in the narration that Harry minds, only that it's probably for the best that Aunt Petunia no longer enters his bedroom as the sight of dead mice would offend her sensibilities (*SS*, p. 88). Hedwig is, by implication, a messy eater, but that only aligns her more with the chaos and mess that will accompany Harry's first entrance into the wizarding world and his sudden knowledge that he is famous. And as a rebellion against the rigidity of order and normality that the Dursleys try to enforce on the world around them, both Harry and Hedwig have chosen a fine one. The catching and eating of mice proves that Hedwig is a wild creature still, free in a way that Harry finds it hard to be when he lives with his relatives and a reminder of the animal world that exists all around humans; "[t]he conspicuous presence" of free wild animals not afraid to associate with humans "can lend a great deal to our biological education" (Haupt, 2009). Harry gets an education in biological realities that the Dursleys try to tidy away and ignore, much like they do Harry himself.

Hedwig is, likewise, an outer sign of Harry's fitness to be a wizard; she is the cause of the strange looks that Muggles aim at Harry when he is wandering through King's Cross Station in a desperate attempt to find Platform 9¾ (*SS*, p. 90), and she enters Hogwarts' Great Hall along with all the other owls, whether or not she has a message for Harry, to spend some time with him in the mornings and eat breakfast from his plate (*SS*, p. 134). She is also the bearer of his messages to Hagrid, accepting Hagrid's invitation for tea, and to Charlie Weasley when Harry, Ron, and Hermione are attempting to solve the problem of Hagrid's dragon (*SS*, p. 236), tying Harry into a web of friendship and aid that encompasses members of his eventual adopted family, the Weasleys. Like Harry, she is a prisoner of the Dursleys in the summer between his first and second year (*CoS*, p. 3), a creature with the right to freedom who is forcibly padlocked into her cage. Harry shares half his food rations with her despite his own near-starvation (*CoS*, p. 22). She thus, alone of any of the other human or non-human beings in the series, shares Harry's home life and his suffering. While Rowling's depiction of the Dursleys' abuse is arguably not realistic nor meant to be—more a "Cinderella existence" (Blakeney, 1998) than a serious study of the consequences of child abuse—this shared bond of suffering is one of the reasons propelling the growing friendship between Harry and his owl.

From the beginning of *CoS*, Hedwig appears more regularly, and is more openly loyal and affectionate to Harry. She helps to fetch his birthday presents (*PoA*, p. 11) and flies to find him at the Leaky Cauldron after Harry has to run away from Privet Drive due to blowing up Aunt Marge (*PoA*, p. 40). She is not a simple pet or toy that Harry can do whatever he wants with, despite his stowing her in the luggage rack on the Hogwarts Express; when she brings him a letter from Hagrid and he accidentally ignores her, she nips him hard and then feeds herself from Neville's breakfast rather than Harry's (*PoA*, p. 201). Harry does not get angry with the nip; he simply thanks Hedwig for her part in delivering the letter. While it is not clear if Hedwig understands the thanks—her reaction to Harry's words is simply not recorded—it is clear that Harry expects her to. Much as we never get a clear account in the novels of how owls learn to deliver letters, if it is inherent magic or training or a combination, we never get a clear account of how intelligent wizards generally perceive them to be, but Harry at least treats Hedwig as though she can fully understand and appropriately incorporate his thanks. This is different from the "Good girl!" that Harry might give a dog who had obediently performed a commanded task. Harry engages with Hedwig on a level more like another human being.

And, although her reaction on the delivery of Hagrid's letter mentioned above is not in the narrative, another one is. When Hedwig returns with his long-awaited letter from Sirius in *GoF*, Harry is distressed by the notion of Sirius returning to Britain as a fugitive and refuses to provide food for Hedwig after her journey, telling her that she'll have to eat in the Owlery instead. Hedwig, insulted, makes sure to hit him with a wing as she takes flight (*GoF*, p. 200). Ron and Hermione, in the room with Harry at the time, give no indication that they find her reaction odd, although whether they believe that Hedwig alone among owls is intelligent is hard to determine. At the very least, however, they do not seem to consider Harry's treatment of Hedwig as coddling her too much, unlike their reactions to Hagrid's pets. An owl is placed even above dogs here, since Hagrid's Fang is portrayed as cowardly, slobbery, and untrained, not nearly as desirable a companion as Hedwig (*SS*, p. 139). Since the only other dog appearing in the series on a regular basis is an Animagus, and even before his revelation as a transformed human is believed to be a supernatural creature, the Grim (*PoA*, p. 83), there is no "boy's best friend" to challenge Hedwig for Harry's affections. Owls have entered, and at least half-created, a space of companionate relationship with humans that other animals in the series do not inhabit.

Even Hedwig's species may have something to do with this. Rowling is on record as admitting on Pottermore that she "made a few elementary mistakes when it came to [her] depiction of Hedwig" (n.d.), notably the fact that snowy owls in the wild do not make sounds. Yet snowy owls are devoted parents (Angell, 2015), and this may well play into the bond that Hedwig and Harry share. This bond does not always seem parental, but with Hedwig named after the patron saint of orphans and the sense of devastation that Harry feels at her death in the seventh book, it is clearly familial. As snowy owls must hunt often because they require abundant food (Angell, 2015), sharing the suffering imposed by Harry's family starving him would have been even harder for Hedwig than for most species of owls. Yet she maintains her bond to Harry until the end of the series. It is no coincidence that Harry's family or potential family is removed from his life one by one (the Dursleys by their distaste for him; his parents, Sirius, Dumbledore, and Hedwig by death), until at the end of the seventh book he finds solace in marrying Ginny Weasley and raising children of his own. Harry's growing losses isolate him and drive him into working harder to defeat Voldemort; that must of necessity include removing Hedwig, and points to her importance in his life.

Other Owls

Other owls in the series do not play as central a role as Hedwig, but they still have personalities of their own and are given characteristics beyond the delivery of post. One example is Errol, the Weasleys' ancient owl. Although he is somewhat mocked by Ron as an example of hand-me-down possessions, like Scabbers (*PoA*, p. 40), Errol is neither an unwanted pet foisted on Ron nor a traitorous Animagus in disguise, but an essential part of the family. That the Weasleys continue to use him when he is old and exhausted is more a sign of their poverty than of cruelty. And like Hedwig, Errol is an owl of a specific species whose characteristics match his wild counterparts, although decided on later than Hedwig was. Rowling discovered that the owl she had envisioned Errol as was the Great Gray Owl (n.d.), a species known for an ability to live to thirteen years even in the wild (Angell, 2015), and thus indeed capable of becoming as old as Errol appears.

Pigwidgeon, the owl gifted by Sirius to Ron, exasperates the Weasleys for other reasons. He is a Eurasian Scops owl (Erickson, 2005) who is hyperactive and sometimes refuses to deliver letters in a prompt manner. Ron also dislikes the fact that Ginny gives him his name and he refuses to answer to anything other than Pigwidgeon or Pig (*GoF*, p. 54). He annoys other owls, including Hedwig when he delivers the birthday letter Harry receives the summer after Sirius gives him to Ron (*GoF*, p. 37). However, this reveals that he has his own distinctive personality—stubborn and highstrung—and is not a simple mechanism for delivering the post. Pigwidgeon is a substitute for Errol, then, only insofar as he makes it possible for Ron to send letters and packages to Harry that Errol is probably unable to deliver anymore. Neither are the Weasley owls identical to Hedwig. Knowingly or not, Rowling used some of each species' noted traits, if mainly the size in the case of the Scops owl, and in doing so connected the humans of the wizarding world to the living world that is *not* magical.

This statement is worth emphasizing. Rowling's wizards seem, at first, to live a less instrumental and modern life, one more in touch with "nature." After all, they use little technology (the primary example in the books being the Hogwarts Express), and that not more recent than the nineteenth century. They live with more animals than modern humans tend to, including, in Hogwarts, the magical creatures of the Forbidden Forest, and, with werewolves, large predators that can kill a human. Fireplaces, house-elf servants, broomsticks, and cauldrons conjure up more "natural" images of warming oneself, doing chores, transportation, and cooking than doing these chores by machine. Since this world is not one that has had an Industrial Revolution, or at least has only adopted parts of the muggle one, it might seem that the humans in Rowling's books live a less instrumentalized life.

But this is not so. As previously mentioned, the Wizarding World is more heavily human-exceptionalist even than the muggle one. Part of this is likely because there is little critical thinking, reflection, or comparison being done between wizards and outside human groups; as Waldau says that anthropology can show the meta-narratives of cultures by comparing familiar cultures with different ones (2013). The lack of such comparisons cuts short one avenue of critical thinking by which wizards could compare their attitudes toward animals with muggle ones. Part of this lack is because most wizards seem to accept the position of other species in their world, no doubt because it is convenient for them. Hermione's efforts to establish S.P.E.W and free house-elves are fruitless, with Ron complaining that since house-elves like their servitude, her desires to help them are actually contrary to what the elves themselves want (*GoF*, p. 198). Even Hermione gives in in the end and eats the food made by house-elves, and when she is in full "elf-freeing" mode, her strategy is to stealthily leave clothes around in the hope that the elves will pick them up and be accidentally freed, rather than actually *speaking* to the elves and attempting to understand their needs and desires (*OotP*, p. 230).

Hermione, although much more progressive than other wizards in many ways, still comes from the human-dominated, mostly human-exceptionalist, muggle world. This leads her to care about the plight of other creatures, but also to assume she knows best, and to discount the chance to receive input from those she wishes to help. In this, she resembles other wizards who do not believe input from muggle-borns even when they receive it, and accuse them, for example, of stealing wands and magic from purebloods after Voldemort takes over the Ministry (*DH*, p. 214). This is an outrage fervently opposed by Harry and other protagonists of the story, but very few people want to join Hermione in her quest to free the house-elves. This is the darker side of human exceptionalism: even when a chance comes up to listen to other creatures, few will take it. Those who are involved in animal studies must continuously check themselves and consider their own responses critically, both when dealing with non-human animal cultures and with marginalized human ones and their views of animals.

With this fact in view, it is all the more remarkable that owls are *not* treated like naughty pets and confined to cages, or like house-elves and confined to homes, or like centaurs and confined to certain preserves such as the Forbidden Forest. They are allowed to fly free, and in fact treated almost like independent agents; they can find a person whose name is on a letter across immense distances and without training that we know of. They eat at table, punish their human companions for infractions against the owl's independence and good nature, and exercise the ultimate freedom, flight, "the greatest of all birds' blessings" (Montgomery, 2009, p. 98). Windrow says that living with an owl entails sacrifices, including having to put paper in many different places in case his owl, Mumble, chose to defecate there (2013, p. 205). But if this sacrifice exists in the *Harry Potter* world (perhaps one should shudder to imagine what the outside of the Hogwarts Owlery looks like, unless house-elves clean there as well), the wizards seem more than content to put up with it. The only owl we ever see in a cage for more than a short journey is Hedwig, and that is mostly through the Dursleys' insistence on keeping her imprisoned in case someone thinks it abnormal to have a pet owl. The cage is also the scene of Hedwig's death, as Harry clutches it behind him while fleeing on Hagrid's motorbike from the Death Eaters (*DH*, p. 52). Without free flight and her wings to protect her, Hedwig loses the power to defend herself. Humans cannot adequately defend owls, the way they can "protect" the house-elves and other kinds of magical creatures under their "care." The cage, a symbol of their domination, proves as much a weight on Hedwig's survival as a shackle on a prisoner. Erickson notes that owls are not fully natural animals when in cages, since "owls are wild, natural birds requiring a wild, natural life. In cages they simply cannot do all the things their bodies were designed for and their spirits require" (2005).

This, of course, leads to the question that inspired this article: can other animals, and magical creatures that may be more human-shaped, actually find their way into the owl's challenging, freer space without having the advantages of the connection that the wizards obviously feel with their owls?

Hope for the Future

The answer, at least if one looks at the surface narrative of Rowling's books, is "no." Despite Dobby's freedom, most of the other house-elves continue to object when freed from their servitude, and Kreacher reforms but remains a servant (*DH*, p. 165). There is no sign in the epilogue of *Deathly Hallows*, mostly focused on the children of the Potter and Weasley families and their journey to Hogwarts, that things have changed permanently; we do not know whether there is still a centaur Divination professor, let alone whether the current students at Hogwarts feel more respect for Hagrid, or whether any werewolf can teach there, or whether prejudices against serpents as a symbol of Slytherin House have lessened. We can feel reasonably certain that Hermione would not employ an unpaid house-elf without knowing if she has made any headway in persuading *other* wizards that they should not own one. But there are owls present with the children as they move toward the train (*DH*, p. 603).

However, the existence of owls in the narrative does offer more hope than if *all* animals in the story were caged—either literally or by the expectations of the wizards who own them, live with them, and work with them. Rowling's wizarding world is decidedly not more progressive than the human-dominated world we live in, rather regressive in contrast, but it has this grace: Freedom is *possible*. Currently, the work of animal studies, long, tiring work that has to challenge countless basic Western cultural assumptions, is confronting more and more demands from our own lives that even beloved animals not be an inconvenience. Bradshaw's study of cats makes him worry whether cats, who in the early twenty-first century became more popular as pets in the UK and the U.S. than dogs (Rogers, 2006), can actually survive as human pets without major genetic changes, considering demands that cats be quiet, restrained, perfect for apartment living, more social with other cats and humans than their usual temperament permits, and otherwise almost objects in animal form (Bradshaw, 2013, p. 282). Large concentrations of unpopular birds such as crows, although created by humans' own activities (especially with regard to garbage), have prompted almost hysterical fears of disease and rages to kill them in towns like Auburn, NY (Montgomery, 2009, p. 226). Many owners of parrots and other captive birds keep them in cages without ever releasing them to fly or even allowing them into larger cages or aviaries for exercise (Low, 2006). That we want animals around but also want to not put up with the inherent inconveniences that come from owning living, breathing beings restricts their freedom and our own.

In this context, then, the freedom allowed Rowling's owls is remarkable. True, the narrative does not dwell on the likely results of being around many non-housebroken birds, but neither does Rowling tend to prioritize telling the reader about the bathroom habits of her human characters. But they are allowed to come and go as they please; to exercise their wings, their natural means of locomotion, rather than being automatically put in a cage as most pet birds are; and to express their emotions, opinions, and attitudes without being punished in the way of a misbehaving dog. True, it may be hard to envision how to discipline a misbehaving owl. Falconers with over forty years of experience in dealing with raptors believe that birds *cannot* be bullied or disciplined in any useful way; instead, the "education of a falconer is a chastening process during which you learn to be polite to an animal" (Bodio, 2015, p. 5). But that would not necessarily keep humans from trying to bully an owl. That the wizards in Rowling's books—even Harry, who has not grown up around them—adopt the polite attitude toward owls so easily speaks of at least one chink in their armor of human exceptionalism, one space where they can let animals through and exist freely with them free.

Whether it would work for certain with other animals, or beings, is an open question. However, there is at least one other animal in the series who seems to have a similar amount of freedom: Fawkes, Dumbledore's phoenix. He is not often portrayed as soaring freely through the castle, but he does fly into the Chamber of Secrets to rescue Harry and Ginny from the basilisk (*CoS*, p. 313), and he resides on a perch in Dumbledore's office rather than in a cage (*CoS*, p. 206). He also disappears after Dumbledore dies, with only his voice lingering to sing a phoenix song at the funeral (*HBP*, p. 573), and this seems to be the expected course of things. No one speaks of trying to capture or "recapture" Fawkes, or try and force him to return and accept another owner or companion. While Fawkes is not mentioned as delivering post or being a predator like the owls are, he does share the obvious and similar traits of being a bird, of being able to fly, and of having a close relationship to the human he is most associated with. Since there are no other phoenixes mentioned so prominently in the series, it is hard to say if others would be treated like him, better, or worse. But he is, in this case, a definitively magical creature who has escaped the prejudice that most of the wizarding world seems to suffer when it comes to other magical creatures like centaurs, werewolves, and house-elves.

In the end, it may be the symbolic value of birds that separates them from so many other non-human animals in Rowling's stories and guarantees them better treatment. That birds can fly is an obvious fact; that many people feel there is something wrong with caging a bird may be a less obvious fact, given that many owners of pet parrots and the like do exactly that. However, that attitude is alive and well among Rowling's wizards, who, like the Weasleys, seem to either not use cages for their owls on a regular basis or, like Harry, regard the cage as a sad necessity and a prison, to be used more because of the demands of uncomprehending Muggles than because an owl "belongs" there. Rowling's owls have their freedom to come and go, their feeding habits either indulged or ignored by the narrative, their companionship to humans and even their right to protest ignoble or ignorant human treatment fully supported. If elves, snakes, or cats were such a symbol of freedom, of the desires that so many humans nourish to take to the sky themselves, then perhaps they would also be treated better.

Conclusion

Rowling's owls do not, in the end, offer either unlimited freedom for any non-humans in Rowling's worlds or unlimited promise that things will get better for them. But they do show that, even in a world where the seat of wizarding Britain's government displays a fountain in its Atrium blatantly showing magical humans' domination over several other kinds of magical creature (*OotP*, p. 117), there are a few places where wizards and audience alike can breathe the freer air of a more-than-human world (Abram, 1997). Their literal, literary bodies carry, then, this symbolic value most strongly: the places humans have, unwittingly, left open and unconquered, places that a next generation of Hermiones in the books, and critically-thinking, open-minded muggles in our world, may step into and grant greater freedom still to those beings that inevitably share our world with us.

REFERENCES

Abram, D. (1997). *The Spell of the Sensuous: Perception and Language in a More-Than-Human World*. New York, NY: Vintage Books.
Angell, T. (2015). *The House of Owls*. New Haven, CT: Yale University Press.
Berger, J. (1992). "Why Look at Animals?" In *About Looking* (pp. 3–28). New York, NY: Vintage Books.
Blakeney, S. (1998, November 7). "The Golden Fairytale." *The Australian*. Retrieved from http://www.accio-quote.org/articles/1998/1198-australian-blakeney.html.
Bodio, S. (2015). *A Rage for Falcons: An Alliance Between Man and Bird*. New York: Skyhorse Publishing.
Bradshaw, J. (2013). *Cat Sense: How the New Feline Science Can Make You a Better Friend to Your Pet*. New York: Basic Books.
Bradshaw, J. (2011). *Dog Sense: How the New Science of Dog Behavior Can Make You a Better Friend to Your Pet*. New York: Basic Books.
Calvez, L. (2016). *The Hidden Lives of Owls: The Science and Spirit of Nature's Most Elusive Birds*. Seattle: Sasquatch Books.
Erickson, L. (2005). "The Owls of *Harry Potter*." Retrieved from http://www.lauraerickson.com/page/owls-of-harry-potter/.

Garrard, G. (2004). *Ecocriticism*. Abingdon-on-Thames: Routledge.
Haraway, D. (1989). *Primate Visions: Gender, Race, and Nature in the World of Modern Science*. Abingdon-on-Thames: Routledge.
Haupt, L.L. (2009). *Crow Planet: Essential Wisdom from the Urban Wilderness*. New York: Little, Brown.
Low, R. (2006). "Making Life Better." Retrieved from https://www.parrots.org/reference-library/making-life-better.
McKibben, B. (2003). *The End of Nature: Humanity, Climate Change, and the Natural World*. London: Bloomsbury.
Montgomery, S. (2009). *Birdology: Adventures with Hip Hop Parrots, Cantankerous Cassowaries, Crabby Crows, Peripatetic Pigeons, Hens, Hawks, and Hummingbirds*. New York: Free Press.
Rogers, K. (2006). *Cat*. London: Reaktion Books, Ltd.
Rowling, J.K. (2012). *Harry Potter and the Chamber of Secrets*. London: Pottermore, Limited.
Rowling, J.K. (2007). *Harry Potter and the Deathly Hallows*. London: Bloomsbury.
Rowling, J.K. (2000). *Harry Potter and the Goblet of Fire*. London: Bloomsbury.
Rowling, J.K. (2005). *Harry Potter and the Half-Blood Prince*. London: Bloomsbury.
Rowling, J.K. (2003). *Harry Potter and the Order of the Phoenix*. London: Bloomsbury.
Rowling, J.K. (2012). *Harry Potter and the Prisoner of Azkaban*. London: Pottermore, Limited.
Rowling, J.K. (2012). *Harry Potter and the Sorcerer's Stone*. London: Pottermore, Limited.
Rowling, J.K. (n.d.) "Owls." Retrieved from https://www.pottermore.com/writing-by-jk-rowling/owls/.
Tolkien, J.R.R. (1966). "On Fairy-Stories." In *The Tolkien reader* (pp. 33–90). New York: Ballantine Books.
Waldau, P. (2013). *Animal Studies: An Introduction*. Oxford: Oxford University Press.
Windrow, M. (2013). *The Owl Who Liked Sitting on Caesar: Living with a Tawny Owl*. New York: Farrar, Straus, and Giroux.

Dangerous Depictions of Adoption in Rowling's Wizarding World Narratives

TARA MOORE

This message was disseminated to participants in the role playing site *Hogwarts Online*: "It has come to the attention of the site administrators that there have been an unusually high number of adoptions taking place … it appears that people are engaging in adoptions a little haphazardly without thinking about the details" (Callaghan, 2016). Role players engaged in virtual adoptions give little thought to the actual adoption communities that exist around the globe, but they might be forgiven for appropriating the adoption plot. Their queen, J.K. Rowling, has based nearly all of her narratives on histrionic adoption storylines. In case *Hogwarts Online* players are too tempted by the narrative power of the adoption plot, the site administrators offer this advice: "Very few school-aged students would have two dead parents and no relatives to live with. […] It would make little sense for someone who just graduated from school to adopt someone, either" (Callaghan, 2016). One can begin to imagine the creative family structures conceived by *HO* students. The role players have been trained by Rowling's narratives to see adoption as a conduit to drama.

For a franchise that has such an impact on young readers, the *Harry Potter* narratives do a terrible job at representing the adopted child. Progressive trends have been supportive of the adoptive family construction for nearly three decades. Even simple good manners should lead to a warm acceptance of the adoptive bond. However, by looking at the novels, the recent scripts, and *Pottermore* stories, it becomes clear that Rowling's world repeatedly belittles the authenticity of the adoptive family. The ever-expanding narrative has been carried away by the icon of the magical orphan, and the representation of adoption has been a casualty.

In my initial readings as a young graduate student, I did not ponder the use of the trope too heavily other than to acknowledge its reliance on the Victorian orphan story. Now, as my children begin to make forays into the world of *Harry Potter*, I read the novels with a new eye. I am a parent of three daughters, two biological and one who was adopted, and I wonder how my children will posit themselves within the franchise's ever widening narrative. As an adoptive mother and fan, I find myself grouped with characters like Petunia Dursley and Mary Lou Barebone; some ugly literary representations of the adoptive mother. I hold out hope that children affected by adoption will see a glimmer of joyful family life in the hints of adoptive mothers like barky but loyal Augusta Longbottom and the barely-narrated Andromeda Tonks. I wonder about the effects of depicting adoption as a titillating horror, and how the evils of fictive adoption will resonate with my daughters and the millions of children like them who immerse themselves in the series.

Adoption in the Harry Potter Novels

The literary traditions present in Rowling's fictive adoptions may cause many readers to brush aside protests about how the novels portray adoption. Perhaps it is easier to see Harry as an orphan on a quest than as an adopted child residing in a hostile adoptive family. The plucky orphan narrative so common in folklore informs Rowling's fiction. As an orphan with magic, he serves as an icon of power, a fantasy for children who might prefer to daydream about the freedom of life without adults and their rules. It is worth noting that, in many cases, the characters billed as orphans are actually part of adoptive families. Harry's birth parents are dead, but his participation in a kinship adoption, or kinship care, as it is referred to in Great Britain and Canada, means that he is no longer an orphan. In fact, of all of the so-called orphans in Rowling's stories, only one does not speedily transition into an adoptive family.

Despite the challenges I will explore in greater detail, Harry's narrative has been used to help adopted children. Hunt (2006), a play therapist, has written about a case study in which an eight year old had been adopted by her grandmother following the death of her mother and the earlier abandonment of her father. This child carried around a *Harry Potter* book and clearly used Rowling's orphan narrative to play through her own real-life situation, a practice seen as a healthy development in the girl's bereavement (Hunt, 2006). Hunt's case study shows that adopted children can be highly aware of the nuances of an adopted protagonist's status; these readers are certainly more attuned than authors and mainstream culture to what it means to create a character who was adopted. An American family business named Transfiguring Adoptions produces discussion points chapter by chapter through the first two *Harry Potter* books. The goal is to use the books to open discussion about being part of an adoptive family. According to the web site, "Most foster parents are NOT prepared to handle specialized behaviors brought on by trauma, sexual abuse, PTSD, malnutrition and other issues that are present in nearly all foster or adoptive children" ("Transfiguring," n.d.). The extreme stereotypes of the novels give children and parents an engaging way to examine their own adoption networks.

The Shortfalls of Harry's Adoption

The Dursley family could certainly have used some counseling and open conversation about their family dynamics. If they had, they would doubtless have learned about the challenges of establishing attachment with an infant put into their care. According to Gray (2012), attachment is the exclusive parent-child relationship that forms as a result of thousands of positive interactions that make a child feel secure in their parents' care. Attachment differs from bonding, and it allows children to feel good about themselves and consider the feelings of others. A child who has attached in infancy is much more likely to adapt to new settings and new caretakers because they know they can trust loving adults. Children who do not have the opportunity to attach will feel the need to look after their own interests and will fail to see their parents as a source of security and comfort.

These considerations are rarely depicted in narratives that suggest lack of attachment. For example, Shasta in C.S. Lewis's *A Horse and His Boy* has been raised by an abusive fisherman that Shasta claims he has never loved. Since the fisherman is willing to sell Shasta as a slave, it is likely that the man has mostly viewed the boy as equity rather than as a son. Without a trusting, loving parental relationship, it is unlikely that a real child in Shasta's situation could speedily adapt, as Shasta does, to being honorable, honest, caring, and willing to accept care. When children are adopted, parents are counseled to nurture the attachment process, hoping the child can smoothly attach to their new caregivers. An unattached child cannot trust their parents, they may horde food, and they may show violent and self-destructive behaviors. This same consideration affects the fictional portrayal of Harry Potter's childhood. Lily and James's careful parenting during Harry's first year certainly would have resulted in attachment, stabilizing Harry's early development. However, it is possible for a child to lose the ability to attach if they suffer neglect or are shifted to new caregivers (Gray, 2012). The new parents can neutralize a child's previous ability to attach if they are neglectful or chilly in their reception of the child (Gray, 2012).

Petunia and Vernon somehow maintained a toddler Harry, but we do not see the results of attachment or any healthy parenting for the child we should be thinking of as their younger son. Instead there is nothing healthy about Harry's adoptive family: they neglect him, berate him, and force him to endure the equivalent of solitary confinement. When we meet the nearly eleven year old Harry in *SS*, he lives in a house where the parents avoid using his name ("I'm warning you now, boy"), refuse to add his photographs to those of their other son, express distrust of him ("That car's new, he's not sitting in it alone"), and speak openly about their disdain for him (Rowling, 1997, p. 24, 22). In *DH* we learn, in case we were not sure, that Harry parts from the Dursleys "at the end of sixteen years' solid dislike" (Rowling, 2007 p. 36).

In *OotP*, Vernon adds extra vitriol to his typical opening-of-the-novel-tirade: "Why we ever kept you in the first place I don't know, Marge was right, it should have been the orphanage, we were too damn soft for our own good" (Rowling, 2003 p. 39). Such words thrown at an adopted fifteen year old would have intense psychological consequences, especially because nothing is ever said or done to apologize for what is in effect a lifelong attitude. In this series, the thrill of the evil adoptive parent has replaced the role of the folk tale's evil stepmother. The fact that many readers do not question Harry's relative normalcy despite the Dursleys' parenting attests to mainstream culture's lack of information about real children and real adoption. While we might enjoy the extremes of behavior, we should also question how Harry could have developed his social and ethical skills given his past. If Harry were a real child, he might respond to his lack of attachment with survival behaviors of manipulation and violence (Taft, Ramsay, & Schlein, 2015) rather than developing the honorable goal of saving all of magical Britain.

Readers do not see any evidence that social workers are involved in Harry's adoption. Instead, magic is at work in the transfer of guardianship. Dumbledore simply decrees that Harry will go to the Dursleys to maximize Lily Potter's sacrificial protection, even though Harry would have been guaranteed a happier childhood in a wizarding home. The kinship adoption is not presented as a more ethical choice; it is a matter of magic. The bond of blood charm requires that Petunia choose to accept Harry as her own: "She may have taken you grudgingly, furiously, unwillingly, bitterly, yet still she took you, and in doing so, she sealed the charm I placed upon you" (Rowling, 2003, p. 836). Given Lily's awareness of her sister's prejudice, it seems unlikely that she would have placed her infant son with Petunia, especially since we know that she and James chose a wizard, Sirius Black, to be his godparent. As a presumed criminal Sirius cannot fulfill his duties, and for some reason it falls to Dumbledore to find a replacement. Dumbledore's plan circumvents any parental authority and takes effect as the result of his all-powerful decree.

Sirius Black's brief period of being an authority in Harry's life, though binding in the magical world—at least as far as Dumbledore and the Hogsmeade permission slip is concerned—does not result in the type of long-term family relationship that a child requires. Harry looks to Sirius for bits of advice and information about his birth family, and he does acknowledge Sirius's authority in his life. These are positive signs of family development. But Sirius does not and cannot fully embrace the role of father. As a wanted man, Sirius cannot make a home with Harry, and in their brief time together, Sirius chooses to be a companion and mentor than a disciplinarian and nurturer. And then the adult male guardian figures keep dying, forcing Harry to mature quickly since, according to Curtis (2016), "Harry ultimately comes to take on the roles of the deceased following their respective deaths" (p. 99).

Cult of the Birth Parent

Currently, language used by adoption professionals like social workers and psychologists encourages the use of the term "birth parent" or "biological parent" and "adoption plan." In general, there is a call for respectful appreciation of the birth parents and the role they will continue to play in the child's life, even if the child has been parted from them through death or the pain of a closed adoption. The idea of the adoption triad is used by adoption professionals to honor the child and legitimize both families that contribute to the child's identity.

Novy (2005) has written about how mainstream culture and even people involved with adoption can be influenced by adoption plots conveyed in literature, film, and other media (p. 1). Novy identifies three mythic stories used to imagine adoption, all of which explore beliefs about the family: "the disastrous adoption [...] the happy reunion [with the birth family, and] the happy adoption" (p. 7). From this list, it seems clear that most of Rowling's works delve deeply into the disastrous adoption motif, with the slight twist in that she also frequently returns to the poignant depiction of the heart-rending reunion—the brief reunion of Harry and his dead parents who love him but cannot return to life to nurture him.

Through Rowling's plot devices, Harry succumbs to a cult of the biological parent. Adopted children should certainly be free to connect with their birth family, or, if that is not possible, to learn about their biological origins. Adoption literature teaches parents to support their child through this development. However, in the *Harry Potter* novels, realigning with the birth family in itself becomes a quest, and Harry's connection to his dead parents is presented as more powerfully nurturing than his current relationship with his live family. Knowing the Dursleys' dursleyness, this seems logical, but its wider implications undercut the viability of the adoptive family and holds up the biological family as the truer entity.

Like many real adopted children before him, Harry discovers that his knowledge about his birth parents is being controlled by adults who wish to manipulate his sense of identity. Openness about a child's adopted status has been the recommended approach since the 1960s (Sales, 2015), but I recall chatting with a student who told me that she had been startled to learn she was adopted when she was ten years old. Harry knows that he does not live with his birth parents, but the Dursleys take care to reshape the information they convey about the Potters, including their magical abilities and the mode of their deaths. Baden (2016) classifies this as a microfiction, a type of identity manipulation that many real-life adoptees have had to endure:

> histories can be altered purposefully, or even accidentally, resulting in adoption stories and pasts that veil or withhold information from adoptees. These adoption stories can also include inaccurate information that was shared to create a fictional story for the adoption stakeholders. For example, generations of adult adoptees (both domestic and international) report being told their birth parents died in car accidents (Free, 2001–2002), thus classifying them as 'true orphans' as opposed to 'created orphans,' and making them more adoptable or desirable.

The Dursleys lie about the Potters' deaths because they want to recast Harry as a muggle child, one that can claim minimal, begrudged space in their home.

Once he gains access to Hogwarts, Harry begins to also gain access to the truth about his birth parents' lives, including their deaths. This engagement easily equates to a real child's natural interest in their family of origin. Although he has been adopted by his extended family, his proximity to his aunt and uncle fails to offer Harry the access to his birth parents that kinship adoptions tend to engender. Instead of introducing Harry to their memories of Lily and James Potter, the Dursleys malign them and fail to make their memory a part of their parenting.

Harry relies on the magical world for an introduction to his birth parents, but this introduction is delayed for ten years (from age one to eleven), even though Harry could have benefited from the information throughout his childhood. While his adult mentors casually drop details about his parents and give him keepsakes (like his Invisibility Cloak), these adults generally fail to support Harry's healthy interest in his biological family.

Hagrid's collection of magical photographs in a full album is one of the most thoughtful acts of any adult mentor. Hagrid, who has also been separated from his mother's culture (the giants), may recognize Harry's desire to know his birth parents in a deeper way, beyond a single glimpse, but in a way over which he can control his access, through possession of a photo album. Despite Harry's other connections, it never seems as though the adults give

Harry enough. They offer brief memories, but never exhaustive ones. This lack of information from the adult mentors is simply another example of adults thoughtlessly controlling Harry's access to relevant details he needs to thrive.

Because Harry is given no emotionally healthy and stable adoptive relationships, he embarks on a quest after his deceased birth parents. In a magical blend of wish fulfillment, Harry even has the opportunity to observe his deceased birth parents at several points in the series. In *SS*, he sees his birth parents in the Mirror of Erised, which shows him what he most desires. In keeping with his spying habits, Harry also invades Severus Snape's memories in the Pensieve and prolongs his meddling there to shadow a day in the life of his birth parents. The only reason he feels this deep need is because the adults in his life, adults who knew the Potters, do not make time to share their memories with Harry.

So far, these encounters with the Potters' legacy could easily be seen as a natural, healthy interest in one's birth family. The series takes the relationship with the birth family further, however, giving them the power to continue to nurture and protect Harry, enacting roles that his living family fails to play in his life. In *GoF,* the young wizard actually carries out a conversation with his dead father via the reversal spell cast on Voldemort's wand: "it will be all right … hold on…" (Rowling, 2000, p. 667). Lily speaks to Harry, too, offering him advice and even actual assistance by distracting Voldemort while Harry makes his escape. In the final book, Harry is able to raise his parents again, along with Sirius Black and Remus Lupin, to walk with him through a horde of dementors and toward his self-sacrifice in the Forbidden Forest. Once again his dead parents express support and love for Harry, either through their characterized actions—Lily looks at Harry "hungrily"—or through their thoughtful, nurturing language, saying just the type of thing a child might fantasize his parents would say (2007, p. 699).

As far as the plot is concerned, having parents that nurture him beyond the grave should tender Harry some satisfaction. He now has concrete knowledge of what his relationship with his birth parents might have been like had they lived. The problem is, the relationship is idyllic. Their appearance is simultaneously heart-warming and heart wrenching. However, it also presents their love as the truer sort of love, one that Harry has been unable to find elsewhere in his young life. Harry has no need to deepen his relationship with the Dursleys because his dead birth parents offer him the nurture of a family. Nguyen (2011) has argued that this fascination with the dead Potters makes the series anti-therapeutic because the tale focuses on "holding on to lost objects" rather than healing (p. 4). Lily and James represent a parental ideal because they are frozen in that essential moment of superlative, eternal parting. They clutter the field, leaving only room for the "friendship family" that grows around Harry in the form of Ron, Hermione, the Weasleys, and the imperfect male guardians who pass through Harry's life. Moreover, the "friendship family" replicates the relationships that Harry sees his father sharing with his friends, so clinging to Ron and Hermione is another way to cling to James. While his friendship families are sometimes beautiful, they are never fully parental.

Other tales of adoption haunt the edges of Harry's story. We learn that Neville Longbottom is being raised by his paternal grandmother. The infant Teddy Lupin is orphaned during the Battle of Hogwarts and is raised by his grandmother Andromeda Tonks, with a healthy connection to his parents' friends, who also serve as an extended family. Both of these women raise their grandsons from infancy; so, while they are biological grandmothers, they are the legal and de facto mothers to the boys. From the short glimpses we see of Augusta Longbottom, we know she has high expectations for her child, but she is also extremely supportive of him. In contrast, fourteen year old Ariana Dumbledore briefly participates in a kinship care relationship with her older brother Albus after she accidentally kills their mother. Ariana has special needs and difficult behaviors that defy her carers' abilities, and she only remains with Albus Dumbledore for a few weeks before she is killed.

Of these orphaned children in the tale, all quickly move into kinship adoptions except for the large exception: Tom Riddle, Jr. His orphan tale has been likened to that of Oliver Twist, even to the point that "both characterizations depend upon the innate goodness or wickedness of the character" (Warshick, 2009). Unlike the other children, Riddle spends his childhood in an orphanage, and his behaviors of cruelty and manipulation do in part represent a possible outcome of institutionalization.

The Birthland Tour in Cursed Child

It is especially heartless that Harry's biological aunt Petunia seems uninterested in sharing any details about her sister's life, and the family does not appear to travel to visit any of the places related to the Potters' lives. In adoption language, children adopted internationally may make a pilgrimage to their country of birth, a trip called a birthland tour. The tours are especially a rite of passage for children from South Korea and China, but they are also possible for any location so that the child can come to better understand the culture of their biological family. The intense feeling that Harry has when he enters Godric's Hollow replicates the event of a birthland tour for him, except he has to squeeze in an appreciation of the town while pursuing his main goal of collecting information about horcruxes and how to destroy them. His emotional attachment to his first home is strong. He is excited, his heart beats "in his throat" as he takes his first glimpse after apparating there, all because he was "return[ing] to the place where he had had a family" (2007, p. 321). The fact that this is his first visit seems almost incredible. None of his caring mentors have thought to apparate with Harry to show him this valuable piece in his story, not even Dumbledore who also hails from Godric's Hollow and has close family buried in the town cemetery.

It is telling, then, that the "eighth story," *Harry Potter and the Cursed Child*, includes a dream sequence in which Petunia Dursley has taken Harry to Godric's Hollow to see his parents' graves. Not only does dream-Petunia belittle the act of connecting with the Potters' graves, she also lies about Lily's past: "Lily tried—bless her—she tried—it wasn't her fault, but she repelled people—by her very nature. [...] And your father—obnoxious man—extraordinarily obnoxious. No friends. Neither of them" (Thorne, 2016, p. 205–6). The adult Harry, who is well aware of his parents' social circle, is dreaming this, so he knows the facts of his parents' personalities from more reliable sources. However, the adult is still affected by the child's wish to make a pilgrimage to the place where his biological parents lived; his subconscious knows that Petunia, had she been convinced to take such a step, would hardly have used it to build her relationship with her adopted son: "Go on then, lay down your grotty little flowers and then let's go. I already hate this poxy little village" (Thorne, 2016, p. 205). Once again, the adoptive family is depicted as a caricature.

The script does allow Petunia one redeeming moment. Readers learn that Dudley has kindly passed on Harry's baby blanket because Petunia had kept it up until her death. According to Harry, "I think—believe—Petunia wanted me to have it, that's why she kept it" (Thorne, 2016 p. 40). The language shows that Harry is choosing to be gracious in his estimation of Petunia's motives. He may not technically think that she kept it for him, but he chooses to believe and pass on the narrative that she did. She certainly could have shared the blanket with him as a child, when he most needed access to his biological family, but instead the blanket becomes a plot point in *Cursed Child*, as Albus learns to understand his father's fears and vulnerability enough to know that on the anniversary of his parents' death Harry will examine the blanket and find the message Albus leaves there while he is trapped in Harry's past.

In the climax of *Cursed Child* the ensemble cast all accompanies Harry on an intense birthland tour only possible in the realm of fiction. They all meet in 1981 Godric's Hollow and observe Harry and his parents on the last day of their life together. After defeating the threat to his 2020 present, Harry chooses to stay a few moments more to watch his parents' deaths. This is a particularly touching scene, one simply dripping with schadenfreude. Ron and Hermione attest that they will stay too ("We'll all watch") to support

Harry through his harrowing time, and the stage direction suggests that the audience too stands there with them, to observe the deaths, but, moreover, to observe Harry processing the deaths (Thorne, 2016, p. 295). As Harry collapses at the sight, the stage directions highlight the audience's voyeurism of this intense emotional climax: "*And we just watch*" (Thorne, 2016, p. 297).

The script introduces one deeply buried adoption tale: that of Delphi, another child of two dead parents (Voldemort and Bellatrix LeStrange) who desperately desires to reconnect with her birth father. We do not hear much about how Delphi has been raised other than that it is in isolation by Euphemia Rowle who has been paid to house Delphi, but who does not like her. It is unclear if this paid arrangement is an actual adoption or a type of Death-Eater foster situation. When we meet her, Delphi is already an adult, but the lack of love during her childhood—in another case of a hateful adoptive/foster family—has driven her into a cult of the birth parent with a far more sinister twist. Since she has not derived her identity from her foster/adoptive mother Euphemia, she will seek out her birth father through time and build an identity through him. She does so by learning to fly like Voldemort and by designing an evil scheme that is perfectly in keeping with what he had planned for magical Great Britain. Once again the wizarding franchise relies upon a hostile adoption to forge a character who instigates and motivates the plot.

Blighted Adoption in Fantastic Beasts

The wizarding world's brand of adoptive relationships take on a gothic element in *Fantastic Beasts and Where to Find Them*. While the script's main narrative is that of Newt Scamander and his introduction to New York and a community of friends, a secondary narrative belongs to Credence Barebone. Credence was adopted and now helps his mother in her cause to unmask a secret world of witches, but he also yearns to rejoin the wizarding world that he knew as a young child. Because of his mother's fanaticism, Credence learned to suppress his hidden magical abilities to the point that he became an Obscurial, a child who creates an uncontrollable, self-destructive dark force called an Obscurus.

The original screenplay first introduces the New Salem Philanthropic Society by focusing on Mary Lou Barebone's speech against the danger of witches in New York. This scene also introduces "Mary Lou's three adopted children, adults Credence and Chastity, and Modesty (an eight-year-old girl)" (Rowling 2016a, pp. 13–14). Here the children's adoptive status is made to stand out and define them as less than full children. In effect, the stage cues accurately capture the relationship between Mary Lou and her children. It does not appear that the family is built on love; instead, it seems to have been assembled to serve as a machine for Mary Lou's cause.

Abuse also fractures the Barebone family. When Credence comes home late, he knows without being told that he must hand his belt to Mary Lou so that she can beat him with it. In fact, the narrative includes three scenes where Mary Lou either belts or attempts to belt Credence. In the third scene, Credence pleads with her, and she responds with an attack on the legitimacy of their family: "I am not your ma! Your mother was a wicked, unnatural woman!" (Rowling, 2016a, p. 204). Graves later reveals that he can tell that Credence has magical ancestry but Graves believes that he is a Squib. It appears that Mary Lou has adopted Credence in an attempt to redeem him from the magical world. Her form of mothering flies in the face of adoption wisdom. She does not embrace her child's biological family and culture, nor does she affirm her affection or her place as her child's mother. In effect, this form of parenting posits adoption as an adult weapon used to further adult aims at the expense of the child.

Mary Lou creates a space that collects children, either her adopted children or the street children who do her bidding in exchange for food. The film shows the Barebones living in a spare building, the Second Salem Church, complete with an embroidered banner, loft, and gothic door. While there are no crosses, these other visual details rework the space as a metaphor for a Christian church. Children and adults move slowly in this space, physically expressing their constant fear of Mary Lou. Although Mary Lou lives in and works out of the Second Salem Church, there is nothing overtly Christian about the Society she runs. It is worth noting that Mary Lou's character is a mishmash of Christian action and imagery. She is dressed like a contemporary Puritan, she hands out tracts, and she feeds street children. Instead of Christian evangelism, however, Mary Lou is interested in spreading her anti-witch gospel. She epitomizes judgment and severity, traits made most clear by the physical abuse she directs toward her son. The depiction of Mary Lou's not-quite-Christianity paired with her harsh parenting can be read as Rowling's revenge on the Christian voices who have spoken out against the *Harry Potter* series since its inception.

Because of this visual aesthetic and the more sinister cruelty of his story, Credence's tale is a gothic version of Harry Potter's story. Credence repressed his magical abilities or was otherwise overlooked, so he was ignored by the American wizarding school Ilvermorny and his witch birth mother's magical society. Audiences can wonder what would have happened to Harry if he had never gotten his letter from Hogwarts but instead listened to the Dursleys' oppressive commands to be normal. In contrast, Credence has been adopted by a fanatical Muggle who actively works to destroy his birth family's culture.

Since his family is blighted by his mother's cruel cause, Credence seeks out acceptance. He believes he has found it in Graves/Grindelwald who he foolishly turns to as a father figure. Credence wants to rejoin the wizarding world, to find the type of tolerance he should have had if he had felt secure enough to reveal his magical abilities. Instead, he has been so oppressed by his mother and her intolerance that he has become an Obscurial with an incredibly powerful, but uncontrolled Obscurus waiting to break forth to show his anger and oppression. In the end, it is Credence's lack of parental guidance—his mother has abused him and he can no longer trust Graves— and his potent frustration that causes him to release the Obscurus. In the climactic scene, he nearly accepts Newt and Tina's offer of help, but he is attacked by MACUSA aurors and appears to be destroyed.

Although Newt Scamander's visually appealing animals steal the show, it is Credence's story that is actually the backbone of the conflict in *Fantastic Beasts and Where to Find Them*. As such, Credence's tale becomes yet another example of how Rowling relies on hostile adoptions to motivate her plot.

Beyond the Books

We may see critics talking about Credence's orphanhood, just like many critics have found literary depth in the presentation of Harry's orphanhood; however, I argue that by seeing these characters as members of dysfunctional families, ones built through adoption, they represent a literary symbol that can also have weighty burdens for real families affected by adoption. Even if we choose to view Harry, Neville, and Credence as fully fictive, literary interpretations of the adopted child, Rowling's world has expanded beyond that, to a place that is much more focused on the differences between the biological and the adopted child. *Pottermore*'s contribution to the treatment of adoptive relationships is perhaps the most damaging of all. The short work of fiction titled "Ilvermorney School of Witchcraft and Wizardry" constitutes a thoughtless attack on the adoptive family.

This piece of short, summary-style fiction was released in June 2016 on *Pottermore*. It introduces Isolt Sayre, a young Irish immigrant to America who founded the first wizarding school in the colonies. Isolt's aunt Gormlaith had murdered her parents and raised Isolt in isolation so that she could instruct the young girl in Dark Magic. As she matured, Isolt came to know that her relationship with her aunt was not that of a regular kinship adoption; she realized her aunt had murdered the Sayres. The disillusioned young woman runs away to America where she makes the acquaintance of a Pukwudgie she names William. William and Isolt save two young wizards, Chadwick and Webster Boot, whose parents had been killed in the forest by magical creatures, and, shortly after, Isolt meets a muggle man and eventually marries him. Together these four humans establish Ilvermorny, largely to tutor the two boys and a few day students who find their way to the door. Later, Isolt gives birth to twin girls. When Isolt's evil aunt crosses to the ocean to find them, the family must pull together to protect themselves from her evil designs.

The piece of short fiction reiterates that, in Rowling's world, orphanhood serves as a lightning rod to greatness. Isolt is only briefly an orphan before she too, like Harry, participates in a twisted kinship adoption/kidnapping that has a bitter outcome. Gormlaith resembles the criminal kidnapper Mother Gothel in Disney's *Tangled*; both women represent the adoptive mother as the thief, the destroyer of bio-normative family connections. Gormlaith steals Isolt away from her family of origin for her own selfish designs: "Only by stealing the child, Gormlaith believed, could [she] be brought back to the 'right way': raised in the belief that as a descendant of both Morrigan and Salazar Slytherin she ought to associate only with purebloods" (Rowling, 2016b). This depiction of kidnapping is consistently depicted as depraved, and the narrator shares that Isolt is "isolated and mistreated by an aunt she believed to be at least half insane" (Rowling, 2016b). Gormlaith's act of kidnapping certainly marks her as a criminal; taken within the scope of Rowling's penchant for producing orphans and housing them with miserable families, the mother/kidnapper presents a yet another dark counterpoint to the healthy adoptive families that exist so rarely in the Wizarding World.

While the details are minimal, it sounds as though Isolt's upbringing resembled Harry's in its emotional neglect. The other adoption line in this narrative, that of the Boot brothers, results in a more loving relationship. Isolt and James adopt the boys and raise them to be wizards, keenly aware that they will need to nurture the boys' magic even without access to the British school and wandmakers. While Isolt and James seem to prioritize the boys and their needs, the narrator is less affirming of the family.

Adoptive families have long faced negative stigmas and challenges to the "realness" of their family relationship (Weger, 2000; Mial, 1987). From broadcast journalism to retellings of fairy stories to children's literature, media continues to ride roughshod over how language affects people in adoptive relationships (Kline, Karel, & Chatterjee, 2006; Baden, 2016; Moore, 2018).

In this article the subtleties of orphan and adopted status have forced me to stress adoptive relationships, and so I have used the adjective "adopted" more often than I would in other venues. Social workers and adoption counselors challenge the mainstream parlance of "real child" vs. "adopted child." The term "real parents," though commonly used in mainstream British and American society to mean the birth parents, is heavily loaded. Once an adoption has been finalized, the child becomes the real child of the family, and her adoptive parents are her real parents. In pre-adoption training, families are challenged to come up with responses to questions such as, "Is that your real child?" or "Are they real sisters?" Families built through adoption know they will become ambassadors to a mainstream culture that does not comprehend the damage an adjective can cause. How will a child process the idea that they are not their parents' "real" child? Already vulnerable due to past transitions, this language can prompt children to feel less secure in their families, less able to commit to attachment and family permanency.

In defiance of modern social practices, Rowling's narrative about the founding of the American wizarding school repeatedly refers to Chadwick and Webster Boot as Isolt's "adopted sons." The narrator does not permit them to be sons in their own right. Note the language used here: "Some protective instinct told Isolt to save the Horned Serpent cores only for her two adoptive sons" (Rowling, 2016b). While Isolt's protective thinking is heartwarming, there is no need to highlight the boys' adopted status in this line. Isolt has no other sons, so it is not as though the adjective "adopted" has to be used to pinpoint which ones the narrator means. Elsewhere the narrator explains that "Isolt and James considered the Boot boys their adopted sons" (Rowling, 2016b). The narration of the boys' home life would be much more secure if the narrator had explained that the adults considered the boys to be "their sons" without the repetition of the adjective. It is important to Rowling and the plot that the boys are not the biological heirs of Salazar Slytherin like Isolt and her twin daughters; however, the boys' birth family is clearly identified from their introduction, so no confusion is possible. During the story's climax, Rowling introduces Chadwick's cleverness with the following line: "Like all children, Chadwick had heard and understood more than his adoptive parents had ever imagined." Since his biological parents have been dead for years, it seems a strange choice to emphasize this adjective since there is no risk that readers will feel at all muddled.

The semantic slip is not the greatest slight the narrator makes against the bonds of a family built through adoption. When Isolt and her husband fall into a cursed sleep, Chadwick fights the evil aunt Gormlaith while Webster runs inside to rouse their parents. Here the problematic adjective temporarily disappears during the climax, as Webster seeks to rouse "his parents" and Chadwick fights to protect "his family" (Rowling, 2016b). However, while the adjective and its insinuations of not-realness are momentarily abandoned, the plot creates a problem for the boys' sense of belonging. Webster cannot rouse Isolt and James from their cursed sleep. The older child's cries fail to wake the parents. In cutting contrast, when the twin girls wake and start screaming, their voices break the spell binding the adults: "It was this that pierced the enchantment lying over Isolt and James. Rage and magic could not wake them, but the terrified screams of their daughters broke the curse Gormlaith had laid upon them, which, like Gormlaith herself, took no account of the power of love" (Rowling, 2016b). The plot point is problematic because it suggests that the love needed to break the enchantment is somehow missing from the relationship between the boys and their parents. Once the baby girls have awakened the parental love, the offending adjective returns to the climactic fight: "Isolt screamed at James to go to the girls: she ran to assist her adoptive sons, Slytherin's wand in her hand" (Rowling, 2016b).

To be clear, it is the cries of their biological daughters that rouse the parents. The narrative pauses to emphasize the plot point of how "the power of love" has saved the day. With curses flying and children crying in their cribs, this scene is reminiscent of Lily Potter's death and the sacrificial protection that it endows to Harry. The moment passes quickly and is almost dismissible, except that the entire success of the climactic fight is based on an assessment of love that is as a slap in the fact to all adoptive relationships. The boys' love and need was not great enough, the parents' love was not real enough, to break the spell. When I covered this plot point with one of my daughters, she passed swift eleven-year-old judgment: "That's terrible."

The fact that the tale is set in the seventeenth-century is hardly a defense of the hostility toward the adoption relationship. Modern sensibilities abound in the tale of a family that is headed by a woman who dressed like a man to cross the ocean, formed an egalitarian marriage, and sent her husband to tend the crying infants so that she could do battle. Historical accuracy is not a consideration here.

Rowling's writings about magic in North America has been cited as an appropriation of Native American culture, and for good reason (Mills, 2016). When I teach "Ilvermorny School of Witchcraft and Wizardry," my class discusses the ways in which the tale abuses the traditions of native peoples. The historical exploitation of that population has been systematic and wide-ranging and deserves careful analysis. To emphasize the careless approach to others' stories and self-definition, I encourage my students to see that such steps are pandemic in the story. Together we consider how the tale includes discrimination against another vulnerable, stigmatized population: families associated with adoption.

Conclusion

In real life, Rowling has used her celebrity to motivate social action to protect vulnerable children. She is the founder and life president of Lumos, a nonprofit organization that advocates for orphans and children at risk of losing their families. Lumos expresses a subtle argument: communities require resources so that parents do not need to go to the extreme of placing their child in an orphanage, and at risk children need to be given the social support necessary to allow kinship adoptions to keep children out of institutions ("Lumos," n.d.). The web site offers logical support for its stance, including a report on an investigation into Haitian orphanage schemes and child trafficking, with the subtitle, "North American orphanage support places thousands of children at risk" ("Child exploitation," 2017). The investigation shares facts about embezzlers who tempt parents to place their children in their care with claims of education and wellness so that they can attract faith-based North American philanthropy. This and other evidence is used to explain why alternatives to institutionalization are preferable.

Lumos grew out of J.K. Rowling's research into orphanage scandals and her interactions with people who research orphan issues (Lumos, 2016). Potterverse celebrities like Warwick Davis, Evanna Lynch, and Eddie Redmayne have joined Rowling's project, as have a small portion of her fans. Rowling uses a personal video message to explain that she witnessed children in orphanages craving the attention of even a temporary helper; such behavior suggests a lack of attachment that is a direct result of institutionalization. Ironically, Rowling has first-hand experience seeing the effects of what happens to unattached children; the web site overflows with statistics about what is likely to happen to children who grow up without a loving family, and it argues for kinship adoptions as one of the solutions to the problem. In a way, it is as though the nonprofit is working to allay the sins of the orphan and adoption narratives the *Harry Potter* franchise has disseminated around the globe.

It would be fascinating to see the lessons being proclaimed via the Lumos web site work their way into the franchise narratives, but that does not appear to be likely at this time. Rowling's tales are built upon our culture's fascination with abusive, unethical adoptions. This has become a habit, very nearly a narrative crutch. It does not seem likely to be abandoned in future franchise stories. Please allow one small voice from the adoption community to assure you of this: the effects of these narratives are not negligible.

REFERENCES

Baden, A.L. (2016). "'Do You Know Your Real Parents?' and Other Adoption Microaggressions." *Adoption Quarterly*, 19(1), 1–25. doi: 10.1080/10926755.2015.1026112
Callaghan, A. (2016). "Adoptions." Hogwarts Online. http://www.hswcw.com/forums/index.php?/topic/73392-adoptions/.
"Child Exploitation in Haiti's Orphanages Highlighted at Seminal Anti-Trafficking Conference: North American Orphanage Support Places Thousands of Children at Risk." (2017). https://wearelumos.org/news/child-exploitation-haiti%E2%80%99s-orphanages-highlighted-seminal-anti-trafficking-conference.
Curtis, J. (2016). "In Absentia Parentis: The Orphan Figure in Latter Twentieth Century Anglo-American Children's Fantasy" Dissertation. http://aquila.usm.edu/dissertations/322.

Gray, D. (2012). *Attaching in Adoption: Practical Tools for Today's Parents.* Philadelphia: Jessica Kingsley Publishers.

Hunt, K. (2006). "'Do You Know Harry Potter? Well, He Is an Orphan': Every Bereaved Child Matters." *Pastoral Care in Education, 24.* doi: 10.1111/j.1468-0122.2006.00369.x.

Kline, S., A. Karel & K. Chatterjee (2006). "Covering Adoption: General Depictions in Broadcast News." *Family Relations, 55,* 487–498. http://www.jstor.org/stable/40005343.

Lewis, C.S. (1982). *The Horse and His Boy.* New York: HarperCollins.

Lumos (n.d.). https://wearelumos.org/.

Lumos (2016). "J.K. Rowling in Conversation with Eddie Redmayne at Carnegie Hall." https://www.youtube.com/watch?v=ca5HYNFuNQk.

Mattson, D. (1997). "Finding Your Way Home: Orphan Stories in Young Adult Literature." *The ALAN Review, 24.* https://doi.org/10.21061/alan.v24i3.a.5.

Mial, C. (1987). "The Stigma of Adoptive Parent Status: Perceptions of Community Attitudes Toward Adoption and the Experience of Informal Social Sanctioning." *Family Relations* 36, 34–39. http://www.jstor.org/stable/584644.

Mills, A. (2016). "Colonialism in Wizarding America: J.K. Rowling's History of Magic in North America Through an Indigenous Lens." *The Looking Glass: New Perspectives on Children's Literature,* 19, http://www.lib.latrobe.edu.au/ojs/index.php/tlg/article/view/764/709.

Moore, T. (2018). "No Longer an Orphan: Narratives of Adoption in Young Adult Fantasy and Science Fiction." The ALAN Review, 45. 57–66.

Nelson, C. (2001). "Drying the Orphan's Tear: Changing Representations of the Adopted Child in America, 1870–1930." *Children's Literature,* 29, 52–70. doi: 10.1353/chl.0.0797

Nelson, C. (June 2001). "Nontraditional Adoption in Progressive-Era Orphan Narratives." *Mosaic: A Journal for the Interdisciplinary Study of Literature,* 34, 181–197. Retrieved from: https://www.questia.com/library/journal/1G1-76880855.

Nguyen, K. (2011). "The Effacement of Post-9/11 Orphanhood: Re-Reading the Harry Potter Series as a Melancholic Rhetoric." *Poroi, 7,* 1–32.

Novy, Marianne (2005). *Reading Adoption: Family and Difference in Fiction and Drama.* Ann Arbor: University of Michigan Press.

Rowling, J.K. (1997). *Harry Potter and the Deathly Hallows.* New York: Scholastic.

Rowling, J.K. (2000). *Harry Potter and the Goblet of Fire.* New York: Scholastic.

Rowling, J.K. (2007). *Harry Potter and the Sorcerer's Stone.* New York: Scholastic.

Rowling, J.K. (2016a). *Fantastic Beasts and Where to Find Them.* New York: Arthur A. Levine Books.

Rowling, J.K. (2016b). "Ilvermorny School of Witchcraft and Wizardry." Pottermore. https://www.pottermore.com/writing-by-jk-rowling/ilvermorny.

Sales, S. (2015). "Contested Attachments: Rethinking Adoptive Kinship in the Era of Open Adoption." *Child and Family Social Work,* 20. 149–158. doi:10.1111/cfs.12062.

Taft, R., C. Ramsay, & C. Schlein (2015). "Home and School Experiences of Caring for Children with Reactive Attachment Disorder." *Journal of Ethnographic & Qualitative Research, 9,* 237–246.

Thorne, J. (2016). *Harry Potter and the Cursed Child.* St. Louis, MO: Turtleback Books.

Transfiguring Adoptions. (n.d.). Transfiguringadoptions.com.

Warshick, J. (2009). "Oliver Twisted: The Origins of Lord Voldemort in the Dickensian Orphan." *The Looking Glass: New Perspectives on Children's Literature,* 13. Retrieved from: http://www.lib.latrobe.edu.au/ojs/index.php/tlg/article/view/165/164.

Weger, C. (2000). "Adoption, Family Ideology, and the Social Stigma: Bias in Community Attitudes, Adoption Research, and Practice." *Family Relations,* 49, 363–370. Retrieved from: http://www.jstor.org/stable/585831.

Harry Potter and the Paradoxes of Fidelity

Jelena Borojević

Where It Begins

A young mind is a mysterious and unpredictable thing. It is curious, creative, imaginative, and in awe of the world. However, from the moment a child realizes that they are different from an adult, and treated as something not fully developed, they withdraw from the outside world and begin a search for a world of their own—where they will be understood. "If we want to understand our true selves, we must become familiar with the inner workings of our mind" (Bettelheim, 1976, p. 97). Adults do this through research and analysis; children do it through imagination.

This essay focuses on the differences in the portrayal of childhood between *Harry Potter and the Philosopher's Stone* (Rowling, 2014) and its film adaptation *Harry Potter and the Sorcerer's Stone* (Columbus, 2001). Each mode presents its own view of a child's story, and in doing so, focuses on different aspects of a child's life and imagination. The film holds a strong preference for magic, and uses it to depict the story as an escapist fantasy. It thus depicts a journey into a world not completely unlike our own, but certainly one where magic, the one very specific thing that our minds can conjure but our realities lack, is used as a way to escape childhood problems.

The novel, on the other hand, strongly emphasizes the individual trauma within a young mind, as well as the cause of the deep psychological need to escape reality. While the film focuses on the enchantments that lie on the other side of escape, the novel seeks to expose the reason why children would want an invitation to Hogwarts and the world of wizards in the first place. Both mediums depict a childhood enriched by the fantastic; however, because their focal points are so different, so is the emotional outcome for readers and viewers at the end of the story.

As the adaptation theorist Thomas M. Leitch (2003, p. 161) reminds us, "fidelity" is one of the most common fallacies in approaching a novel turned into a film, and a comparison that seeks a 'literal adaptation,' one that expects to find every possible moment in the novel projected in its exact 'original' state onto the big screen, is both belittling to the art of film and unrealistic. This analysis will focus instead on the difference in story atmosphere created by each medium, as well as the psychological states evoked in readers and viewers as a result.

The Context for the Harry Potter Series

When the *Harry Potter* series debuted in 1997, the approaching 21st century, and the technological advancements that accompanied it, created a state of confusion among many parents over how much children should accomplish prior to a certain age. Many parents desired a faster learning progress, which often resulted in "fostering performance anxiety and perfectionism in their children" (Ablard & Parker, 1997, p. 651), while their time to truly *be* children was drastically shortened, and replaced by the need to become successful at a much younger age. Even in the kindest of parents, this created the need for a balancing act between allowing children to play freely, and yet not to the extent that they are completely unaware of the much less forgiving world that exists outside of their imagination. As Jessica Lahey (2014) wrote in *The Atlantic* magazine,

> We may pay lip service to character education and empathy, but our children report hearing a very different message.... A new study from Harvard University reveals that the message parents *mean* to send children about the value of empathy is being drowned out by the message we *actually* send: that we value achievement and happiness above all else [Why Kids Care More About Achievement Than Helping Others, para. 3].

For many young people growing up in the late 20th and early 21st century, there was a deep desire hiding beneath the surface of young minds facing the upcoming Millennium, one that may not have been obvious to many adults: a desire to escape. This in no way implies that children are not brave enough to face a challenging future—far from it! However, in the delicate and often scary period of childhood, children can find it difficult to receive the safety, emotional and existential support they need to encourage their development.

One way to deal with such internal conflicts is to leave, if only temporarily, the reality that hosts them. There are a number of triggers for such a decision (including family problems, bullying, and disorientation), but whatever the cause of their distress may be, an escape must be found from such an environment, both as a method of psychological relief and as a way to step back from reality and see the world in a different light. It took "12 publishing rejections in a row" (*Lit Rejections*, 2012) before someone understood that the story of Harry Potter spoke to both of these realities—the increasing pressures on childhood development at the turn of the 21st century, and a resulting desire for an imaginative escape into a world of fantasy.

The Difficulty with Adaptation

> Though novels and films may seem at any given moment in history of narrative theory to have essentially distinctive properties, those properties are functions of their historical moments and not of the media themselves
> —Leitch, 2003, p. 153].

As the very first film adaptation of the series, and appearing at a time (2001) when Harry Potter mania was still growing, it is understandable that the film version, *Harry Potter and the Sorcerer's Stone*, featured an emphasis on spectacular visual effects in order to keep an audience entertained and, hopefully, eager for the second film. What was lost in this emphasis on the magical dimension of *Harry Potter* was Rowling's naturalistic evocation of the pain and trauma of childhood, a pain and trauma that fed the desire for a magical world.

It is not so much a question of whether the film could or could not have adapted the portrayal of childhood better; it is a question of why it chose not to, and what was created in the process. By placing almost complete emphasis on magic, what the filmmakers didn't notice is that it is precisely in childhood, and the many obstacles which appear in it, that magic is sought as relief.

A Story of Childhood, Lost

What many young readers found so comforting in *Harry Potter and the Philosopher's Stone* were characters who were going through problems in life very similar to their own, and whom they could empathize with precisely because of the naturalism of Rowling's descriptions, but who, as a bonus, also had a means of escape. Young fans may not have Hogwarts in the real world, but they have the imaginative abilities to transport themselves to the world of witches and wizards:

fiction builds on the same cognitive adaptations for attributing thoughts and feelings to other people and ourselves that we use in our daily social life.... One important feature of fictional mind reading is that it intensifies certain patterns of mind reading present in our daily social interactions [Zunshine, 2015, p. 727].

The book begins with an introduction of the Dursley family. As is the case in most families, it only takes a small number of people to have an enormous impact on shaping a child's opinion of themselves, the world around them, where exactly their position in the world is, and how much they can or cannot contribute to it. In Harry's case, the Dursleys were more than enough to abuse, distort, and almost completely ruin a childhood. Harry's initial reactions and communication with people, both at home and in school, were largely shaped by the way he was treated at home. Because this realistic and even satirical description of suburban family life occurs at the very beginning of the book, it creates an instant connection between the reader and Harry, a connection that will be understood and empathized with throughout the entire series.

The film, on the other hand, skips the introduction of a family entirely and instead begins with Dumbledore performing magic, Professor McGonagall transforming from cat to human, and Hagrid arriving on a flying motorcycle. All attention is placed on magic, and because this is the first thing that viewers (including those who haven't read the book) see, magic is presented as the most important part of the story. Very little is known or explained about the baby that is about to be left on the doorstep of the Dursley home, and as a result, the initial emotional bond that forms between the audience and the story isn't with Harry but with the wizards.

While the film starts off with visually impressive magical elements to attract the audience, the book begins with a much more naturalistic tone. By doing this, the author conveyed that, despite the vast detail and creativity of her fictional world, she valued the importance of upbringing and the effect that family arguments and abuse have on a child more than the magic of it; the film's creators, on the other hand, chose the visual excitement afforded by the magical world as the primary value of the first film.

There exists a belief that "readers of novels, unlike viewers of films, expect a certain amount of psychological description and are troubled, even if they do not know why, if it is suppressed" (Leitch, 2003, p. 152). However, viewers of films can be just as demanding of psychological development and explanation. Both mediums can serve the demands of entertainment, but similarly, they are both capable of impressive psychological depth if they choose.

Although the film's introduction differs from that of the novel, it does include some of the book's key sentences, which are exchanged between Dumbledore and Professor McGonagall:

> **McGonagall:** Albus, do you really think it's safe? Leaving him with these people. I've watched them all day. They're the worst sort of muggles imaginable. They really are—
> **Dumbledore:** —the only family he has [SS, 2001].

Much of the *Harry Potter* story relies precisely on these psychologically significant questions: Is family more important than friendship? Are family members by default better guardians than a stranger?

"[F]iction acquaints readers with a wide range of possible problems and solutions, and it allows readers to explore those possibilities with little personal risk in imagined worlds" (Kidd, 2016, p. 2). When the pleasures of fantasy are offered without a grounding in the physical and psychological circumstances that motivate the desire for escape, very little is taken away from the experience other than a brisk escape from repetitive daily routines. In front of an audience which also includes many adults, both the novel and the film had an opportunity to significantly influence the public's perception of children and childhood. In the mind of an adult, *Harry Potter* has the potential to spark an understanding of, or perhaps more accurately, a *memory* of why the world of witches and wizards is, for many children, the equivalent of a sanctuary.

Throughout the novel, in both the sections dealing with the muggle Dursley family, and continuing into the world of Hogwarts, Rowling maintains a focus on the sources of childhood pain and trauma.

Mr. Dursley "didn't approve of imagination" (Rowling, 2014, p. 5), which meant that the only way for Harry to have the ability to dream, imagine, develop his creativity, and create a better world for himself, was to leave the Dursley home. This is one of the many restrictions imposed by adults, both muggle and magical, that will appear in the book. Harry would soon be saved from the clutches of the Dursley family by the magical intercession of Hagrid. Most children in the real world, however, have no guardians beyond those in their own home who will come to their rescue. Instead, because of their parent or guardian's inability to see the world through young eyes, the child's possibilities and development are already limited and restricted to where they are at the moment, and who they are with.

There is also a clear division of social class in the book between Harry and the Dursleys. Dudley delights his mother by learning to say "Shan't" (Rowling, 2014, p. 6), they refer to the family side of Harry's mother as "*her lot*" (p. 7), and remark that "Harry" is a "nasty, common name" (p. 8). All of these remarks hint at the very serious and offensive division in social class between Harry and the Dursleys, despite living in the same home. This early introduction to class prejudice is crucial to understanding the central developmental idea informing Rowling's world view: that children may be born with a certain temperament, but they are not born with arrogance and self-entitlement; it is the environment that curves their personalities this way.

The Dursleys are also an incredibly traditional family who do not like any form of change occurring around them (Rowling, 2014, p. 19), as well as a despicable family who ignore the existence of another child in their home. "The room held no sign at all that another boy lived in the house, too" (p. 19). Their traditional and conservative views on life are equivalent to challenges real world children have to deal with in such homes as well, including, but certainly not limited to, the fight for rights to a young person's sexuality, education, career choice, and freedom from or acceptance of religion.

In fact, the Dursleys go to such extreme lengths to ignore Harry that he lives in a cupboard under the stairs, which is full of spiders (Rowling, 2014, p. 20). The film version does show Harry's living conditions fairly accurately (minus the spiders), but because this scene has been preceded by little background information, the impact of Harry's situation, which in the novel can be seen as blatant child abuse, isn't as shocking, but instead verges on the lines of light-hearted humor. Additionally, because very little screen time is spent on Harry's room under the stairs, the full impact of such abuse at home is not conveyed to the film audience.

The book, on the other hand, specifically states how the Dursley home affected Harry's development. "Perhaps it had something to do with living in a dark cupboard, but Harry had always been small and skinny for his age" (Rowling, 2014, p. 21). This is only one of the book's many examples of how destructive a negative family environment can be on a child; and even worse, how rarely those who are not a regular member of such a household ever notice that something very wrong could be taking place behind closed doors. Although the film does show the existence of Harry's room and his inadequate clothing, it lacks the depth and gravity of Rowling's social realism and instead plays up a comic portrayal of the Dursleys as people more to be laughed at than feared.

In contrast, Rowling was very serious about making sure that the reader understands that Harry could at all times be very close to receiving a beating, and as such, is the potential victim of outright physical abuse: "I accept there's something strange about you," Mr. Dursley tells Harry after the secret of Harry's magical birthright is revealed, "probably nothing a good beating wouldn't have cured" (Rowling, 2014, p. 61). Although this particular line was excluded, the film, like the book, does show Harry occasionally being threatened by Mr. Dursley, as when they enter the car before heading for the zoo, but again with lesser consequences than in the book. In the book, Harry will be confined to the cupboard under the stairs until Christmas (p. 25), while in the film, Harry "won't have any meals for a week" (SS, 2001). In the world of the novel, Harry *has* actually been punished before by spending an entire week in the cupboard (p. 26). Unlike the impression created by the more comical film version, Mr. Dursley's threats in the novel are not empty ones.

Even though Mr. Dursley is very much aware that Harry is likely a wizard, Rowling used the broad term "something strange" to describe Mr. Dursley's thoughts. Many children suffer serious repercussions from their parents for being thought of as "strange." By using a general term and not a direct reference to Harry's magical abilities, Rowling allowed the readers' minds to recall a time when they too may have been considered "strange" in their household; and for many readers, this memory could be easily recollected while reading the book.

Another sentence that is familiar to many children is, "*Don't ask questions*" (Rowling, 2014, p. 21). Any time that Harry might be curious about something, he is quickly silenced. Meanwhile, Dudley can't even count simple numbers and yet is treated like royalty (p. 22). Dudley is also described as quickly breaking most of his birthday presents without any respect for them (p. 33). Despite his ridiculous behavior, Mr. Dursley proudly exclaims that the boy is "just like his father" (p. 23). None of these points are mentioned in the film, and yet all serve in the novel as realistic evocations of the difficulty and trauma of childhood and family life. More importantly, they represent an environment that a child would feel the need to escape from *immediately*.

In fact, the film not only underplays the threat posed by the Dursleys to Harry's health and safety, but occasionally portrays the Dursleys in a more positive light. In the film version of Dudley's birthday, we see Harry instantly heading to the car with the rest of the family and participating in the zoo trip as if this is a normal, annual occurrence. The book, on the other hand, makes it clear that this is actually *the first time* that Harry has ever been taken to the zoo on Dudley's birthday (or at all), and only because the woman who usually took care of him on these occasions, Mrs. Figg, had broken her leg (Rowling, 2014, p. 23).

Even before the appearance of bullies in Hogwarts, the book explains that Harry is often bullied at muggle school "for his baggy clothes and Sellotaped glasses" (Rowling, 2014, p. 25–26). The film never mentions what school life was like for Harry before his invitation to Hogwarts arrived, and because of this, the film viewers have no background information on Harry's current thoughts on school or how he is treated in it. Even Hagrid understands how cruel even magical children can be and quickly stops Harry from getting a toad as a pet in Diagon Alley because, "toads went outta fashion years ago, ye'd be laughed at" (p. 87). This is a very important line because it foreshadows how Neville will be treated at Hogwarts, since his pet is in fact a toad, and thus suggests, unlike the film adaptation, that even Hogwarts may not be the magical sanctuary that Harry hopes for.

Instead, Rowling describes how toxic a school, even Hogwarts, can become to those who fail to follow the often-arbitrary rules of adults. For example, in one of their midnight adventures, excluded from the film version, in which Neville also plays a small role ("Chapter Fourteen: Norbert the Norwegian Ridgeback"), Harry, Ron, and Hermione lose one hundred and fifty points for Gryffindor as punishment. We then read the reaction that followed the four adventurers after destroying their house's high score:

> [Harry] could hear Neville sobbing in his pillow for what seemed like hours.... He knew Neville, like himself, was dreading the dawn. What would happen when the rest of Gryffindor found out what they'd done? [Rowling, 2014, p. 262].

Even though ruining Gryffindor's high score was not intentional, no explanation would have been adequate enough for their peers. Harry finds that "[f]rom being one of the most popular and admired people at the school, [he] was suddenly the most hated" (p. 263).

The film adaptation, on the other hand, provides no foreshadowing of the potentially dark side of Hogwarts; instead, as with the first scene, the film provides a more visual spectacle, with Hogwarts rising from the Great Lake aglow with candlelight, suggesting the magical sanctuary Harry longs for, and creating an atmosphere where Harry would always be admired by his peers for being "the boy who lived." Had it kept this scene, it would have shown how quickly a fall from grace is possible at any age, and in any environment, magical or otherwise. Additionally, by retaining this scene, a very private psychological state in a child would have been presented to the audience.

Throughout the novel, Harry's adult mentors at Hogwarts both display their own Dursley-like prejudices, and offer hard life lessons. She may be an important and beloved part of Harry's future, for example, but Professor McGonagall's description of the Dursleys in the book's opening, "You couldn't find two people who are less like us" (Rowling, 2014, p. 14), shows that members of the wizarding world are aware of and wish to maintain a great difference between themselves and the Muggles. The film doesn't include this line, and thus, initially, makes it seem as if wizards are automatically the "good" side, more inherently tolerant than muggles.

Another important life lesson comes through Dumbledore's words, "Scars can come useful" (Rowling, 2014, p. 15), referring specifically to the scar the infant Harry had received from Voldemort's failed killing curse, but more broadly to the benefits that children can gain from being hurt. It is an affirmation that young minds are capable of learning from negative situations, as painful as they may be, and viewing them as preparation for negative events that will almost certainly occur again in the future.

Although Harry's scar is the most visual symbol of all, he is not the only child in the novel that has been through some form of suffering at a very young age. Ron openly shares that he has had a lot to live up to being the youngest of six brothers, and he mentions that he inherited many things from his older siblings without getting anything new for himself (Rowling, 2014, p. 106). This is very similar to Harry's situation with Dudley, and is the reason why the two boys strike such a quick and close friendship. However, the way that this friendship starts off in the film is quite different.

Rather than bonding over their shared psychological trauma, in the film adaptation, upon seeing the very humble state of Ron's packed lunch, Harry uses his newly inherited money and proceeds to buy *everything* from the snack trolley that arrives near their train compartment at that moment. Although this may be a goodhearted and generous gesture towards Ron, it also satisfies a very particular fantasy about wealth (one that is also very common among adults). Because Harry purchases a generous amount of sweets from the trolley, the film allows viewers to psychologically enjoy the satisfaction of what money can bring, reinforcing the sense of unearned wish fulfillment.

The novel, on the other hand, is much more restrained in how it deals with the presence of wealth. In the book, the woman with the trolley does appear (p. 108), however, the kindness that ensues is quite different from the one shown in the film. Harry is indeed saddened by Ron's poor meal and decides to make a purchase from the trolley. However, he buys "some of everything" (p. 108) and not "the lot" as he does in the film. The novel focuses on the fact that Harry "never had anything to share before" (p. 108).

Ron is not alone in having a difficult problem to deal with while growing up, and it is one that Rowling, through her own life experience, understood very well: living very close to the poverty line. Most of Ron's things are hand-me-downs from his brothers. This includes an old wand, an old rat, and his older brothers' clothes. On the contrary, Harry, although initially living in awful conditions, inherits a small fortune from his parents. Likewise, Hermione is also an only child, and her parents are both dentists, who are likely to have a stable income. Financially, Ron has had a far worse financial start to his school life, which may be why he frequently lacks motivation to do any serious work. Ron's family is described as both poor and having a mother who forgets many things because she is far too busy with so many children to take care of. "'You don't want this, it's all dry,' said Ron. 'She hasn't got much time,' he added quickly, 'you know, with five of us'" (p. 108).

It is endearing to see Ron defending his mother and the mistakes that she makes with his lunch on a regular basis. Rather than condemn her for making something that he doesn't like to eat, as young as he is, he understands that it is simply part of their current everyday life, and that, hopefully, things will be better someday. The film excludes this line and the serious atmosphere that surrounds it.

Ron is also worried that his parents will be angry if he is in any house other than Gryffindor (Rowling, 2014, p. 114). Neville also had to deal with a similar issue on multiple occasions. First, because he was very slow to come to terms with his magic, his family was worried that he may not have inherited the skills of a wizard. Once Neville performed his first bit of magic, although relieved that he was indeed a wizard, his family was also *very* quick to move on to fears of whether Neville was good enough to be accepted into Hogwarts (p. 133–134). The fears of Ron and Neville's families are not concerned with what the boys want, but whether or not their families will be embarrassed while talking about their progress in school with others. However, Ron and Neville are not alone in this.

Interestingly, Draco Malfoy has a similar problem with his father. Instead of worrying about which house he will be put into (since Slytherin is a given for their family), he is worried about not making a valuable contribution to his Quidditch team: "father says it's a crime if I'm not picked to play for my house" (p. 83). Ron and Draco may come from very different family backgrounds, but the fact that they are both pressured to succeed by their parents, and how this is affecting them in school, is not surprising at all. Malfoy may be a spoiled and at times ruthless bully, however, and although this is not a firm excuse for his behavior, like Ron and Neville, he is also a child. His behavior is a result of his own environment back home. Again, Jessica Lahey's (2014) comments on the mixed message given to contemporary schoolchildren is relevant in understanding Harry Potter's appeal to young readers:

> [Students] reported that their teachers prioritize student achievement over caring. Surveyed students were three times as likely to agree as disagree with the statement "My parents are prouder if I get good grades in my class than if I'm a caring community member in class and school…." Empathy is a key ingredient of resilience, the foundation to trust, the benchmark of humanity, and core to everything that makes a society civilized [Why Kids Care More About Achievement Than Helping Others, para. 4&6].

Which brings us to one of the most significant lines in the book, (also used in the film) but which comes across in a very different light across the two mediums, Hermione's warning to Ron and Harry after their failed encounter with Draco led to their discovery of the three-headed dog guarding a mysterious trap door, "We could all have been killed—or worse, expelled" (Rowling, 2014, p. 173). Hermione's words are interpreted in very different ways in the book and in the film. In the film, the line is a comic moment reinforcing Hermione's identity as a bookworm, and conformist rule follower.

Although Hermione is often mocked for it, her fear is in no way exaggerated. Her passion for the best possible education at Hogwarts is two-fold. Hermione is the only witch in her immediate family. If expelled, she would be forced to return to a "regular" life among muggles. Furthermore, instead of only portraying her as an annoying know-it-all, the novel also presents Hermione as a child trying very hard to create a successful future for herself.

The mere thought of being thrown out of Hogwarts is a regret beyond anything Hermione could imagine, and is also the force that pushes her forward in life. Although the movie adaptations of the remaining books in the series make it quite clear that she is so much more than a 'bookworm,' this first adaptation relies heavily early on a more comical caricature of Hermione, so much so that it comes as a surprise to Ron, Harry, and the viewers when she runs off crying after her feelings are hurt.

Throughout Harry's initial training for Quidditch in the book, Hermione continuously helps him with his homework, and even lends him a book on Quidditch to help him prepare (Rowling, 2014, p. 194). Her kindness is not shown in the film. She offers Ron a lot of help with his homework as well, however, "she would never let them copy ('How will you learn?')" (p. 195). Mindless copying is something that Hagrid also sees no point in. "Writin' lines! What good's that ter anyone?" (p. 268). It is impressive how early in her life Hermione understood that repetitive behavior and "writing lines" teaches nothing about life.

However, in the film, a particularly important feature of Hermione's character was excluded during her involvement in the final puzzle before Harry reaches Quirrell in "Chapter Sixteen: Through the Trap Door." In the book, Ron remains on the Chess board after sacrificing himself (his chess piece) so that Harry and Hermione can continue on to the next stage of the puzzle. Mere moments after reading the instructions for the puzzle with bottles, Hermione figures out a way to solve it, leaving Harry with a very bewildered look on his face. And it isn't magic she relies on to do so. "'*Brilliant!*,' said Hermione. 'This isn't magic—it's logic—a puzzle. A lot of the greatest wizards haven't got an ounce of logic, they'd be stuck in here for ever.'" (p. 307). And so would Harry, had it not been for Hermione's help. By completely removing the final puzzle, and leaving Hermione behind to take care of Ron, although the adaptation does show Hermione to be a great friend and someone who will become an even bigger foundation for Ron in the future, it dims the light on her intellectual abilities, and the importance of her passionate studying.

After Fantasy

> "Reality is something the human race doesn't handle very well."
> —Gore Vidal

What the books and the film adaptations of *Harry Potter* have provided are a forum for discussion among children growing up in the 1990s and early

2000s, many of whom have now become scholars themselves, and who finally have a pedestal to describe their experiences and serious existential problems through the experience of *Harry Potter*. And even now, sixteen years after the first film was brought to a worldwide audience, fans can still clearly recall why it was so important to queue for hours in front of a bookstore, for a chance to experience the life of a wizard, and just for a few hours, be relieved of any personal problems that existed outside of those books.

There comes a point in a child's life when they realize that the toys in front of them will soon be replaced by an education system that, in most countries, does not nearly value actual knowledge as much as the competition for grades, percentages, and numbers. The *Harry Potter* books succeeded because, for many children and teenagers, they appeared at a time in their lives when it was precisely these thoughts that were roaming through their young minds.

Fiction, whatever its medium of expression, "influences how we make sense of our real social world. In this sense, reading is not just a way of appreciating or consuming culture, it may also be a practice that allows us to transmit and even shape culture" (Kidd, 2016, p. 13). The same is true for the power and influence that film has on reaching a large number of people and depicting a story. Imagination is the key in finding an explanation for our world, for new ideas in it, and for people who share those ideas and are living through similar lives to ours.

As the adaptation process continued with the *Harry Potter* series, the films began to more fully adopt the naturalistic approach of the novels and more openly explore issues of childhood and adolescent pain and trauma.

For example, in Alfonso Cuarón's adaptation of *PoA* (2004), the focus on magic is greatly reduced and replaced by more naturalistic childhood encounters. Even more evident is the strong focus on a search for identity among the young characters, as well as giving Harry's personality and inner feelings more attention than in the first two films. In the film version of *PoA*, Harry defends the memory of his parents from the insults of Aunt Marge, and he openly threatens Mr. Dursley with his wand, even though he still depends on him for shelter. Because Harry doesn't use any magic against Mr. Dursley, but simply displays the wand as a power which his uncle can't quite comprehend, the wand is the equivalent of children threatening adults with their own inner world when, like Harry, they reach a breaking point and seriously consider running away.

Another superb part of this adaptation concerns the portrayal of the Professor of Divination, Sybill Patricia Trelawney. Her most passionate goal is to teach students to "broaden [their] mind"(*PoA*, 2004). Knowledgeable in her field, but clumsy, awkward, and likely with a difficult past behind her, ironically, she in many ways resembles adults who have grown up in a world of imagination; daydreamers who spent most of their time in their minds and now wish to encourage younger generations to embrace these thoughts.

There is a similar impressive development of a more psychologically naturalistic approach in the film adaptation of *DH1* (2010). Both the novel and the film became progressively darker, representing not only the change in plot, but also the growth of a child coming into and realizing the dark side of the world. As is often the case in real life, jealousy and suspected treachery are more than enough to damage the bonds of a strong friendship. After Ron's abrupt departure, Harry and Hermione find themselves in a moment of loss where magic cannot help them come to a solution. And so, in their short dance together, an example of a psychologically subtle and poignant scene found in this case in the film and not in the book, all that is left is human touch, friendship, and pure emotion. No spells that could alter the thoughts or ambiance.

Especially interesting is the portrayal of another seemingly minor character, the Professor of Muggle Studies, Charity Burbage. She is murdered by Voldermort because of her belief that "the mixture of magical and muggle blood is not an abomination, but something to be encouraged" (*DH1*, 2010). She represents *research*, much like the article you are reading now, that wishes to combine the worlds of fantasy and reality, and use them to balance the world that surrounds and ultimately affects all living beings.

Works of fantasy, such as the *Harry Potter* series, are often stereotyped and belittled as merely escapist. But crucial to the 'escapism' of fantasy in the *Harry Potter* novels is Rowling's naturalistic and sensitive portrayal of the psychological pain and trauma that her young characters want to escape, not just the un-magical world of the muggles, but the pressure of conforming to an increasingly achievement-oriented and status-obsessed adult world. As impressive as *SS* (2001) is on the big screen, sparks of magic, without the full strength of the story, are not enough to convey the psychological complexity of childhood. Even though both the book and the film prove to be great friends in moments of needed escape, reality will still have to be dealt with when the book is closed and the credits have rolled. "'Still famous,' said Ron, grinning at him. 'Not where I'm going, I promise you,' said Harry" (Rowling, 2014, p. 331).

REFERENCES

Ablard, K.E. & Parker, W.D. (1997). "Parents' Achievement Goals and Perfectionism in Their Academically Talented Children." *Journal of Youth and Adolescence, 26(6),* 651–667.
Bettelheim, B. (1976). *The Uses of Enchantment: The Meaning and Importance of Fairy Tales.* New York: Vintage Books.
Columbus, C. (Director). (2001). *Harry Potter and the Sorcerer's Stone* [Motion Picture]. United States: Warner Bros.
Cuarón, A. (Director). (2004). *Harry Potter and the Prisoner of Azkaban.* [Motion Picture]. United States: Warner Bros.

Kidd, D. (2016). "Different Stories: How Literary and Popular Genre Fiction Relate to Folk Psychology and Folk Sociology." Presented at the 2016 MLA Annual Convention, Modern Language Association, Austin, TX, 7–10 January, 2016.

Lahey, J. (2014, Jun 25)". Why Kids Care More About Achievement than Helping Others." *The Atlantic*. Retrieved from http://www.theatlantic.com/education/archive/2014/06/most-kids-believe-that-achievement-trumps-empathy/373378/.

Leitch, T. (2003). "Twelve Fallacies in Contemporary Adaptation Theory." *Criticism 45(2)*, 149–171.

Lit Rejections. (2012, Nov 16). "Best-Sellers Initially Rejected." Retrieved from http://www.litrejections.com/best-sellers-initially-rejected/.

Rowling, J.K. (2014). *Harry Potter and the Philosopher's Stone*. London: Bloomsbury Publishing.

Vidal, G. (1990, Jan 3). *Radio Times*.

Yates, D. (Director). (2010). *Harry Potter and the Deathly Hallows: Part 1*. [Motion Picture]. United States: Warner Bros.

Zunshine, L. (2015). The Secret Life of Fiction. *PMLA, 130(3)*, 724–731.

What Is a Hero?
An Analysis of Legacy Symbolism
Marley Stuever-Williford

J.K. Rowling's series of *Harry Potter* novels was a groundbreaking effort in children's literature, and while there has been much speculation on just *why Harry Potter* has been so phenomenally successful, little critical study has been done on how Rowling engages her audience. Literature is an art form, and the skill and attention to craft that Rowling brings to her work solidifies her place as one of the best-known artists of the 21st century. The core series consists of the seven novels and three spin-off supplemental texts: *The Tales of Beedle the Bard*, *Quidditch Through the Ages*, and *Fantastic Beasts and Where to Find Them*, all three of which are titles that appear in the canonical novels. Beyond these ten books exist films, a play, a fan-made musical, and the website Pottermore.com where Rowling herself has published dozens of blogs, supplemental information, details, and insights into the world of *Harry Potter*. These additional texts serve the purpose of satisfying audience curiosity; Rowling created a world with characters so intriguing and complex that they kept fans of the series speculating and questioning even until now, more than a decade after *Deathly Hallows*' release. When a series is able to accomplish what *Harry Potter* has, it is the task of fans, academics, and historians to examine how it reached this level of success: not just the financial success (with the brand having an estimated worth of $25 billion) (Meyer, 2016), nor even just its cultural success (although it has been translated into 68 languages and is read and beloved all over the world) (Scholastic). This essay aims to analyze the emotional achievement of *Harry Potter*, and how Rowling managed to tell a story that kept fans invested long after they closed the last book.

Rowling as an author is no stranger to the use of literary devices. Authors have compared her work to the "hero's journey" outlined in Joseph Campbell's

Hero with a Thousand Faces (Natov, 2001). She has borrowed character names from Shakespeare, Roman myth, and Arthurian legend. Rowling's use of the motif of "threes," which occurs throughout famous literature, will be discussed at greater length in this analysis. Rowling makes effective use of these tropes and motifs from famous (and often British) literature to instill a sense of familiarity in her work and give something with which the audience can connect. In the case of *Harry Potter*, themes and symbols are used as literary devices that are critical to the emotional through line of the story. There are countless examples of themes and symbols within the narrative, but this analysis will focus solely on the theme of legacy and the connected symbolism. The recurrence of legacy throughout the story keeps the audience invested and helps to give greater character and world depth. The First Wizarding War, which took the lives of James and Lily Potter along with hundreds of unknown witches and wizards, had abruptly ended due to Voldemort's disappearance when the audience first encounters the world of *Harry Potter* (Rowling, 1997). However, the threat of Voldemort still lingered enough for much of the Wizarding world to fear using his name. Just eleven short years after his disappearance, Voldemort begins to regain power and the series effectively becomes a steady build to the Second Wizarding War. Harry Potter and the rest of Dumbledore's Army make it their mission to end Voldemort's reign over the Wizarding public, partly because of the legacy that was left to them by their precursors, the Marauders.

By placing the narrative of *Harry Potter* in a "war story" context, the narrative gains the benefit of its contemporaries and genre companions, specifically other fantasy and science fiction novels and properties that enlist the trope of "The War Just Before." It also raises the stakes for the main cast of the story to withstand the horrors of war that the generation before them failed to do. The details the audience learns of the First Wizarding War strengthen their connection to both the deceased and/or hapless generation of soldiers, and to the youthful, optimistic faces of the Second Wizarding War, which takes place near the end of the series.

Harry Potter finds itself genre-wise among other YA "dystopia," fantasy, and science fiction literature, films, television shows, and video games. Literature and entertainment properties in these related genres are saddled with similar conventions in plot, world-building, and style. *Harry Potter* often breaks genre convention; for example, at the time the first *Harry Potter* novel was written it was unconventional for a fantasy novel to be set in the modern day. Despite the occasional stereotype-bucking, *Harry Potter* still owes a lot to genre and its predecessors in literature and other art forms. The primary concepts addressed in this analysis—"The War Just Before" trope, the prominence of redemption narratives, and the use of trinity structure—have all been addressed in reference to other texts in history.

The War Just Before

The concept of the "War Just Before" has not been established in academic literature, but occurs regularly enough in fantasy and science fiction popular culture to be recognized as a trope on the open source website TVtropes.org. "The War Just Before" is used as a world-building and character-establishing technique, especially in fantasy and science fiction narratives, because the world building needs to be immediate and familiar. The trope dictates that just before the start of the narrative, there was a war that ended badly for society, drained resources, or ended in a loss for the main characters of the narrative. For example, *The Lord of the Rings* series begins decades after the Battle of Five Armies from *The Hobbit* (Tolkien 1937, 1954). In the massive multiplayer online game *Destiny*, the game begins centuries after a multi-species war that pushed humans off Earth and onto a space-station city-state (Staten, 2014). In the television show *Firefly*, both the captain of the Serenity and its first mate were veterans of a war between the Alliance and the Independents of the Unification War (Whedon, 2002). *Battlestar Galactica (BSG)* is set after the first Cylon War (Moore, 2004). In nearly all instances of this trope, "The War Just Before" sets the groundwork for the war or central conflict that will take place in the narrative. It establishes enemies, historical context, and character motivation for those who participated in the First War. In this way, "The War Just Before" makes use of the concept of legacy, either in carrying on the legacy of a previous generation of soldiers, or continuing one's legacy of fighting in wars with the hopes of actually ending the war and becoming a hero. "The War Just Before" is a failed war, at least from the perspective of the protagonists, giving them the motivation to fight for redemption or freedom. It is both a useful world-building technique and character-building exercise, as it places the protagonist in the beginning of the story with already clearly established values and history.

Trinity Structure in Harry Potter

This analysis is built on the foundation created by C. Bell in "Three Is a Magic Number: Trinity Archetypes in Harry Potter," as it expands upon the triad structure outlined in that work. Bell's work focused on the use of the triadic protagonist structure of the story, wherein Harry, Ron, and Hermione embody the Hero, the Anti-Hero, and the Heroine roles that occur frequently in literature and popular culture:

> One of the most salient examples of the trinity protagonist structure in modern literature is that of Harry Potter, Hermione Granger, and Ron Weasley. While many tend

to focus on Harry Potter as the main character of the story, simply because his name happens to appear in the title, it is clear to this author that, in fact, the real protagonist of the Potter series is not Harry Potter, but a triadic and aspect-based single entity made up of three distinct yet wholly symbiotic parts: Hero, Anti-Hero, and Heroine. Removing any one of the three elements and the whole falls apart [Bell, 2011].

The aspects Bell refers to in the above quotation are Power, Love, and Knowledge, characteristics that apply to Harry, Ron, and Hermione respectively and define their roles in the story and in the protagonist triad. These three axes apply not only to these characters but to other trinities in the story as well; the Deathly Hallows, for example, are made up of the Elder Wand (Power), the Cloak of Invisibility (Knowledge), and the Resurrection Stone (Love):

> The Elder Wand is an artifact of pure power, designed to defeat any wand standing against it. The second Hallow—the Resurrection Stone—belongs to the love locus of the triad [...]. The second brother uses the Stone to return a lost love to the world. [...] Lastly, the Invisibility Cloak represents knowledge in the form of wisdom: The youngest brother was the humblest and also the wisest of the brothers, and he did not trust Death. So he asked for something that would enable him to go forth from that place without being followed by Death [Bell, 2011].

These are just two examples of Rowling's use of trinities and triads in the *Harry Potter series*, as noted by Bell. Rowling has established a pattern with this structure to imbue the series with symbolic significance.

The symbolism and structure Rowling uses consistently throughout the series can be expanded to include not only the core triad of Harry, Ron, and Hermione, but other minor characters that have great significance to the plot and major thematic elements. This analysis borrows that model and applies it to Luna, Neville, and Ginny as members of the D.A., and Sirius, Lupin, and James, as well as extends the definitions of Love, Power, and Knowledge within the context of the *Harry Potter* universe.

Discussion

Rowling weaves trinities, threes, and triads throughout her narrative. Bell illustrates numerous uses of trinities in the article mentioned above; the number three provides necessary structure to keep the complex narrative afloat (2011). The triads serve a narrative purpose, with Rowling making value judgments about certain qualities and characteristics and making use of those characteristics. These triads of characters spin out from each other through the cast—the three sisters Bellatrix, Narcissa, and Andromeda; the three bullies Malfoy, Crabbe, and Goyle—but the trinities also exist in variations on themselves, complementing what qualities the others lack. This is where groups of three become groups of six in the main players of Voldemort's initial success and his ultimate downfall; the Marauders and Dumbledore's Army, respectively. This section will aim to argue that Dumbledore's Army adopted the legacy of the Marauders, using complementary characteristics and succeeding where the Marauders failed. First, though, it must be established the importance of legacies in Rowling's narrative, and her use of them to thread together narrative and theme.

Legacy Symbolism

The concept of legacy is critical to unraveling the *Harry Potter* narrative. Legacies give the story a sense of historicity, and symbolic weight to the characters and objects that carry both the narrative and the tradition of the Wizarding people with them. Legacies in the *Harry Potter* universe can be people, places, or objects, and they usually denote important plot points—when Rowling adds a legacy or history to a story element, it is not thoughtless or done solely for world-building. Legacy items and characters signal to the audience something to remember and track through the series. Because of the complex nature of the interconnected narratives in the seven novels, there are dozens of examples of these "legacy items" and characters.

Legacy Characters

Both the main protagonist and the main antagonist, Harry Potter and Voldemort respectively, are given a familial legacy that dates back to some of the most famous names in Wizarding history. Voldemort is deeply connected to his ancestry, which includes Salazar Slytherin, one of the four fabled founders of Hogwarts. In *HBP*, Marvolo Gaunt, Voldemort's grandfather, brags about being one of the last direct descendants of Slytherin and the famous Peverell family (Rowling, 2005). Voldemort's ability to speak Parseltongue is also a legacy trait, rumored to be a genetically passed-down talent of Salazar Slytherin himself (Rowling, 1999). Harry is also related to Peverells; it is suggested in *DH* that Ignotus Peverell was the original owner of Harry's Invisibility Cloak (so capitalized because the Cloak is an item of Wizarding legend), and started the tradition of passing it down through generations (Rowling, 2007). The Cloak was given to Harry Potter via Albus Dumbledore, after Harry's father had died (Rowling, 1998). This makes Harry a legacy character and the Cloak a legacy item. Considering the legendary status of the Cloak, which was considered nothing more than a fairy tale by Wizarding culture, this particular legacy implies a specific fate for Harry. Ignotus Peverell was the brother from the Tale of Three Brothers that outsmarted Death, and then, when he was old enough to pass on, "departed this life as equals" with Death (Rowling, 2007). Harry's ancestry reflects his destiny to defeat Death until he meets it on his own terms. Harry was the first person in history to survive the Killing Curse, and when he faces Voldemort in the Forbidden Forest in *DH*, he walks to his death willingly and knowingly. The Cloak's significance is in the symbolic, peaceful transition from life to death, and although Harry met his death (his first death, anyway) violently and at the hands of a monster, he met that end purposefully, and with no intention of hiding or escaping it. Without the legacy behind the Invisibility Cloak, that symbolism would be lost.

Voldemort and Harry are not the only legacy characters in the story. Sybill Trelawney, the Divination professor at Hogwarts, was the great-great-granddaughter of Cassandra Trelawney, a famous Seer (Rowling, 2003). Sybill's divination talents are frequently questioned, despite even her most casual and ridiculous-sounding predictions coming true. In fact, she does make two genuine prophecies, the first of which was supposedly about Harry and Lord Voldemort. The second prophecy came in a conversation with Harry in *PoA*, about the "servant" who would return to his master (Rowling, 1999). The audience later learns that this prophecy was referencing Peter Pettigrew's return to the side of Voldemort. Sybill only secured the interview to teach Divination at Hogwarts because of her great-great-grandmother's legacy, further cementing the idea that legacy and history is enormously important in the universe that Rowling created (Rowling, 2005). During the interview, Sybill Trelawney made the first prophecy the audience knows of, which is also the prophecy that starts the plot of the entire series:

> The one with the power to vanquish the Dark Lord approaches … born to those who have thrice defied him, born as the seventh month dies … and the Dark Lord will mark him as his equal, but he will have power the Dark Lord knows not … and either must die at the hand of the other for neither can live while the other survives … the one with the power to vanquish the Dark Lord will be born as the seventh month dies…. [Rowling, 2005].

Severus Snape, at this point in the timeline, is a Death Eater and overhears the prophecy and relays it to Voldemort. The child that Voldemort marks as his equal is Harry Potter, prompting Voldemort to track down Harry's family in an attempt to kill Harry and prevent the realization of the prophecy. Sybill Trelawney's legacy of Second Sight in her family places her in the wrong place at the wrong time, and seals the fate of Lily and James Potter. The history behind this character is made to be essential to the plot, and not just incidental to the character.

Legacy Places

Legacies can signal important places in the narrative as well as important characters. Some of the most notable places in the *Harry Potter* universe have an immense history and mark the spot of major plot developments. Godric's Hollow, the birthplace of Godric Gryffindor, was also home to some of the world's most famous Wizarding families; the Dumbledores and the Potters both had homes there, and it was the final resting place of Ignotus Peverell (Rowling, 2007). 12 Grimmauld Place was the home to "The Noble and Most Ancient House of Black," to later become the headquarters for The Order of the Phoenix, the secret society dedicated to defeating Voldemort and his Death Eaters (Rowling, 2003). The Chamber of Secrets, hidden beneath Hogwarts castle, was created by Salazar Slytherin to house his monstrous Basilisk, claimed by Voldemort to commit murder and create his first Horcrux, as well as the place where the first Horcrux was destroyed by Harry (Rowling, 1999). These spaces, dripping with history both legendary and gory, indicate the necessity of legacy in the series. Rowling uses space to infuse the series with a sense of past. Wizarding history is ancient, varied, and the context given by a place's legacy imparts to the audience the significance of Wizarding history to current events.

Legacy Objects

It is rare in the *Harry Potter* universe to encounter an item that is relevant to the overall plot but does not come with a history or backstory. Like the aforementioned places and people, objects with historical significance or those that have been passed down through generations indicate plot consequence.

One of the first of these items we encounter is Harry's wand, which via a shared wand core with Tom Riddle's wand, links the two characters together both symbolically ("the wand chooses the Wizard, Mr. Potter"), and narratively—the shared wand core saves Harrys life in a number of duels with Voldemort (Rowling, 1998). The series makes a concerted effort to compare these two characters. Both Harry and Voldemort were orphans, and neither was aware of his magical background. Both characters were popular in school, had the same talent for talking to snakes, and as mentioned by the memory of Riddle in *Harry Potter and the Chamber of Secrets*, even look somewhat alike (Rowling, 1999). The phoenix-core wand that Harry and Voldemort share is one other similarity that indicates an intertwined destiny.

Voldemort and Harry also have a distantly shared ancestry. Through the Deathly Hallows—the Elder Wand, the Invisibility Cloak, and the Resurrection Stone, we learn that both Harry and Voldemort were descendants of the Peverell brothers of legend. The Elder Wand has a legacy not of familial generations, but is instead passed on through a bloody history of powerful wizards and witches murdering each other to take control of it. The Resurrection Stone ended up set in Marvolo Gaunt's ring and passed down through his family line. Voldemort stole the ring and made it a Horcrux, and then Dumbledore came into possession of it, destroyed the Horcrux that lived within it, and passed the Stone on to Harry in his will, making it a legacy item for both Voldemort and Harry. The Invisibility Cloak, as mentioned above, belonged to the third Peverell brother and traced Harry's history to this common ancestor with Voldemort (Rowling, 1998, 2005, 2007).

There is a near endless list of similar objects throughout the series. The Marauders Map, several of Voldemort's Horcruxes, the Sorting Hat, Gryffindor's sword, and the other items in Dumbledore's will all come with a similar sense of historicity. Legacies are everything in the *Harry Potter* universe. History is not incidental to the most crucial pieces of the narrative; those pieces are important *because* of their history and link to the old Wizarding culture, wars, or traditions. Rowling uses this theme of legacy literally through use of these "legacy objects" and figuratively. She crafts a redemption narrative out of the theme that the past is not only relevant, but omnipresent in the events that unfold for our heroes.

The Triads

In Bell's piece entitled "Three is a Magic Number: The Trinity Archetype in Harry Potter," he establishes that the core protagonists Harry, Ron, and Hermione, all reign over their domains of Power, Love, and Knowledge respectively. Harry's role is to take action; Hermione's role is to plan and problem-solve; Ron's role is to keep the group grounded and connected through their love and compassion for one another (Bell, 2011). Examples of these roles exist continually throughout the series, but the most clear and obvious example occurs in the first novel, leading up to Harry's first conscious encounter with Voldemort. To protect the Sorcerer's/Philosopher's Stone, the professors of Hogwarts create trials to prevent outsiders from making their way to the Stone. Harry, Ron, and Hermione make it through the first three trials together and without incident. However, when they come upon the enchanted chessboard, these characters begin to exhibit their special skills and what their roles will be for the remainder of the series.

Ron sacrifices himself in the game of chess they three have to play in order to progress to the Stone: "'Yes ...' said Ron softly, 'it's the only way.... I've got to be taken'" (Rowling, 1998). Ron's willingness to sacrifice himself for the safety of his friends and the progression of their mission is a defining moment for his role as the Love axis of their triad. Then comes Hermione's trial, where she is faced with a logic puzzle and solves it, allowing Harry to progress and Hermione to go back and get help for Ron. Hermione dominates the Knowledge axis in this instance, as an eleven-year-old girl who cleverly solves a logic puzzle designed by Professor Snape, a man easily three times her age. Hermione, however, cannot progress past this point in the trials, and leaves Harry to face Voldemort alone (somewhat alone, at least. Voldemort was, at the time, living on the back of Professor Quirrell's head). Here is where Harry exercises his axis, the axis of Power. Harry is expected, time and time again throughout the series, to face Voldemort head-on. It is not that Harry has any particular skill that brings him to these climactic moments, but rather that he chooses to face them and despite whatever the odds may be, does what needs doing. In this case, Harry procures the Sorcerer's Stone simply by *wanting it*, in quite a literal sense. Dumbledore equips the Mirror of Erised with the power to bestow the Stone on whomever may want it, but does not wish to use it (Rowling, 1998). Simply by entering the arena with the *desire* to stop Voldemort gives Harry what he needs to stop Voldemort. The roles are further solidified in the end-of-the-year house points that Dumbledore issues to all three of them:

> Yes, yes well done Slytherin, well done Slytherin, however recent events must be taken into account, and I have a few last minute points to award. To Miss Hermione Granger, for the cool use of intellect when others were in great peril, 50 points. Second to Mr. Ronald Weasley, for the best played game of chess that Hogwarts has seen these many years, 50 points. And third to Mr. Harry Potter, for pure nerve and outstanding courage, I award Gryffindor House 60 points [Rowling, 1998].

A few key phrases from this quote congratulate Hermione for her "cool use of intellect" and Harry for "pure nerve." In the cases of all three of these characters, Rowling establishes from the first novel exactly what roles they need to fulfill to defeat evil and win the war, though this was only the first battle and merely delayed Voldemort's return to power.

There exists, too, a secondary, complementary triad within the cast of Dumbledore's Army. The other three characters that accompanied Harry to the Ministry of Magic in *OotP*, in what they thought was a mission to save Sirius, embody a triangular structure with similar, related axes. Harry, Ron, and Hermione represent Power, Love, and Knowledge, while Ginny, Neville, and Luna represent Skill, Courage, and Wisdom.

Neville is the character that earns the House Cup for Gryffindor in their first year, as Dumbledore awards his house points last (emphasis added): "And finally, it takes a great deal of *courage* to stand up to your enemies, but a great deal more to stand up to your friends. I award 10 points, to Mr. Neville Longbottom" (Rowling, 1998). Dumbledore is referencing the moment where Neville tries to prevent the trio from leaving the Gryffindor common room in the middle of the night, knowing that the three were up to something dangerous. Neville is unable to prevent them from leaving, but the act of trying is what marks him as unquestionably brave. Neville's brand of courage is most closely associated with the Love axis. Neville's bravery does not beget any additional power for him as a character, but it does show his depth for caring. After Harry, Ron, and Hermione leave school to track and destroy Horcruxes, Neville leads the D.A. in a makeshift hideout in the Room of Requirement. There he cares for students fleeing the cruelty of the new Hogwarts administration:

> Room of Requirement, of course! Surpassed itself, hasn't it? The Carrows were chasing me, and I knew I had just one chance for a hideout: I managed to get through the door and this is what I found! Well, it wasn't exactly like this when I arrived, it was a load smaller, there was only one hammock and just Gryffindor hangings. But it's expanded as more and more of the D.A. have arrived [Rowling, 2007].

The Room of Requirement becomes an effective refugee camp that Neville manages, and he welcomes Harry, Ron, and Hermione to the resistance he has been leading in their absence.

While Neville leads the resistance through his courage and caring, Ginny fights with her exceptional skill and embodies the Power axis of the secondary triad. Ginny is repeatedly referred to as "talented" and is by every measure, a powerful young woman. Ginny's skills for hexes is noted by her older brother George:

> **George Weasley:** Yeah, size is no guarantee of power. Look at Ginny.
> **Harry Potter:** What d'you mean?
> **George Weasley:** You've never been on the receiving end of one of her Bat-Bogey Hexes, have you? (Rowling, 2003)

Ginny's skill is equated here with power. She is also a talented flyer, taking Harry's place as Seeker on the Gryffindor Quidditch team when he is suspended. Ginny's charisma and talent make her powerful, but in a way that contrasts sharply with Harry's power. While Harry's accomplishments are described as "dumb luck," and "pure nerve," Ginny has skill that affords her power.

To complete this triad, Luna contributes a different kind of knowledge that complements Hermione's intellect. Luna's defining characteristic is wisdom. Per Bell:

> "Wit beyond measure is a man's greatest treasure" is the motto of Ravenclaw House. This is usually applied to Ravenclaws in terms of them being smart, but there is an element of wit that has less to do with intelligence and more to do with intelligence *applied*. Applied intelligence is the very definition of *wisdom*. Luna is wise; she is the voice of reason for the group. Luna looks at the world in ways other people do not, and she sees things no one else sees (which, of course, occasionally includes nargles) [Bell, 2016].

Luna is gifted with intuition and calm, understanding wisdom in the face of bullying and ostracization. There's a quote that describes this quality in Luna perfectly: "Luna was once again demonstrating her usual knack of speaking of uncomfortable truths; he had never meet anyone quite like her" (Rowling, 2003). Luna's ability to process complicated emotions and speak them without awkwardness is a hallmark of her Wisdom, and her connection to the third axis of Knowledge.

All of these characters had to engage these characteristics to not only survive the Second Wizarding War, but to take down Voldemort permanently. While all six of the D.A. members (under the limited definition) survive to the end of the series, none of the six Marauders (under the extended definition) do.

The Failure of the Marauders

Each member of the Marauders possessed the same axes of the triads as their younger counterparts, but each also failed to exercise those characteristics at crucial points in the First Wizarding War. This section details those crucial moments in which a different decision, or a better embodiment of a role, would have resulted in a different outcome.

James/Harry

The James Potter/Harry Potter connection is easy enough to make. They are described as being nearly identical, save for Harry having his mother's eyes. Both are stars of the Gryffindor Quidditch team, making them well-liked and popular athletes—the real-world analog would be the "captain of the football team" archetype. Severus Snape, though considerably bitter about his history with James and undoubtedly biased, often compares Harry and James, calling Harry "just as arrogant as [his] father … strutting about the castle." Even Sirius sees the similarities, and Ron's mother Molly accuses Sirius of treating Harry like an adult because he thinks he has his best friend back. Harry and James both possess the role of the action-taker. Harry is constantly taking action, even when it poses a significant danger to himself (especially then). James had a similar history of breaking rules and seeking out dangerous situations, and eventually became a member of the Order of the Phoenix. However, James failed his role as the Power axis of his group, by going into hiding with his wife and son. This decision cannot be earnestly criticized, as any reasonable person whose family was in danger from a mass murderer would likely make the same choice. However, James' role was not to hide from death or danger, but to face it willingly. James' choice not to take action sealed his fate. He and his wife were caught off guard when their location was revealed to Voldemort, leaving them powerless to stop him.

Sirius/Ron

Sirius was James and Lily's first choice as Secret-Keeper to hide their location from Voldemort. At the last minute, Sirius requested they make Peter Pettigrew their Secret-Keeper, incorrectly assuming that Voldemort would never suspect Pettigrew and that Voldemort's chances of finding the Potters would die with Sirius. Ironically, this was Sirius' attempt to sacrifice himself for his friends. If the Secret-Keeper died, the location of the Potters would no longer be secret, and Voldemort could get to them. Sirius assumed Voldemort would kill him to reveal their secret, but the secret would remain safe with Pettigrew. Instead, Pettigrew betrayed the Potters to Voldemort and Sirius was left saddled with the guilt of losing his two closest friends. Sirius, like Ron, was willing to sacrifice himself to protect his friends. In that way, he captures the Love axis in his character. Unfortunately, not being able to make that sacrifice was his failure—he was unable to fulfill his role in protecting James and Lily because of his incredible love for them.

Remus/Hermione

Remus Lupin and Hermione Granger have a lot in common in how their stories are meant to parallel real-world prejudices. Hermione's status as a muggle-born woman makes her subject to slurs and assumptions by "pure-blood" witches and wizards. Authors have addressed this narrative device as a parallel to real-world racism, calling the term "Mudblood" a racial slur (Layman, 2017; Möller, 2014; Walters, 2015). Remus is a werewolf, even more ostracized from the Wizarding community and seen by many as little more than an animal. Remus' illness has been compared by one author to HIV/AIDS, particularly at the height of the AIDS epidemic in the 1980s (Green, 2008). Hermione and Lupin are subject to paranoia and xenophobia in Wizarding communities, with the animosity toward both muggle-borns and werewolves increasing drastically at the height of the Second Wizarding War. Both characters are considered to be the clever ones in their group, but Remus fails in the Knowledge axis at a crucial moment. Remus assumes, along with everyone else, that it was Sirius who betrayed the Potters and then killed Peter Pettigrew. Remus' intellect fails him and leaves him tortured by the thought that the man he trusted could turn out to be a crazed murderer and servant of Voldemort.

Peter/Neville

Peter Pettigrew and Neville Longbottom are framed similarly in the narrative, especially in the context of how the other characters treat them. Upon the first description of Peter the audience ever hears, Professor McGonagall calls him a "foolish boy," with no exceptional talent for magic and a habit of "hero-worshipp[ing]" James Potter and Sirius Black (Rowling, 1999). Pettigrew is the "tag-along" member of the Marauders, edging his way in by following the others around. McGonagall's description gives insight into the dynamic between Pettigrew and the other Marauders, as well as Pettigrew's reputation with the Hogwarts professors. Neville suffers a similar reputation in his early years at Hogwarts. He is the center of several embarrassing mishaps in his first year, notably losing control of his broom on the first day of flying lessons, and his poor skill as a wizard is repeatedly referred to by Severus Snape: "possibly no one's warned you, Lupin, but this class contains Neville Longbottom. I would advise you not to entrust him with anything difficult. Not unless Ms. Granger is hissing instructions in his ear" (Rowling, 1999). Neville is also not often considered part of the core team, at least not until after the scene in the Ministry of Magic in *OotP*, but Neville had always existed on the margins of the trio of Harry, Ron, and Hermione. He was present for the first sighting of Fluffy, the three-headed dog that guarded the Sorcerer's Stone; he joined Harry, Ron, Hermione, and Draco in detention in the Forbidden Forest where Harry comes face-to-face with Voldemort for the first time since his parents' deaths. Neville's presence for these significant moments in the storyline without directly impacting them leave him to occupy a similar position as Pettigrew: almost part of the group, but just not quite (at least for the first three or four novels).

As established above, Neville's defining quality of Courage is most aligned with the Love axis of the triangle. The significant difference between Neville and Pettigrew, the difference that results in Neville's ultimate success and Peter's ultimate downfall, is the kind of love that these characters feel and how it affects their bravery. Neville's bravest moments come with concern for the safety of his friends. The attempt to prevent them from leaving the common room in *SS*, his accompanying them to the Ministry of Magic to try to rescue Sirius, and the refugee camp he designs and runs in the face of the Carrows were all acts of immense bravery as a direct result of his capacity for love.

To contrast, Peter Pettigrew's brand of love was sycophantic, desperate love in an effort to earn the admiration of his peers. He attached himself to James Potter because the warm glow of attention and praise that James received as one of the more popular students in school was attractive to Pettigrew's inferiority complex, which was the result of taunting by other students and professors alike. Pettigrew's love drove him to powerful characters: first James, then Voldemort. However, the courage that was required of him to stop Voldemort failed him nearly instantly, driving the secret of the Potters' whereabouts right into the hands of Voldemort. Pettigrew died, quite literally, at the hand that Voldemort created for him.

Lily/Ginny

The Lily/Ginny connection is more difficult to pin down, partially because Lily Evans-Potter is not exceptionally fleshed out within the narrative. These two characters have aesthetic similarities, though, such as the red hair and the black-haired, Quidditch Captain boyfriend on their arm. Both of these women are described in terms of their Skill, which is Ginny's axis of Power. Slughorn described Lily Evans as one of the most talented students he ever had and took a special interest in Ginny for her talent, as well. Both were unique inductees into the "Slug Club," i.e., the band of students to whom Slughorn gave special treatment. Ginny and Lily were unique in that they both were invited to the Slug Club on the merit of their skill and not, as with the other students in the Slug Club, because of a family tie to a famous, rich, or powerful witch or wizard. Because the Skill axis is an extension of the Power axis, one could argue that Lily's failure was the same as her husband's: her choice to go into hiding rather than fight on the frontlines doomed their family. Ginny, conversely, was an underage witch during the Battle of Hogwarts, and despite explicit instructions by her mother to remain hidden, ran into battle anyway.

Severus/Luna

Severus Snape was relentlessly bullied in school, especially by James Potter and Sirius Black. His greasy hair and lonesome demeanor made him an outsider in his school, just as Luna's "scraggly" hair and unusual dress and behavior made her an outsider. Severus and Luna are also the only two non-Gryffindors in either group. However, where Luna's wisdom allowed her to overcome cruel taunts and eventually make friends, Severus turned the cruelty inward. He absorbed it and became violent and sadistic. He invented a spell that nearly killed Draco Malfoy when Harry used it. He called Lily an offensive slur, and of course, his critical failure was joining the Death Eaters. When Severus overheard Sybill Trelawney's prophecy about the Dark Lord's equal, he told Voldemort about it and inadvertently signed the death warrant of Lily Potter, his only friend. Luna and Severus illustrate two paths for children who suffer bullying. Severus' character is sympathetic, but his actions are not excusable.

Conclusion

What Rowling is trying to impart with these character similarities is a sense of bitter tragedy from the players in the First Wizarding War. All of the Marauder-era characters failed in their roles in some way, leading to death, imprisonment, and grief. James, Sirius, Remus, Peter, Severus, and Lily leave behind a legacy of failure, though a sympathetic one. In each of these instances, especially considering the youth of these characters during the war (all of whom were around twenty-one years old when Voldemort first fell from power), one can understand and even empathize with the characters on a deeply emotional level. James and Lily only wanted to protect their son. Sirius only wanted to save his friends. Remus only wanted to keep his friends close. Peter was afraid to die. Severus was emotionally bruised from years of torment. None of these young people were ready or willing to commit themselves to ending the war, much less accept their roles as heroes of the war. Despite all of these characters having the qualities that Rowling deems most necessary to be heroes, Power, Knowledge, Love, Skill, Wisdom, and Courage, they acted in the interest of preserving what they had rather than the interest of fighting for it. The members of Dumbledore's Army accept their role as heroes as soon as they fly to the Ministry of Magic, and some even earlier than that, and use their respective talents and qualities in harmony with one another to end the war and save the world.

References

Bell, C. (2016). "Heroes and Horcruxes: Dumbledore's Army as Metonym." In C. Bell (Ed.), *Wizards vs. Muggles: Essays on Identity and the Harry Potter Universe*. Jefferson, NC: McFarland.

Bell, C. (2011). "Three is a Magic Number: The Trinity Archetype in Harry Potter." *Journal of Literature and Art Studies, 1*(3), 209–218.

Layman, L. (2017). "Magically Empathetic: An Investigation of Theory of Mind and Empathy in the Harry Potter Series." Retrieved from UTC Scholar: http://scholar.utc.edu/cgi/viewcontent.cgi?article=1087&context=honors-theses.

Möller, C. (2014). "Mudbloods, Half-Bloods and Pure-Bloods: The Issues of Racism and Race Discrimination in J.K. Rowling's Harry Potter." Retrieved from Lund University Humanities and Theology: http://lup.lub.lu.se/luur/download?func=downloadFile&recordOId=4285141&fileOId=4285142.

Moore, R. (Director). (2004). *Battlestar Galactica* [Motion Picture].

Natov, R. (2001). "Harry Potter and the Extraordinariness of the Ordinary." *The Lion and the Unicorn, 25*(2), 310–327.

Rowling, J. (1999). *Harry Potter and the Chamber of Secrets*. New York: Scholastic.

Rowling, J. (2007). *Harry Potter and the Deathly Hallows*. New York: Scholastic.

Rowling, J. (2000). *Harry Potter and the Goblet of Fire*. New York: Scholastic.

Rowling, J. (2005). *Harry Potter and the Half-Blood Prince*. New York: Scholastic.

Rowling, J. (2003). *Harry Potter and the Order of the Phoenix*. New York: Scholastic.

Rowling, J. (1999). *Harry Potter and the Prisoner of Azkaban*. New York: Scholastic.

Rowling, J. (1998). *Harry Potter and the Sorcerer's Stone*. New York: Scholastic.

Saussure, F. d. (1966). *Course in General Linguistics*. New York: McGraw-Hill.

Staten, J. (2014, September 9). Destiny. Activision.

Tolkien, J. (1937). *The Hobbit: There and Back Again.* Crows Nest, New South Wales: Allen and Unwin.
Tolkien, J. (1954). *The Lord of the Rings.* Crows Nest, New South Wales: Allen and Unwin.
Walters, T. (2015, May). "Not So Magical: Issues with Racism, Classism, and Ideology in Harry Potter." Retrieved from NMU Commons: http://commons.nmu.edu/cgi/viewcontent.cgi?article=1045&context=theses.
Whedon, J. (Director). (2002). *Firefly* [Motion Picture].

About the Contributors

Alison **Baker** is a senior lecturer in early childhood studies at the University of East London. Her research interests include cultural representation and picture books, and she is researching for a Ph.D. on white working-class children in children's fantasy fiction, focusing on *Harry Potter*, Philip Pullman's *His Dark Materials*, Jonathan Stroud's *Bartimaeus* trilogy and Michael De Larrabeiti's *Borribles* trilogy. She has published on girls' horror comics, reading experiences of white working-class teachers and trainee teachers' experiences of introducing culturally representative picture books in multicultural classrooms.

Dr. Christopher E. **Bell** is the director of graduate studies and an associate professor of media studies at the University of Colorado in Colorado Springs. He teaches theory and methodology courses in critical analysis of popular culture, rhetorical theory, representation theory and mass media. He also serves as chair of the Southwest Popular/American Culture Association's Harry Potter Studies division.

Jelena **Borojević** is a Ph.D. candidate at the Department of English Language and Literature, University of Novi Sad. Her thesis is concerned with mythopoetics in the works of J.R.R. Tolkien, Philip Pullman and J.K. Rowling. She is the editor in chief of *The Lilith Review*, and the assistant editor for fiction at Arcadia Press. She contributed to *Critical Insights: The Hobbit* (Salem Press) with her chapter "The Hobbit: A Mythopoeic Need for Adventure." Additionally, she is also interested in fan studies, popular culture, and the modern representation of fairy tales.

Dr. Lauren **Camacci** is a post doctoral teaching fellow in communication arts and sciences at the Pennsylvania State University. She is rhetorical critic and critical masculinities scholar, working primarily on popular culture, mid–20th-century American history, and the U.S. presidency. She completed a dissertation that examined mid-century American masculinity during the Nixon presidency. Along with her other scholarship, she is very active in Harry Potter Studies, through both research and service.

Dr. Elizabeth Morrow **Clark** is a professor of history at West Texas A&M University, where she teaches modern European history. She has research interests in twentieth-century diplomacy, memory, and nationalism. Her publication "Dzięki temu, ja jestem: Polish memories and narratives of trauma and national identity" in *Rocznik*

Antropologii Historii/Anthropology of History Yearbook (2018) investigates war trauma and post-generational memory, themes she also pursues in Harry Potter Studies. She has escorted student groups to Poland, Germany, and the Wizarding World of Harry Potter in Orlando. She has served as vice-chair of the Harry Potter Studies division of the Southwest Popular/American Culture Association since its inception.

Soma **Das** is researching in children's literature with CIRCL, Reading University, UK, as an MRes student. She presented a paper and was a panelist at the *Harry Potter* conference held in London. Her research interests include literature, media and cultural studies. She has past experience in media and communications from organizations such as a quango in Westminster, The Royal Society of Arts & Manufactures (The RSA) and, the University of Sussex. She completed her MA in media and cultural studies from the University of Sussex and, BA (Hons.) in English literature from St. Stephen's College, Delhi University.

Kate **Fulton** is an associate professor of psychology at San Juan College in Farmington, New Mexico, and a licensed clinical mental health counselor in Colorado and New Mexico. She teaches courses in introductory psychology, human development, personality and abnormal psychology. She taught a *Harry Potter* learning community for four years with Dr. Alicia Skipper, pairing English composition and psychology classes with a *Harry Potter* theme.

Tolonda **Henderson** is an instruction and reference librarian at George Washington University where they are also earning an MA in English. They regularly participates in the Harry Potter Studies section of the Southwest Popular and American Culture Association, contributing papers on such topics as the memorials to the Potter family (2017) and disability in the Harry Potter series (2016).

Dr. Tara **Moore** teaches young adult literature and technical writing at Elizabethtown College, a liberal arts college in central Pennsylvania. She has published two books about Christmas: *Victorian Christmas in Print* (Palgrave) and *Christmas: The Sacred to Santa* (Reaktion). Her work has also appeared in *The ALAN Review*, *Victorian Periodicals Review*, and *Victorian Literature and Culture*. Her research interests include two fairly different topics: representations of killer girls in dystopian fiction and adoption in children's and young adult novels.

Camilla **Schroeder** is writing her Ph.D. thesis on the English-language translations of Grimms' fairy tales at Kingston University while teaching English literature and German. She has previously finished her MA in publishing at Kingston University. She has given several papers at conferences, including: "E.T.A. Hoffmann and the Brothers Grimm: The Sandman-Motif in Modern German Gothic Fiction" (Reflected Shadows, Kingston University), "Animalising the Male and Silencing the Female: Cursing in Grimms' Fairy Tales" (Cursing Conference, Museum of Witchcraft and Magic), and "The Genrefication of 'Cinderella'" (All about Cinderella, University of Bedfordshire). Furthermore, she has an upcoming chapter on English language translations in a collective volume about the works of Kai Meyer.

Dr. Alicia **Skipper** holds a BA in English from Coastal Carolina University, a master's degree in English from University of North Carolina Wilmington and a Ph.D.

in literature from Arizona State University. She is a professor of English at Bakersfield College where she teaches composition and literature courses.

Dr. Keri **Stevenson** is an assistant professor of English at the University of New Mexico–Gallup. Her research has focused on kinship with animals, particularly birds, in literature; she has put together a bird-focused composition reader called *Feather by Feather*, presented on falconry memoirs at the ASLE (Association for the Study of Literature and the Environment) conference at Detroit in June 2017, and on skylarks and other avian conduits of kinship in George Meredith's writing at the Hawaii International Conference on Arts and the Humanities in January 2018. In addition, she presented on atheistic kinship with animals in Terry Pratchett's writing at the SWPACA Conference in February 2018.

Samantha J. **Vertosick** is a Ph.D. candidate focusing on children's and young adult literature alongside LGBT studies at the Indiana University of Pennsylvania. Another sample of her work can also be seen in Melissa Edmundson's edited collection *The Gothic Tradition in Supernatural*. She calls Pittsburgh home, and is a part-time instructor at Westmoreland County Community College.

Marley **Stuever-Williford** has a B.A. in communication with a media studies emphasis from the University of Colorado, Colorado Springs. Her previous work in *Harry Potter* studies includes a presentation at the Southwest Popular/American Culture Association conference and as a panel chair for the 2017 Page23 Lit Con at Denver Comic Con.

Index

Adams, Douglas 64
Alexander, Lloyd 66
Amidala, Padme 13
Asimov, Isaac 66
Aunt Marge 83–84, 101
Auntie Muriel 84

Baggins, Bilbo 80
Barebone, Chastity 18
Barebone, Credence 7, 9, 17–19, 140–141
Barebone, Mary Lou 17–19, 131, 139–140
Barthes, Roland 61
Bettleheim, Bruno 22–23, 28
Black, Sirius 11, 25, 27–29, 72, 83, 94–95, 110, 117, 123–124, 133–134, 136, 171–172
Brown, Lavender 56
Buckbeak 72, 88
Burbage, Charity 158

Camacci, Lauren Rose 61
Cattermole, Mary 101
Chang, Cho 52
Cinderella 10–11, 13, 103
Cole, Mrs. 13, 86–87
Creevey, Colin 26, 30
Crookshanks 105, 116, 120

Delacour, Fleur 44, 46
Delphi 63–65, 113, 138
Dick, Philip K. 63
Diggory, Amos 63
Diggory, Cedric 26–29, 62–65
Dobby 26, 84, 106, 126
Doge, Elphias 84
Dumbledore, Albus 13, 26–31, 33, 39, 61, 71–72, 81, 84–88, 96–97, 106, 109–110, 113, 123, 127, 133–134, 137, 150–151, 154, 162, 165, 168–169, 175
Dumbledore, Ariana 41, 137
Dumbledore, Kendra 97
Dumbledore, Percival 97
Dursley, Dudley 10, 33, 35–39, 42, 138
Dursley, Petunia 10, 37, 82, 110, 131, 133, 138

Dursley, Vernon 10, 37, 82, 133, 151–153, 158

Einstein, Albert 68
Evans, Lily 99, 174
Everett, Hugh III 71

Fang 122
Fawkes 127
Feynman, Richard 70–71
Filch 106
Finnigan, Seamus 81, 106
Firenze 47–48
Fluffy 88, 173

Gaiman, Neil 30
Gareth 66
Gaunt, Marvolo 97, 168
Gaunt, Merope 13–14, 87, 97
Gaunt, Morfin 15, 84, 97
Genette, Gerard 61
Gernsback, Hugo 68
Gloop, Augustus 36–37
Goldstein, Tina 18
Granger, Hermione 1, 8, 15–17, 26, 41, 46–48, 50–52, 55, 61–62, 64–66, 69, 71, 74, 76, 77, 81, 88–89, 98–102, 105, 107, 116, 121–122, 124–125, 154, 156–157, 163–164, 168–169, 172–173
Granger-Weasley, Hugo 64
Granger-Weasley, Rose 62, 64
Graves, Percival 141
Grindlewald, Gellert 18, 98, 141
Gryffindor, Godric 167

Hagrid, Rubeus 11, 44, 70, 82, 85–89, 98–99, 106–107, 112–113, 116, 119, 121–122, 125, 134, 150
Hawking, Stephen 69
Hedwig 25–26, 105, 120–123, 125
Hero's Journey 13–14
Highfield, Roger 69
Hills, Matt 1

Index

Hinton, Charles Howard 66
Hitler, Adolf 111

Invisibility Cloak 12

Jenkins, Henry 1
Jones, Hestia 38

Kreacher 26
Krum, Viktor 44, 64

L'Engle, Madeline 61, 66
LeStrange, Bellatrix 17, 29, 96, 113, 139, 164
Lestrange, Roldophus 65, 113
Lewis, C.S. 66, 70, 132
Link, Kelly 60, 71
Lockhart, Gilderoy 109
Longbottom, Augusta 17, 131
Longbottom, Neville 7, 9, 15–17, 19, 33, 35, 39–42, 56, 65, 97, 99, 106, 122, 137, 141, 153–154, 156–157, 169–170, 173
Longstocking, Pippi 15
Lovegood, Luna 7, 9, 15–17, 19, 26, 41, 170–171
Lovegood, Xenophilius 15–16
Lumos Foundation 7
Lupin, Remus 24–25, 29–30, 81, 110, 136, 172, 175
Lupin, Teddy 81

Mad-Eye Moody 81
Madam Malkin 108
Malfoy, Astoria 62, 92
Malfoy, Draco 7, 56, 62, 65, 70, 84–85, 88, 92–93, 98–99, 103, 106, 111, 156–157, 164, 174
Malfoy, Lucius 93, 95, 112
Malfoy, Narcissa 7, 82, 92, 164
Malfoy, Scorpius 62–64, 92, 101
McGonagall, Minerva 39, 48, 56, 71, 82–83, 105, 150–151, 154
Messrs Moony 110
Mirror of Erised 12
Mlodinow, Leonard 68

Nagini 25, 41–42
Nigellus, Phineas 99
Ninth Doctor 73
Norbert the Dragon 106

Obscurial 19
Ogden, Bob 97
Olivander 108

Padfoot 110
Paikea 17
Parkinson, Pansey 56,
Patil, Padma 44–57, 64, 113
Patil, Pavarti 44- 57, 113
Pettigrew, Peter 110, 172–173, 175

Peverell, Ignotus 166
Pigwidgeon 123–124
Pitkin, Walter 68
Potter, Albus 31, 50, 62–64, 70, 138
Potter, Harry 7–17, 19, 21–31, 33, 35–40, 45, 48–49, 51–53, 55, 59–70, 72–73, 76–77, 80–81, 84–89, 93–103, 105–113, 116–117, 119–125, 127, 131–136, 141–142, 150–152, 154–155, 157–158, 162–166, 168–171, 173–174
Potter, James 10, 12, 23, 110, 136, 142, 162, 166, 171–172, 174–175
Potter, James Sirius 31, 62, 70, 94
Potter, Lily 10–11, 23, 25, 38, 99, 110, 133, 136, 144, 162, 166, 172, 174–175
Potter, Lily Luna 31, 62
Prang, Ernie 109
Prince, Eileen 98
Prongs 110

Quirrell 90

Radcliffe, Daniel 78
Redmayne, Eddie 145
Riddle, Tom, Jr. 7, 9, 12–16, 39, 69–70, 81, 84, 86, 96, 117, 137, 167
Riddle, Tom, Sr. 13
Rosmerta 83
Rowle, Euphemia 139
Rowling, J.K. 7, 21, 60–61, 71–73, 76, 84–89, 94, 96, 103, 117, 120, 124, 127–128, 130–131, 134, 144–145, 149, 152–153, 155, 161, 164, 167–168, 174

Sagan, Carl 69
Scabbers 120, 123
Scamander, Newt 18, 139
Shakespeare 70, 85
Shunpike, Stan 109
Skywalker, Luke 13–14
Slughorn, Horace 33, 35, 39–40, 42, 81, 84, 86–87, 93
Slytherin, Salazar 94, 96–97, 142, 167
Snape, Severus 25, 65, 82, 93, 97–98, 136, 166, 173–174
Swanson, Kj 73

Thomas, Dean 26, 81
Thorne, Jack 60
Tiffany, John 60
Tonk, Andromeda 131, 137, 164
Tonks, Nymphadora 24–25, 30, 110
Tonks, Ted 112
Trelawney, Sybil 47–48, 84–85, 97, 158, 166, 174
Tyler, Rose 73

Umbridge, Dolores 64,101

Voldemort 7, 9–12, 14–15, 17, 19, 23, 25–26, 28, 30, 33, 40, 42, 53–54, 62–65, 70–71, 82,

86–87, 89, 94–97, 99–101, 106, 113, 116–117, 123, 125, 136, 139, 154, 162, 165–166, 169, 172, 174

Wallace, Charles 66
Weasley, Arthur 82, 93, 95, 104
Weasley, Bilius 81
Weasley, Bill 46
Weasley, Charlie 40
Weasley, Fred 24–25, 30, 62, 110
Weasley, George 24, 110, 170
Weasley, Ginny 31, 41, 50, 53, 123–124, 127, 164, 169–170, 174
Weasley, Molly 7–8, 28, 171
Weasley, Percy 25
Weasley, Ron 8, 15–17, 26, 41, 48–52, 61–66, 76, 81–82, 84, 93, 95, 99–102, 104, 109–110, 116, 121, 124, 154–157, 163–164, 168, 172–173
Webb, Caroline 103
Wells, H.G. 66–68, 74
Willis, Connie 66
Winky 84–85, 106, 108
Wormtail 96, 110

www.ingramcontent.com/pod-product-compliance
Ingram Content Group UK Ltd.
Pitfield, Milton Keynes, MK11 3LW, UK
UKHW042014140426
5217IPUK00015B/1160